T0148979

The Living Thoughts
of Gotama the Buddha

This new and expanded edition of *The Living Thoughts of Gotama the Buddha* is made possible by a grant from the Wisdom Foundation. One of the most significant books dealing with the Buddhist tradition, this classic work is the first in the Wisdom Foundation Series, which seeks to promote spiritual values throughout the world.

The Living Thoughts
of Gotama the Buddha

Ananda K. Coomaraswamy

and

I. B. Horner

FONS VITAE

Originally published by Cassell and Company, Ltd., 1948

"Buddhism" reprinted from *Religion in the 20th Century*
Edited by Vergilius Ferm
Published by Philosophical Library, Inc.

With appreciation to Shelly and Morgan Ward for photography.

This new and expanded edition published by
Fons Vitae
49 Mockingbird Valley Drive
Louisville, Kentucky 40207
www.fonsvitae.com

THE WISDOM FOUNDATION SERIES

© 2001
All rights reserved,
including the right of reproduction,
in whole or in part, in any form.

Printed in the United States of America

ISBN: 1-887752-38-2

Library of Congress Control Number: 2001087453

CONTENTS

Contents

The Publishers wish to express their indebtedness
to the Pali Text Society and to the Oxford
University Press for permission to include
quotations from *Gradual Sayings, Woven Cadences,
Minor Anthologies* and *Kindred Sayings.*

ABBREVIATIONS[1]

A.	Anguttara-Nikāya
AA.	Commentary on Anguttara
BG.	Bhagavadgītā
BU.	Bṛhadarañyaka Upanishad
Comy.	Commentary
D.	Dīgha-Nikāya
DA.	Commentary on Dīgha
Dh.	Dhammapada
DhA.	Commentary on Dhammapada
E.R.E.	Encyclopaedia of Religion and Ethics
G.S.	Gradual Sayings
HJAS	Harvard Journal of Asiatic Studies
It.	Itivuttaka
ItA.	Commentary on Ittivuttaka
J.	Jātaka
KhA.	Commentary on Khuddakapāṭha
K.S.	Kindred Sayings
M.	Majjhima-Nikāya
MA.	Commentary on Majjhima
Miln.	Milindapañha
Min. Anth.	Minor Anthologies of the Pali Canon
RV.	Rig-Veda
S.	Saṃyutta-Nikāya
SA.	Commentary on Saṃyutta
Sn.	Suttanipāta
Thag	Theragāthā
Ud.	Udāna
UdA.	Commentary on Udāna
Up.	Upanishad
Vn.	Vinaya-Piṭaka
Vism.	Visuddhimagga

[1] All references to Pali works are to the Pali Text Society's editions, except in the cases of *Vinaya* and *Jātaka*, the roman-letter editions of which were published by Williams and Northgate, 1879-1883, and by Trübner & Co. (and Kegan Paul, Trench, Trübner & Co. Ltd.), 1877-1897, respectively.

PRONUNCIATIONS

In Pali the vowels are pronounced as follows :

The short *a* as *a* in *at*
The long *ā* as *a* in *father*
The short *i* as *i* in *pin*
The long *ī* as *ee* in *been*
The short *u* as *u* in *put*
The long *ū* as *oo* in *tool*
The long *ē* as *a* in *table* (always long)
The long *ō* as *o* in *bone* (always long).

The consonants are mostly as in English; but *g* is always hard, and *c* is always *ch* as in *church*. The consonants *ṭ*, *ṭh*, *ḍ*, *ḍh*, *ṇ*, *ḷ*, are linguals and are formed by bringing the upturned tip of the tongue in contact with the back of the palate.

BIOGRAPHY
of
Ananda Kentish Coomaraswamy

T HE PRESENT WORK WILL BE A BOON TO BOTH SCHOLARS AND THOSE
seeking the Buddhist path. What makes the book offered
here so important is that Coomaraswamy not only knew
Buddhism inside and out; he also knew Christianity in the same
way. This made it possible for him to write and translate in the
proper equivalent terms, as well as to explain what the Buddha
said in equivalent terms as would be used by mediaeval
theologians. Unfortunately, just as many Christians have little
interest in the penetrating wisdom of the mediaeval theologians,
so also many Buddhists are little interested in the deeper meaning of the Buddhist texts. With much of the somewhat superfi-
cial Buddhism introduced into this country, his book acts as a
solid corrective in making clear the true nature and teaching of
the Buddha.

Dr. Coomaraswamy (1877-1947) was one of the most
penetrating scholars to live in the 20th century. The son of a Sri
Lankan father and an English woman, he was raised and educated
in England, receiving his Doctorate in Science at London
University. He initially went to Sri Lanka (then called Ceylon)
to further his studies in geology, and his geological surveys of
the country are still considered a standard. However, it soon
became clear to him that Ceylon was being culturally devastated
by the inroad of modern western ideas. As a result, he progressed
from the realm of social action to that of the arts, and from the
arts into the realm of theology. His text on mediaeval Singhalese
art is still a classic and has been republished several times. His
History of Indian and Indonesian Art is likewise still considered
authoritative and has been published in several languages.

He had an extraordinary gift for languages, having taught
himself Icelandic when in high school in England, and in his
sixties was able to carry on a conversation in this tongue. He
knew some thirty-six languages and once stated that to say one
knows a language means one must know its history, its poetry,
and be able to read it without a dictionary. It goes without saying
that he rapidly picked up Pali and Sanskrit, which gave him access

to the Buddhist texts in Ceylon as well as the fundamental Sacred Hindu texts. At the same time he studied in great depth the Church Fathers and the writings of mediaeval theologians. His set of the works of St. Thomas Aquinas is heavily underlined and cross-referenced with Hindu and Buddhist equivalents. He was a prolific scholar, with a bibliography of well over 900 titles, dealing with all aspects of his varied career. Other books dealing with Buddhism are his *Buddha and the Gospel of Buddhism* and *Hinduism and Buddhism*, which was the published lecture series that he gave at the Jewish Theological Seminary in New York.

He died in 1947, having retired from his position at the Boston Museum of Fine Arts and his teaching responsibilities. It was his intention to return to India and to eventually take *Sanyas*, or to become a monk, but God saw fit to make this impossible.

His knowledge of Buddhism was nothing short of extraordinary. He had spent time in China and Japan furthering his studies, but had never been to Tibet (which was at that time a closed land). He did, however, have a close relationship with Marco Pallis (author of *Peaks and Lamas*) and as a result had a deep understanding and respect for Mahayana Buddhism. Pallis once suggested he learn Tibetan, but he declined, saying he knew enough languages and was too old to learn a new one.

—*The Publishers*

FOREWORD

BUDDHISM

—Ananda Kentish Coomaraswamy

I. *History* :

THE BUDDHIST SCRIPTURES SPEAK OF THE BUDDHA—GOTAMA, thus distinguished by his family name from former Buddhas and Buddhas yet to come—as having been a man who, in his last birth, attained the goal of Full Awakening (*sambodhi*) and Despiration (*nirvāna*) for which he had prepared himself in the course of the long series of his residences in "former habitations." The recorded events of his life as a *Bodhisatta* before the Great Awakening are largely, however, the echoes of much older myths; and the recorded teachings of the later life are to a very large extent transpositions and reaffirmations of the older Brahmanical doctrines pertaining to the Ancient Way that he claims to have followed; and these facts, taken together with those of the Buddhology of the canonical texts make it entirely possible that what he represents is really another revelation to men and gods (he is always the teacher of both) of the Eternal *Avatar* and Light of lights, who is spoken of as Fire and Sun.

As a historical person, the exact date of Siddhatta's birth is uncertain; it may be 483 B.C., but it is hardly possible to say more than that the Buddha's life-span of eighty years, of which thirty-five precede the Awakening, or *Nirvana*,[1] covers the greater part of the fifth century B.C. The Bodhisatta was born at Kapilavatthu as the son of king Suddhodana and his queen Mahā Māyā, thus not as a Brāhman but as a *Khattiya*; this incarnation taking place by a deliberately willed descent from the Tusita heavens in which the future Buddha Maitreya now resides. In referring to him as a "prince" it must be understood that while he must have been brought up in luxury, the "kingdom" was really sort of a republic with a royal president, and that the "parliament-procedure" of Buddhist monastic assemblies was

---

[1] "Nirvana" has long been a naturalized English word, and is therefore employed in this Sanskrit form, rather than the Pali *nibbāna*. All other terms cited in their Pali forms.

really modelled on that of the secular councils.

The Bodhisatta's birth was miraculous; as such it was already compared by Hieronymus to that of the Christ, and it may also be mentioned here that the Christian legend of St. Josaphat ("Bodhisatta") is really the story of the Buddha's life. The child already bore the marks of a "Great Person," and it was foretold of him that he would become either an emperor or a World Teacher; in effect, he was "both king and priest," and could speak of himself as a "Brahman," not by birth, but in the full sense of the word, by knowledge, and of himself as a king in leadership. He was married to his cousin Yasodā, and had a son, Rāhula, who later on received ordination and so became his spiritual son in the sense in which the Buddhist monks are "Sons of the Wake."

On the day of the child's birth the Bodhisatta for the first time came into contact with the fact of the universal liability of all men to sorrow, old age, sickness and death; and thereupon determined to devote himself to the search for a "medicine" for this sickness unto death, all the more dangerous in that men are ever striving to forget their misery; to devote himself, in other words, to the quest for a kind of knowledge and a way of life that might ensure to those who would practise it a state of inviolable happiness and an assurance of immortality. So the Bodhisatta, not yet a Buddha, or "Wake," abandoned his home and all family ties, as many had done before him, as many have done since and still do. He became the disciple of Brahmanical teachers, finding much, but not all that he sought for. He practised the most extreme austerities, and had his own followers. But he found no help, and decided to follow the Middle Way between the extremes of luxury and self-mortification; his disciples then abandoning him. At last the time was at hand: taking his seat at the foot of the Bodhi-tree, at the navel of the earth, with his back to the tree facing the east, he firmly resolved never to rise again, though the flesh should wither on his bones, until the goal should be reached. Then follows the conflict with *Māra*, the principle of Love and Death, who claimed the sovereignty, and would not "let go"; the Bodhisatta's victory is a recension of the ancient Vedic myth of the conquest of the Dragon, *Namuci*, "Holdfast," Death. Then, passing through ever deeper and deeper states of consciousness, and recalling his "former habitations," the Bodhisatta at last obtained that complete understanding of Causal Origination, and that Awakening after which he is called the Buddha, "Wake."

At first the Buddha hesitated, fearing that none would be found able or willing to grasp the hard-won truths; but persuaded by Brahmā and moved by pity, he became an itinerant teacher, preaching the First Sermon ("The World is on Fire"), or more literally "Setting in Motion the Wheel of the Eternal-Law" (*dhamma*), before his former disciples, in Benares, and thereafter gradually winning from all classes of society an ever-increasing following of disciples, known as *bhikkus* (mendicants or almsmen) or *samaṇas* (ascetics, workers), composing the Buddhist order or community (*sangha*) of monks; many of these became *Arahants* ("Worthies," *digni*) and having accomplished their Nirvana can be referred to as "Awake" (*buddha*), like their Great Teacher, who nevertheless remains uniquely *the* Buddha of the Age. An order of nuns, parallel to that of the monks, was later established; it is expressly admitted that women are no less capable of spiritual attainment than are men.

After the Buddha's death, which is thought of as the shattering of the bodily investment, his teachings, at first transmitted orally (and by no means therefore inaccurately), were brought together in the books of the Pali canon. These embrace the *Tipiṭaka* (i.e. *Vinaya*, five *Nīkāyas*, and *Abhidhamma*), *Dhammapada*, *Itivuttaka*, *Udāna*, *Sutta Nipāta*, *Thera-therīgatha* and a few others. Of the extra-canonical Pali texts the most important are the *Milinda Pañha*, *Jātaka*, and still later Buddhaghosa's commentaries, in particular the *Visuddhi Magga*. English versions of all these have been published by the Pali Text Society. The earliest of these books may date from the second century B.C., the latest from the fifth A.D. In the present writer's opinion their fundamental consistency justifies the view that the Canon at least is a reliable report of what had actually been taught; he puts no trust in the kind of "higher criticism" that tries to distinguish what the Buddha "must" or "ought" to have said from what he is reported to have said. In any case they are a reliable source for the content of "Early Buddhism." Differing schools of interpretation had arisen already within a few centuries of the Founder's death; of these, the *Sautrāntikas*, as their name suggests, seem to have been the most orthodox.

The first great impetus to the spread of Buddhism in and beyond India proper was given by the renowned Emperor Asoka (272-232 B.C.), who was not only himself a practising Buddhist and famous for the rock-cut and monolithic pillar Edicts in which he both expressed his own repentance for previous wars of conquest and enjoined on his subjects the earliest practise of Buddhist ethics, but also for having dispatched Buddhist missions to more distant lands, and in particular by his son Mahinda to Ceylon, where Buddhism more or less in its earliest form has survived to the present day. Later rulers amongst the Kuṣāḥas, Guptas and others likewise supported Buddhist doctrines and institutions; but it must not be supposed therefore that there was ever a "Buddhist India" in any exclusive sense of the words or that Buddhism effected any changes in the outward forms of Indian society. The Buddhist layman is a Buddhist in faith and conduct, not by virtue of any kind of institutional revolution; just as, also, in the case of Buddhist art, which flourished from the second century B.C. onwards, there is iconographic adaptation, but no Buddhist style or technique different from that of contemporary Brahmanical or Jaina art.

Before the beginning of the Christian era the Buddhist Order was no longer one of merely itinerant monks, but one of monastic communities living in monasteries, the larger of which were at the same time universities. One of the greatest of these was that of Nālandā, well known by its remains and by the accounts of it given by the Chinese pilgrim Hsuan Tsang. In India proper, Buddhism during the Middle Ages gradually declined; surviving, after the destruction of Nālandā by the Moslems about 1200, only in Nepal, Sikhim and Bhutān. Meanwhile as a result of colonizations and of missions, Buddhism side by side with Hinduism, or sometimes therewith combined, already long established in Ceylon, spread eastwards from India to Burma, Siam, Cambodia, Malaya, Sumatra, Java and even to parts of Borneo and the Philippines, and survives to the present day in Burma, Siam, Cambodia and (with Hinduism) in Bali. As the result of royal alliances and missions Buddhism became the religion of Tibet; and mainly as a result of the visits of Chinese pilgrims to India, and partly also by the settlement of Indian teachers in China, Buddhism and Buddhist art spread throughout the Far East, China,

Korea and Japan. Practically all the Buddhist texts were accurately translated by bodies of qualified scholars, and these Tibetan and Chinese sources still retain their independent value. The total number of Buddhists in the world has been estimated at something like a fifth of the world's population.

The main divisions of Buddhism are those of the *Hīnayāna* and *Mahāyāna*, respectively the "lesser" and the "Great" Way or Vehicle; sometimes also, but rather inaccurately called "Southern" and Northern," the *Hīnayāna* having best survived in Ceylon. The scriptures of the *Hīnayāna* are in Pali, those of the *Mahāyāna* in Sanskrit. As known from existing texts, the *Mahāyāna* develops from the beginning of the Christian era onwards; and as a whole is a scholastic, metaphysical, epistemological and also theistic and devotional aspect of Buddhism. It would take more than the whole of the present article to summarize its history. The most important texts are those of the *Mahāvastu*, ostensibly, the *Vinaya* of one of the older *Hīnayāna* sects; the *Lalita Vistara*, in which the Buddha's divinity is strongly emphasized; the various *Prajñāpāramitās*, of which the famous *Vajracchedikā* ("Diamond-cutter"), which became the leading text of the *Shingon* school in Japan, is the briefest; the *Samādhirāja*; the *Suvarṇaprabhāsa*; the *Laṅkāvatāra*; the *Saddharmapuṇḍarīka* ("Lotus of the True Law"); the *Karaṇḍavyūha*, in which the doctrine of the *Ādi* Buddha is developed, and the subject of a long series of sculptures at Borobudur; and the *Amitāyurdhyāna* and many other *Sūtras*; all of these range from the 2nd to fifth centuries, and the majority exist in Tibetan and Chinese as well as Sanskrit versions. The names of the great *Mahāyāna* doctors are Nāgārjuna, Aśvaghoṣa, Aryadeva, Sāntideva, and the brothers Asanga and Vasubandhu.

II. *Doctrine and Way:* The basic and essential doctrines, ostensibly and probably stated really in the Buddha's own words, are enunciated in the *Hīnayāna* Pali Canon. The doctrine in its briefest form is one of causality (*hetuvāda*); all phenomea are parts of a beginningless causal series,—"this being so, that becomes; this not being so, that does not become." Other statements are: "Of all things causally come to be, the Buddha has told the cause"; "Whatever has had a beginning must also cease (i.e. "death is certain for all born beings")"; "Just this is what I set forth, Ill, and the ceasing of Ill"; "All things composite are transitory"; "All beings are nourished by food, all are composite."

The great importance of the principle of causality for what is really a medical diagnosis, is this, that if no cause of "Ill" (*dukkha*, the misery of existence subject to origination, change and decay) could be pointed out, no way of putting an end to this intrinsic infirmity of "life" or "becoming" (*bhava*) could be found. The cause of Ill is "Ignorance" (*avijjā*); that is, our congenital blindness to the true nature of the phenomenal world of which we are a part and to which, for so long as we do not realize its "vanity" (*suññatā*), we are bound by our "desires" (*kāma*) and "thirst" (*taṇhā*) as if to a mirage. The very notion of "possession" (*mamatā*, "mineness") is a delusion, for "it is of the very nature of all things dear and attractive to be various, that we must be bereaved of them, and to change. How, then, is it possible to 'have' them? Birth and death are not merely the first and last events of life, but of its very substance. The characteristics of life are misery (*dukkha*), transience (*anicca*), and the absence-of-any-persistent individuality (*anattā*). Ignorance is the "original sin" because of which beings are born. This does not mean that a Buddhist could wish he had never been born, or might commit suicide; birth as a human being is the supreme opportunity for making an escape from all the necessity of ever being born again.

Life as a psycho-physical process is one of combustion, requiring the continued supply of physical and mental food or fuel if its feverish heat is to be maintained; the fires are those of passion, malice, and delusion (*ragā*, *dosa*, *moha*). But if their fuel is withheld by detachment from all pursuits, the fires no longer "draw" (breath); and the result of that "despiration" (*Nirvana*) is precisely that reduction of temperature and state of nonchalance on which all true and stable happiness depends; we find, accordingly, the words *nibbuto* (despirated) and *sītibhūto* (cooled) in constant apposition. The word *Nirvana* (Pali *nibbāna*) itself has led, perhaps, to more misunderstandings than any other Buddhist term. Certainly, it implies a "death" of some sort: the fire is "quenched" and "goes out." But if we are to avoid the great error involved in any rendering of *Nirvana* by such words as "annihilation" (which would be to beg the whole question of the meaning of the Buddhist "immortality," and contrary to the Buddha's express repudiation of all "annihilationist" heresies) it must be observed that the reference of *Nirvana* (or *Parinirvana*) to physiological death is only a special case of its general meaning; the common references are to the *completion* of stages in a continued life,—each of the transformations of which involves the arrest of or death to a previous condition and a going on in some other and superior condition. For example, when first Yasodā sees Prince Siddhattha she aspires to be his wife, and refers to that *end* of her girlhood as a *Nirvana*,—not an extinction (though she will be a girl no more) but a consummation and a fulfillment; and, similarly, the successive stages in the training of a royal stallion (analogous to the training of the human individual) are referred to as so many *Parinirvanas*, which is as much as to say that the colt is dead, the steed perfected. Thus we "rise on stepping stones of our *dead* selves"; and when the word *Nirvana* is used absolutely with reference to the Great Awakening of any *Arahant*, this is merely the last step, and implies that the whole work of self-naughting has been accomplished. This is the end of all becoming and beyond all states of being; when "all has been done that there was to be done" (*katam-karaṇīyam*), and the heavy burden of existence has been dropped, there is no more a return to any conditioned existence in which to be at all one must be *so*, or *such*. This end and *summum bonum*, equally so for men and the highest of the personal gods (whom we should now call angels), is attainable either (and preferably) here and now, or at the point of death, or hereafter from whatever position in heaven one may have earned by the practice of moral or habit of intellectual virtues. For so long as the goal has not been reached there remains the possibility of an ultimate fall from even "the summit of contingent being" (*bhav' agga*).

It is often asked: What is the condition of the Buddha, or Arahant, after death? And although annihilation is expressly denied ("to say of a monk thus set free [*vimutta*] that he neither knows nor sees would be improper," D.II.68; after death, the Buddha "is," though neither here nor there, Mil.72), it is always answered that words (inasmuch as their application is only to things that have beginnings and ends) are inadequate, and that none of the phrases "is" or "is not" or "Is and is not" or "neither is nor is not" is applicable,—even in this life, indeed, a Buddha is beyond our grasp, and how much more so when the body is no more. Further discussion of what is therefore "untold" is refused. It is just because of the limitations of "logic" that there must be (as also in Christian theology) a resort to the *via negativa* even when referring to the most positive reality; for example, it can be told what liberation is *from*, but not what an absolute independence *is*. The arrest of becoming (*bhava-niroda*) is *Nirvana*; and what this implies can only be illustrated by analogies (*upamā*) such as that of "the way of a bird ion the air, leaving no track." The ultimate reality is "void" (*suñña*) of any psychic (*attanīya*) essence, and of all defects that pertain to it; hence, the "Void" is synonymous with *Nirvana*.

The great work to be done is, then, one of self-naughting; one of the eradication, root and branch, of the notion (*māna*) "I and mine,"—*denegat seipsum*. For all suffering is bound up with the concept, I am this, or that; and to have laid down this burden is a beatitude than which there can be no greater. [1] Of all the delusions that men are attached to the greatest is that of their conviction of the constancy and reality of their "name and shape" (*nāmarūpa*), Ego (*aham*), or "self" (*attā*)—Behmen's "that which thou callest 'I, or myself'"—with which the "untaught many-folk," animists (then, as now) identify themselves; and the most dangerous aspect of this belief is that of the identification of Self not with the visible body (an evident inconstant) but with the invisible "soul" of which the persistence throughout our life, and even thereafter, is

---

[1] It may make this more intelligible if we point out that the modern psychologists have asserted in almost the same words that the concept or postulate of individuality is "the very mother of illusions" and that any person would be "infinitely happier if he would accept the loss of his individual self"; "individuality and falsity are one and the same." Cf. also St. Paul's "I live, yet not I"; the O. Fr. "morir vivant"; and Islamic "Die before ye die" and "dead man walking"; Angelus Silesius' "Stirb ehe du stirbst." "How can that which is never in the same state be said to 'be' anything?" (Plato, *Cratylus* 439 E). Almost always and everywhere it has been realized that our life is a dream from which we may sooner or later *wake*.

assumed. A great part of the Buddhist teaching is therefore devoted to the destructive analysis of the postulated (*sammuta*) "self" or "soul" (*attā*) or "being" (*sattā*); and it must be clearly understood that this is no mere matter of being "unselfish" but one of a quite literal self-denial—of which "unselfishness" in the ethical sense will be only a natural consequence and symptom.

The psycho-physical "self" is a bundle of five "stems" or composite of five "elements": visible body (*rūpa, kāya*) and invisible sensibility (*vedana*), recognition (*saññā*), constructions (*sank hārā*),[1] and consciousness, discrimination or valuation (*viññāna*); or more briefly, of body with consciousness, the latter term then including the other four components which correspond to the "soul" with its contents. Whoever would not be deceived must know this composite "as become" (*yathā bhūtam*), viz. as a causally determined process of which the peculiarities exhibited at any given moment are the consequences of past events, this man So-and-so being the "inheritor" of past acts (*karma*); the composite is not "ours" because "we," who are "swallowed up in it," cannot say "let it be thus, or thus" but must take it as it is. It is demonstrated that the contents and the whole of this "self" are inconstant, never the same from one moment to another; "the life of a mortal lasts for so long as it takes one thought to succeed another"; and the analysis invariably ends with the words, "That's not mine, I'm not that, that's not my Self."

These words are a negative definition of the Self that I *am*.

Once at least the analysis is followed by the injunction, "Make the Self thy refuge, or resort" (*kareyya saraṇ' attano*, S.III.143), familiar also in the Buddha's well known saying, "Make the Self your lamp, the Self your refuge" and paralleled in the concept of a Self to be sought for as opposed to that of a self to be rid of. It is evident that the Self thus referred to cannot be equated with the unreal, composite, mortal self that was analyzed and by which we are overburdened already. It must be realized, if the Buddhist formulae are to be understood, that just as in every

---

[1] Here, the notions, postulates, beliefs, opinions and *idées fixes*—e.g. "progress"—that are the convictions of individuals or parties; but in other context, more generally any or all of the composite things that "become."

other traditional metaphysics, "there are two (selves) in us," and that the one word *attā* (Sanskrit, *ātman*) may refer to either of those "selves" according to the intention of the context; just as the one word "soul" may refer either to the fleshly "life" or the "Spirit," i.e. "Soul of the soul"; or as "self" may refer to the outer and "selfish" man or to the inner and "selfless" Man, the "Man in this man"; we have already made this distinction by printing, in accordance with a well established convention, on the one hand "self" and on the other "Self" with the capital.

Buddhist references to the Self are explicit; for example, "Self is the Lord of self, Self self's goal." The Great Self (*mah' attā*) or Fair Self is distinguished from the petty or foul self, and is the latter's judge or conscience; the two selves are at war with one another, until self has been tamed or conquered. So it is asked, "With which self (*ken' attanā*) does one reach the Brahma-world?" and to this there are variously formulated answers, e.g., "with the purified Self," "with Self made-become," "with Self Brahma-become) or (Brahmā-become," as the sense may require). The Buddha knows the Brahma-world, and all the roads that lead to it, as one who was born and bred there. But it cannot be said of the Self that it "is" or "is not," or "is and is not," or "neither is nor is not"; and here "self" is synonymous with the *Tathāgata* (Truthfinder), i.e. the Buddha.

The Way (*magga*, an old word implying the following of footprints), not indeed of the Buddha's invention, but an "Ancient Way" reopened, has been taught, but it is for everyman individually to "swelter at the task" until it has been accomplished; it is followed for the sake of what has not been, because it cannot be, taught. Until the "end of the road" has been reached, the pilgrim remains a learner (*sekho*), but having reached it, becomes an "untaught" (*asekho*), i.e. adept or expert; short of "World's End," not to be reached "by paces" but within you, there will be no escape from Ill. At this point the meaning of "Faith" emerges. Those who have not yet "heard" hold all sorts of mostly false "beliefs" (*diṭṭhi*, views), and it is only because of his *faith* in the authority of one who *has* reached the goal that a man will be led to adopt the homeless life of the *peregrin* for the sake of an end as yet unseen; only if we believe in the credibility of a witness do we act accordingly, especially if the action demands a great renunciation. On the other hand, if the adept, who has actually reached the goal, is no longer "faithful," no longer a disciple "walking by faith"; "gnosis (*ñāṇam*) is better than faith."[1]

The practice of virtues, notability of generosity, by the householder leads to rebirth in the happy heaven worlds, not of itself to liberation; the household life at best is a "dusty path," involved in worldly cares. The Way taught by the Buddha and that, by a variety of images, leads overland to World's End, or overseas to the Farther Shore, or upstream to its Source, or downstream to the Sea in which the rivers "lose their names and definition," or in any case to the attainment of higher and higher conditions of existence and at last (whether now or hereafter) to an end beyond all conditions, is the life of "Walking with God" (*brahma-cariya* or *dhamma-cariya*) to which the Buddhist monk commits himself under a Master. The monastic discipline regarded as a training in self-control by Self is a life of purification (*sujjhana*,—katharsis, *via purgativa*) from all that is not-Self, and especially from all those foul issues or fluxes (*āsava*) by which Self is outwardly contaminated. The following of the Way, in addition to the avoidance of all worldly attachment and all incontinence, sexual or other, requires a practice of the virtues ordinarily demanded by any monastic rule of moderate severity. But the procedure is by no means only negative; it is one at the same time of ethical and intellectual development; i.e. in Buddhist terms, one of the "fostering" or "making become" (*bhāvanā*) of desirable qualities, the work of self naughting coinciding with that of the "making-become" of the Self, one whose self has been "cast off" (*atta-jaho*) being equally one whose Self has been "made-become" (*bhāvit' atto*). This "making become" is a deliberate and controlled procedure, to be sharply distinguished from the unregulated "becoming" that is characteristic of any mere existence and from which a deliverance is sought. "Making become" is essentially a way of contemplative practice (*jhāna*, Sanskrit *dhyāna*, becoming in Chinese *ch' an*, and in Japanese *zen*),—ethical and intellectual, because in fact liberation has these

[1] "Habent illa duo certam veritatem: sed fides clausam et involutam, intelligentia nudam manifestam": St Bernard on *Consideration*, V.3.6.

two logically distinct aspects, and should be realized in both ways, that is to say as regards the will (*ceto-vimutti*) and as regards the understanding (*paññā-vimutti*).

The ethical contemplation consists in the practice of the four *brahma-vihāras* or "godly states,"—a willed pervasion of the entire universe and an extension to all living beings whatever and wherever of feelings of love, sympathy, tenderness and impartiality,—desiring, "May every living thing become a beatified Self" (*sukhit' attā*). Needless to say that this devotion includes the love of one's enemies; against whom, whatever the provocation, no monk may feel anger. The practice of the "godly states" is a purification of the heart and establishes the habit of perfect clarity.

On the other hand, the contemplations (*jhāna*), four in which an objective image persists and four "without image," are attainments of degrees or stations of consciousness (*viññāna*) in the hierarchy of states of being beyond that in which the practitioner normally functions; synthesis (*samādhi*) being a state of unified consummation reached on any one of these levels. The states of contemplation are analogous to the stations of "mystic experience," but differ in this respect, that the contemplative (*jhāyī, dhīra, yogī*) is only considered proficient (*kusala*) when he is able to reach, remain in or abandon any one of them and to pass from one to another in either direction *at will*. Each degree of this ladder is a liberation of its kind, but all, with their respective advantages and disadvantages, come short of the final goal by the very fact of their relativity; no Comprehensor would wish to remain in any one of these states for ever. Miraculous powers (*iddhi*) such as that of walking on water or passing through solid obstacles are accidental results of contemplative practice, but are not to be sought for their own sake, nor may they be publicly exhibited.

There are also what may be called mediations, or rather "recollections" (*satī*) than contemplations. In the "recollection of death" (*maraṇasatī*—"memento mori"), practised sometimes in the presence of a decaying body, one pays attention to the liability of all things and all men to change and decay and on the inexpressible brevity of life under any conditions. In the "recollection of former births" (*jāti-sara*), which at the same time is a recollection of past aeons (*kappa*), one recovers to the degree of one's ability (possessed absolutely only by a Buddha) the memory of all stages of the long road that has been travelled in past aeons and in the course of which more tears have been shed than would fill the sea. This recollection introduces us to the difficult subject of "reincarnation," and here it must be made very clear, what has been recognized by many scholars but has been rarely understood, that Buddhism knows nothing of a "reincarnation" in the presently accepted sense of the rebirth of an identical "soul" in another body on earth; explicitly, "there is no being (*sattā*) that passes over from one body to another as a man might leave one village and enter another." What takes place is the reintegration of a consciousness (*viññāna*) under conditions predetermined by past actions (*karma*), which are only to be regarded as those *of* the new consciousness in the sense of possession by inheritance. What is transmitted and regenerated is aptly symbolized by the lighting of one fire from another; what is renewed is not an entity but a process. The ignoramus thinks, "*I* was in the past, am now, and shall be in the future"; but in reality the "former habitations" that one remembers were no more than one's present encienté anything but the five-fold aggregate "that I am not, nor is it mine"; and no enlightened monk would be so foolish as to say that "in time past I was So-and-so, or am now, or shall be So-and-so." The expressions "I" and "my," and "a being" (*satta*) are merely *conventions* and *façons de parler*, permissibly used by a Buddha or any enlightened monk in everyday life for practical purposes, but are not to be taken for assertions of a corresponding reality. There is, thus, a clearly realized distinction of pragmatic (*sammuti, vohāra*) from absolute (*paramattha*) truth, of which the latter alone is really valid, "one, without a second." A man of knowledge "does not worry about what is unreal" (*asati na socati*); —i.e. "himself," or anything else that "is not my Self."

One further point respecting the realization of the saint's intrinsic "purity," of which the familiar *exemplum* is the old likeness of the smooth lotus-leaf that is not wetted by the water it grows in and rests upon: in the same way Freedman (*vimutto*) is uncontaminated by human qualities, i.e. by any of the contraries on which experience rests and between which our ethical choices are made; he knows neither likes or dislikes, and is as little stained by virtue as by vice. The making of choices as between good and evil is an absolutely indispensable means of procedure, but of no more use to one who has arrived than a boat to one who has "crossed over" and is now safe ashore; all attachment, whether to vice or virtue, is a barrier to the taking of the last step.

As the Buddha often points out, he teaches his Law (*dhamma*) always in terms of the mean (*majjhe*), avoiding both extremes (*antā*); refusing to say, for example, of things, that they "are" or "are not" or of apparent identity that it remains in the sequence of cause and effect "the same" or "not the same"; so much depends on what we mean by "is" and what by "same." The most interesting application of the principle of the "Middle Way" is to time: the moment without duration that separates past from future embracing the whole of any existence, which is no longer the same but another as the flux of the moments continues without a break. The moment (*khaṇa*, "glance") remains the same; it is we who change. Eternity is not in time, but now; it follows that this indivisible now is man's ever-present opportunity, that gateway of immortality that the Buddha "threw open" by his "Turning of the Wheel of the Law" (*dhamma-*, or sometimes *brahma-cakka*), and at which the disciple "stands knocking."

The *Mahāyāna* is often sharply contrasted with the *Hinayāna*; but in the present writer's view the *Mahāyāna* represents a perfectly orthodox and by no means "degenerate" expansion of doctrines already enunciated in the Canon; those, for example, of the Middle Way, the Void, the Moment, and that of the distinction of pragmatic from ultimate truth; there is little difference between Buddhaghosa's canonical position in the fifth century and that of the *Sūnyavadins* or *Mādhyamikas*. The difficulties inherent in the *Mahāyāna* dialectic arise from the universally recognized truth, that *Trasumanar significar* per verba *non si poria*; all the discussions of actions without an agent, knowledge without a knower, and impossibility of the knower knowing himself (as the finger cannot touch itself) revert to this. In the end, one becomes aware of the impossibility of *knowing* anything,—objects, because they never stop to be, our own reality, because this is not an object. Relative knowledge of the "facts of experience" in terms of subject and object—implied by the "consciousness" that in the parable of the raft is indispensable as means but of no further use when the end has been reached—is bound up with and appropriate to the existential nature that presupposes it; but it is a veritable ignorance when envisaged in the light of absolute understanding (*pañña*) that is not derived from objects perceived. *This* knowledge is not *of* the Suchness or Truth (*tathatā*) but *is* the Truth. As such the Truth, already synonymous with "Buddha," "Dharma," "Brahma," is all-inclusive, the infinite not other than the *finite*, and this is the sense of the famous aphorism, "*Samsara* and *Nirvana* are one and the same." That the relative is thus never really out of touch with the absolute at the same time leaves room for the cult of images and relics as supports of contemplation and for the concept of Buddha's compassion or grace (*karuṇa*). It would be an error to realize *only* the transitoriness of the existent, or *only* the timelessness of *Nirvana*; negation and affirmation are both no more partial than partial truths, between which the Middle Way is one of silence. One who has reached the end holds no views, "in him there is no assumption, and no rejection"; this had already been enunciated in the Canon. One learns to think of "oneself" and other "things" in terms of process; and having outgrown a belief in their positive entity, understands also that it cannot be said that they have no existence whatever; and when at last the problem "is" or "is not" no longer presents itself, and can no longer be asked, there remains no distinction of the resultant gnosis from the residual gnostic; this is the Buddhist "peace that passeth understanding."

III. *Buddhology:* Who was the Buddha? In a statistical sense, the question is meaningless: "useless," as he himself says, "to ask my name or parentage,—I wander in the world a nameless no-body." This represents a "return,"—if we bear in mind that according to the old doctrine of which the Buddhist teachings are only a new version, "this one who is neither born nor dies, the eternal, hath not come anywhere nor become anyone." Asked from another point of view (as in the *Upanishads*, "Which is the Self?"), the question, Who? can only be answered in terms of the impersonal epithets that must be many if only because there are so many points of view from which That can be regarded. Amongst all these, very many are the old names that were those of *Agni* or the Sun in the Vedic tradition; and it must not be overlooked that the name of the future Buddha, *Metteya*, itself implies a "scion of Mitra", i.e. of the Sun or Fire, that "Eye in the World" that is one of the Buddha's well known designations. Amongst the names that he shares with the great Brahmanical divinities are those of Supreme Person, Great Hero, Dispenser, Physician, Charioteer, and God of gods; in his own words, he is freed from all those conditions that might make him a god (angel), spirit, daimon, or human being, one amongst others; he is a Buddha, and as such out of all categories; just as all others "gone home" can no longer be accounted for.

However, the most significant of the terms in which the Buddha is referred to are those of *dhamma-bhūto* and *brahma-bhūto*, "become the Eternal Law" and "become Brahma," which occur repeatedly in apposition. The Buddha says of himself that "He who sees me sees the Eternal Law, and he who sees the Eternal Law sees me"; and he refers to himself and is referred to as "He whose name is Truth" (*saccam*). Now, for the essentially Brahmanical audiences to whom the Buddha preached (and we must put ourselves in *their* position if we want to understand him who always preached *ad hominem*) these principal names had all along been those of one and the same essence, an essence, moreover, identical with that of the immanent Self in all beings. That the Buddha himself is this Self, that his is the very nature that should be served (*bhatti*, Sanskrit *bhakti*) and made-become within you is suggested by the appellations *Vissantara* and *Vessantara*; and it is more than once asserted that "the wakened Self is the Wake" (*buddh' attā yeva buddho ti*). Buddhahood, then, represents a potential goal finally attainable by anyone who takes upon himself the vows of a *Bodhisatta* and fulfills them. In some cases a *Bodhisatta's* final release may be delayed by the very nature of his resolve to function as a Savior "until the last blade of grass shall have been set free."

The universality of the Buddha-nature is explicit in the *Mahāyāna*, where also in the elaborated pantheon we find the conception of an *Ādi* (primal) Buddha, of whom all other

Buddhas ("human" or "contemplative") and *Bodhisattvas* are the diversified manifestations, while the *Tārās* (feminine Saviors) who are their consorts represent their "Wisdom" and correspond in all their forms, notably in that of the supreme *Prajñāpāramitā*, to the Christian *Sophia*.

In the epithet "Brahma-become," *brahma*- is grammatically ambiguous, but in apposition to *buddha*, and in many expressions synonymous with *dhamma*-, cannot be understood to mean Brahmā, the supreme *personal* deity of the age. For not only has the Buddha already in former births, before he was a Buddha, been a Brahmā or Mahābrahmā, but, great as the glory and long as the life of a Brahmā may be, it is repeatedly emphasized that the knowledge and understanding of even a Brahmā are very limited if compared to those of a Buddha; the Buddha is a teacher of Brahmās, not they his; and he is explicitly "far more than a Mahābrahmā." It is emphasized that merely to have reached the empyrean Brahma-worlds, however great a reward, is not the "final escape"; in former lives, as a *Bodhisatta*, the Buddha had taught only the Way to these worlds, but as a Buddha, "Brahma-become" himself, he knew and taught the way of the final escape from all circumstantial existence in any mode, whether human or divine.

IV. *Cosmogony*: The scheme of the succession of cycles is not only of great intrinsic interest, but is to be envisaged as the tremendous background against which the whole drama of liberation is enacted. "There are these four incalculable aeons (*kappa*): those of involution, state of involution, evolution, and state of evolution." These all together make a Great Aeon (*mahākappa*); our world, having long ago evolved, is now in a cycle of involution, i.e. dissolution, and will finally be destroyed either by fire, water or wind; such destructions extend as far as to the Brahma-worlds, in which all living beings remain latent until the evolution of worlds begins again from the highest level affected by the dissolution; then beings descend from the *Ābhassara* to the lower Brahma-worlds, and in due course to lower and lower realms as these appear in descending order of progressive materialization. This whole beginningless process constitutes the "conflux" (*saṁsāra*) or cycle of becoming (*bhava-cakka*) of which the Buddha is omniscient and from which he teaches the way of escape; the Freedman (*vipamutto*), *Arahant*, "transcends the aeons"; the Eternal Law with which the Buddha identifies himself as "intemporal."

v. *In conclusion*: Some of the greatest European "mystics" have asserted that "God is properly called 'Nothing' " (*nihil*): Meister Eckhart speaks of the freedom of the Godhead "in its nonexistence." It would be difficult to distinguish this "nihilism" (which is only another aspect of the Scholastic "realism") from the Buddhist "nihilism" that equates *Nirvana* with the "Void" and at the same time asserts that this "unborn, unmade, unbecome, incomposite *is*, and were it not, there would be no way to escape from the born, the made, the become and composite." In other words, the "Vacancy" into which the Freedman escapes is "empty" not by privation inasmuch as it does not contain any of those "things" that are themselves privations and of which the veritable non-entity has been realized by the Freedman who now "transcends the aeons"; the "rest" and "peace" that are synonymous with *Nirvana* and beyond our understanding are, literally, man's holy day and *vacation*, open here and now to anyone whose work of self-naughting has been perfected, or if not now, then hereafter, when the task has been completed, and all potentiality has been reduced to act (*kata-karaṇīyam*).

Buddhaghosa can say that *Nirvana* is a passing away or destruction (*khaya*) :

> For there is Ill, but none to feel it ;
> For there is action, but no agent ;
> And there is peace, but none enjoys it ;
> A way there is, but wayman none

but he is equally careful to say, and equally orthodox in saying, that there is no passing away or destruction of anything but of passions, defects, and all possible delusions. As Meister Eckhart says, "Behold the soul divorced from every aught," or, again,

xxxii

"The soul must put itself to death." These are "hard sayings"; but it must be realized that such a "mystical theology" as this, like that of Dionysius, cannot be grasped apart from the "ascetic theology" that it involves. The Way is "for those whose wants are few," and only for them. The Forerunner asks us to abandon all our "great possessions," material and mental goods, vices and virtues together, to follow him to an end of the road beyond all values whatever, to the realization of an Eternal Worth that is not a value, but on which all values depend. The Buddha might have said with Meister Eckhart that "What the tyro fears is the expert's delight."

FOREWORD BIBLIOGRAPHY

Most valuable are the texts and translations published by the Pali Text Society, together with *The Sacred Books of the Buddhists* published by the Oxford University Press. Mrs. Rhys Davids' many books on Buddhism are of high value but must be read with reservations. Amongst other works available in English may be cited: Vols. X, XI, XIII, XVII, XIX, XX, XXI, XXXV, XXXVI, XLIX of the *Sacred Books of the East* (Oxford); Vols. 3, 28-30 and 37 in the *Harvard Oriental Series*; E. B. Cowell, ed., *The Jātaka* (Cambridge, England, 1895-1907); E. H. Johnston, *The Buddhacarita* (Calcutta, 1935-6); and The *Saundarānanda* (Oxford, 1928, 1932); E. W. Burlingame, *Buddhist Parables* (New Haven and Oxford, 1922); E. Foucaux, *Le Lalita Vistatara* (Fr. tr.), (Paris, 1884, 1892).

I. B. HORNER, *The Early Buddhist Theory of Man Perfected* (London, 1936).

A. K. COOMARASWAMY, *Hinduism and Buddhism* (New York, n.d.).

A. B. Keith, *Buddhist Philosophy* (Oxford, 1923),—best for the Mahayana.

I. BABBITT, *The Dhammapada . . . with an Essay on Buddha and the Occident* (Oxford and New York, 1936).

SIR C. N. E. ELIOT, *Hinduism and Buddhism* (London, 1921).

J. LEGGE, *A Record of Buddhistic Kingdoms . . . by Fâ-Hien* (Oxford, 1886).

J. Beal, *Life of Hiuen-Tsang by Hwui Li* (London, n.d.), and *Buddhist Records of the Western World . . . Si-Yu-Ki of Hiuen Tsang* (London, n.d.).

D. T. Suzuki, *Açvaghosa's Discourse on the Awakening of Faith in the Mahāyāna* (Chicago, 1900); *Outlines of Mahāyāna Buddhism* (London, 1907).

_____, *The Lankāvatara Sūtra* (London, 1932).

_____, *Studies in the Lankāvatara Sūtra*, London, (1930).

_____, *Essays in Zen Buddhism* (London and Kyoto, 1928-1934).

W. Gemmell, *The Diamond Sutra* (London and New York, 1913).

L. D. Barnett, *The Path of Light . . . Bodhicharyāvatāra of Sānti-Deva* (London, 1909).

Bendall, *Cikṣāsamuccaya of Cāntideva* (Petrograd, 1902).

_____, *Buddhist Texts from Japan* (Oxford, 1881).

E. H. McGovern, *A Manual of Buddhist Philosophy, I. Cosmology* (New York and London, 1923).

L. de la Vallée Poussin, *The Way to Nirvāna* (Cambridge, Eng., 1917), and (in French) *L'Abhidharmakosa of Vasubandhu.*

Th. Stcherbatsky, *Buddhist Logic* (Leningrad, 1932). (Paris and Louvain, 1923-1931).

G. Tucci, *Indio-Tibetica* (Rome, 1932-1941).

Marco Pallis, *Peaks and Lamas* (London and New York, 19— etc.)

W. Y. Evans Wentz, *Tibetan Yoga and Secret Doctrines* (Oxford, 1935).

J. Bacot and H. I. Woolf, *Three Tibetan Mysteries* (London and New York, n.d.).

Lama Yongden, *Mipam* (London, 1938).

LIFE OF THE BUDDHA

Reduce to meekness the wild motions of the will, and make it thy care to tame the cruel beast. Thou art bound to the will ; strive to unfasten the bond that cannot be broken. The will is thy Eve.

St Bonaventura, *De conversione.*

THE STORY OF THE BUDDHA'S LIFE IS WELL KNOWN AND need be only briefly summarized ; its span of eighty years covers the greater part of the fifth century B.C., but the exact dates of his birth and death are uncertain. Prince Siddhattha, the only son of king Suddhodana of the Sākiya clan and of his queen Mahā Māyā, was born at Kapilavatthu, the capital city of Kosala, a district extending from southern Nepal to the Ganges. In saying " king " (*rājā*) it must not be overlooked that most of the " kingdoms " of the Ganges Valley at this time were really republics over which the " kings " presided ; the procedure followed in the Buddhist monastic convocations corresponded to that of the republican assemblies and to that of the trade guilds and village councils.

Until the Great Awakening Siddhattha is still a Bodhisatta, although this is the last of the countless births in which he had already developed those supreme virtues and insights that lead to perfection. As a Buddha, the " Wake " is sometimes referred to by his family name of Gotama or Gautama, and this serves to distinguish him from the seven (or twenty-four) previous Buddhas of whom he was more truly the lineal descendant. Many of the Buddha's epithets connect him with the Sun or Fire, and imply his divinity : he is, for example, " the Eye in the World," his name is " Truth," and amongst the most characteristic synonyms of *Buddha* (the " Wake ") are the expressions " Brahma-become " and " Dhamma-become." Many of the details of his life are direct reflections of older myths. These considerations raise the question, whether the " life " of the " Conqueror of Death " and " Teacher of Gods and men," who says that he was born and bred in the Brahma-world and who descended from heaven to take birth in Mahā Māyā's womb, can be regarded as historical or simply as a

I

myth in which the nature and acts of the Vedic deities Agni and Indra have been more or less plausibly euhemerized. There are no contemporary records, but it is certain that in the third century B.C. it was believed that the Buddha had lived as a man amongst men. It is not proposed to discuss the problem here, and, although the writer is inclined to the mythical interpretation, references will be made to the Buddha as if to a historical person.

Prince Siddhattha was brought up in luxury at the court in Kapilavatthu and kept in total ignorance of the old age, sickness and death to which all mundane beings are naturally subject. He was married to his cousin Yasodā, and had by her an only son, Rāhula. Soon after Rāhula's birth it was realized by the Gods that the time had come for Siddhattha to " go forth " and take up the mission for which he had prepared himself in many previous births that he had for the present forgotten. Orders had been given that whenever he rode out through the city from the palace to the pleasure park, none sick or aged and no funeral procession might appear in public. So man proposed, but the Gods, assuming the forms of a sick man, an old man, a corpse, and a religious Mendicant (*bhikkhu*), appeared. When Siddhattha saw these, to him strange sights, and learnt from his charioteer, Channa, that all men are liable to sickness, old age and death, and that only the religious Mendicant rises superior to the distress which suffering and death occasion in others, he was deeply moved. Straightway he resolved to seek and find a remedy for the mortality that is inherent in all composite things, in all that has had a beginning and must therefore come to an end. He resolved, in other words, to discover the secret of immortality, and to make it known to the world.

Returning home, he informed his father of this determination. When he could not be dissuaded, the king set guards at all the palace gates, and endeavoured to keep his son and heir at home by force. But at night, after taking a last look at his sleeping wife and child, he summoned his charioteer and, mounting his stallion Kanthaka, came to the gates, which were silently opened for him by the Gods, and so rode away. This was the " Great Going Forth."

In the deep forests the prince cut off his royal turban and long hair, unsuitable to a religious Mendicant, and dismissed his charioteer. He met with Brahman hermits, under whose guidance he led the life of a contemplative. Then, leaving them, he devoted himself alone to the "Great Effort"; at the same time a company of five Mendicants became his disciples, and served him, in the expectation that he would become a Buddha. To this end he now practised far more severe mortifications, and brought himself to the very verge of death by starvation. Realizing, however, that the consequent weakening of his bodily and mental powers would not lead to the Awakening (*bodhi*) for the sake of which he had abandoned the worldly life, he again took up his bowl and begged his food in villages and towns like other Mendicants. At this, the five disciples abandoned him. But the time for his Awakening had come, and from his dreams the Bodhisatta drew the conclusion, "This very day I shall become a Buddha." He ate food into which the Gods had infused ambrosia, and rested during the day. When evening came, he approached the Bodhi tree, and there, at Earth's centre, with his face to the East, he took his seat, where every former Buddha had been seated at the time of his Enlightenment; immovable, he determined so to remain until he had realized his purpose.

Then Māra (Death)—the old Vedic Ahi-Vṛtra-Namuci, "Holdfast," overcome in the past by Agni-Bṛhaspati and Indra, but never really slain—perceiving that "the Bodhisatta wants to liberate himself from my dominion," would not let him go, and led his armies against him. The Gods were terrified and fled in alarm; the Bodhisatta sat there alone, with only his own transcendent virtues for bodyguard. Māra's assault with weapons of thunder and lightning, darkness, flood, and fire, and all the temptations presented by Māra's three beautiful daughters, left the Bodhisatta literally unaffected and unmoved. Māra, unable to recover the throne to which he had laid claim, could only retire. The Gods returned, and celebrated the prince's victory; and so night fell.

Entering into ever deeper states of contemplation the Bodhisatta obtained successively the Knowledge of Former Births, Divine Insight, the Understanding of Causal Origination, and finally, at dawn, the Full Enlightenment or "Awakening" (*sammā-sambodhi*) that he had been seeking, and so, ceasing to be a Bodhisatta, became a Buddha, the "Wake." A Buddha is no longer in a category, but inconnumerable; no longer "this man So-and-so," no longer anyone, but one whose proper name it would be in vain to ask, and to whom are appropriate only such epithets as *Arahant* (" Worthy "), *Tathāgata* (" True-come "), *Bhagavā* (" Dispenser "), *Mahāpurisa* (" Great Citizen "), *Saccanāma* (" He whose Name is Truth "), and *Anoma* (" Un-fathomable "), none of which is the designation of an individual. The explicit synonyms " Dhamma-become " and " Brahma-become " are particularly noteworthy ; for the Buddha expressly identifies himself with the Eternal Law (*dhamma*) that he embodies, and the expression " Brahma-become " must be taken to imply an absolute theosis, if only because the Buddha had been a Brahmā and Mahā Brahmā already in previous births and because in any case the gnosis of a Brahmā is inferior to that of a Buddha. Here and now in the world the Buddha had attained that Liberty (*vimutti*), Despiration (*nibbāna* = *nirvāṇa*), and Immortality (*amatam*), the Way to which he would henceforth proclaim to all men.

But now he hesitated, knowing that the Eternal Law of which he had become the bearer, and with which he identified himself, would be hard indeed for other-minded and worldly men to understand ; he was tempted to remain a Solitary Buddha, enjoying by himself the hard-earned fruits of an age-long quest of which the goal had been reached at last. If we are to form any conception of the Buddhist Nibbāna it will be almost indispensable for us to understand the quality of this " enjoy-ment " ; it was " the supreme beatitude of one who had rejected the notion ' I am ' " ; of one who had utterly " denied himself," and so " laid down his burden." This was Māra's last and subtlest temptation : that it would be folly to abandon this hard-won felicity and to return to ordinary life in order to preach a Way to men who would neither hear nor under-stand. But at the Buddha's hesitation the Gods despaired ; and their highest, Brahmā Sahampati, appeared before him, lamenting that " The world is lost ! " and pleading that there were in the world at least some people of comparatively clear vision who would hear and understand his teaching. For their sake the Buddha consented, announcing that " the Doors of Immortality are open." Accordingly, he set out to spend the remaining forty-five years of his natural life in " Turning the Wheel of the Law," that is to say, in the preaching of the liberating Truth and of the Way that must be followed if

the ultimate purpose and meaning of life (" man's last end ") is
to be attained.

The Buddha went first to the Deer Park in Benares, to the
five who had been his first followers. He preached to them the
doctrine of the Middle Way between the two extremes of self-
indulgence and self-mortification : that of the liability to
suffering that is in all born beings, the cause of which—appetitive
desire (based on ignorance of the true nature of all desirable
things)—must be eradicated if the symptom is to be cured ;
and that of the " Walk with Brahma " which leads to the end
of sorrow. Finally he taught them the doctrine of the liberation
resulting from full comprehension and experience of the
proposition that of one and all of the constituents of the mutable
psycho-physical individuality that men call *I* or *myself* it must
be said, " that is not my Self" (*na me so attā*)—a proposition
that has very often, despite the logic of the words, been mistaken
to mean that " there is no Self." The five Mendicants obtained
Enlightenment, and there were now six Arahants in the world.
When the number of Arahants, " freed from all bonds, human
and divine," had risen to sixty-one, the Buddha sent them forth
to preach the Eternal Law and the Walk with Brahma, and
empowered them to receive and ordain others ; so there came
into being the Buddhist congregation (*saṅgha*) or order of
Mendicants, composed of men who had abandoned [1] the household life and " taken refuge in the Buddha, the Eternal Law,
and the Community."

On his way from Benares to Uruvelā the Buddha fell in with
a party of young men picnicking with their wives. One of
them, being unmarried, had brought with him his mistress ;
but she had run off with some of the young men's belongings.
They were all looking for her, and asked the Buddha if he had
seen her. The Buddha replied : " What think ye ? Were it
not better ye sought the Self (*attānaṁ gaveseyyātha*), rather than
the woman ? " (*Vin.* i. 23, cf. *Vis.* 393). This answer, accepted
by the young men, who subsequently become the master's
disciples, is of the utmost significance for our understanding
of the Buddhist doctrine of self-denial. We find the very

---

[1] This abandonment is literally a going into exile (*pabbajjā*) : the Buddhist
view being like Meister Eckhart's, that those poor souls who settle down at home
and serve God there are in error " and will never have the power to strive for
or to win what those others do who follow Christ in poverty and *exile*."

Master in whom the work of self-naughting has been accomplished recommending others to seek for the Self—an apparent contradiction that can only be resolved if we clearly distinguish between the " selves " referred to—one to be naughted, one to be cultivated.

At Uruvelā the Buddha resided for some time at the hermitage of a school of Brahmanical fire-worshippers, and performed two notable miracles : in the first he overcame and tamed the furious Serpent (ahi-nāga) that lived in their fire-temple ; and in the second, when the Brahmans could neither split their wood nor light their fires, he did these things by his supernormal powers (iddhi). The final outcome was that the Brahman master Kassapa and all of his five hundred followers decided to " Walk with Brahma " under the Buddha, and were received by him into the Order.

The Buddha then proceeded to Gayāsīsa, accompanied by all those, to the number of a thousand, who had by now become his disciples. There he preached the famous " Sermon on Fire." All sensation, all sensibilia (for example, the tongue and its tastes, the mind and its thoughts), are on fire—the fire of appetite, resentment, and delusion (rāgo, doso, moho), birth, ageing, death, and sorrow. This sermon is of particular importance for the understanding of Nibbāna (" Despiration ") in its primary sense : the " going out " of these fires which—with the empirical " individuality " (atta-sambhava) of which they are the " becoming " (bhava)—cease to " draw " when their fuel is withheld. It is also of special interest because of its very close correspondence to James iii. 6 where " the tongue is a fire . . . and setteth on fire the wheel of becoming " (ὁ τροχὸς τῆς γενέσεως) just as in the Buddhist context " the tongue is afire " (jivhā ādittā) and " life " is the " wheel of becoming " (bhava-cakka). In the New Testament context the formulae are more likely to be of Orphic than of Buddhist origin, but there may be older common sources underlying both formulations.

The Buddha went next to Rājagaha where he preached to King Bimbisāra of Magadha and an assembly of Brahmans and Householders, calling first upon Uruvelā Kassapa to explain why he had abandoned his ritual fires. Kassapa having borne witness, the Buddha preached, and the whole company obtained the " Eye for the Eternal Law," that is, they understood that " Whatever has had a beginning must also come to an end."

It must never be forgotten that this apparently simple formula, more familiar in the form,

Of whatever originates causally, the Truth-finder hath told the cause,
And of all these things the Great Ascetic hath likewise explained the cessation.

(*Vin.* i. 41, etc.)

is actually a valid epitome of the Buddha's doctrine and a sufficient means (if one is prepared to act up to all that it implies) to the attainment of Immortality and the ending of all sorrow. Its primary application is, of course, to the understanding and eradication of the causes of the " becoming " of all the mortal ills that the passible " individuality " is heir to : the passing away of appetite, resentment and delusion and consequent arrest of " becoming," are one and the same thing as Despiration and Immortality, ultimate Felicity (*S.* ii. 117, iv. 251, v. 8 ; *Sn.* 1095).

In the course of his wanderings, the Buddha returned to Kapilavatthu, his birthplace ; and accompanied by a host of Mendicant Arahants begged his food in the streets, where he was seen from the palace windows by Rāhula's mother. To his father's protests the Buddha replied that this had been the rule of all past Buddhas. Suddhodana became a lay disciple, and on his deathbed became an Arahant, without ever having abandoned the household life. In the meantime the Buddha, accompanied by his two chief disciples, Sāriputta and Moggallāna, and giving his begging bowl to the king to carry, visited Rāhula's mother. She came to him and clasped his ankles and laid her head on his feet ; and the king told him that when she had heard that her husband had taken the yellow robes, she also put on the yellow robes, and ate only once a day and followed all the rules of the Buddha's life. Rāhula's mother sent her son to his father, telling him to ask for his inheritance, he being now the heir to the throne. But the Buddha, turning to Sāriputta, said " Give him the monastic ordination," and Sāriputta did so. So Rāhula received a spiritual inheritance. But Suddhodana was deeply hurt, and said to the Buddha, " When thou didst abandon the worldly life, it was a bitter pain, and so is it now that Rāhula has done the same. The love of a son cuts into one's skin and to the very marrow. Pray grant that in future a child may not be ordained without his father's and mother's consent." To that the Buddha agreed.

In the meantime, the merchant prince Anātha Piṇḍika had become a lay disciple, and, having purchased at great price the Jetavana Park at Sāvatthi and built there a magnificent monastery, invited the Buddha to take up his residence there, and he did so, making this his headquarters for the rest of his life. The Jetavana, indeed, is a " place never abandoned by any of the Buddhas " (*DA.* 424 ; *BndvA.* 298) ; and naturally the " Fragrant Pavilion " (*gandha-kuṭi*) in which he resided there became the archetype of the later Buddhist temples in which he is represented by an icon. The Buddha was not always in actual residence ; this was simply his permanent home, and it is in this connection that the question of an iconography first arises. For the question is asked (in the *Kālingabodhi Jātaka*), by what kind of a symbol or shrine (*cetiya*) may the Buddha be properly represented, so that offerings can be made to him in his absence. His answer is that he can only be properly represented during his lifetime by a Great Wisdom Tree (*mahā-bodhi-rukkha*), and after his death by bodily relics ; he deprecates the use of " indicative," i.e. anthropomorphic, icons, calling them groundless and imaginative. It is, in fact, the case that in " early " Buddhist art the Buddha is represented only " aniconically " by his evident " traces " (*dhātu*), viz. either by a Bodhi-tree, by a " Fragrant Pavilion," by a " Wheel of the Law " (*dhamma-cakka*), by Footprints (*pada-valañja*), or by a reliquary Cairn (*thūpa*), and never by a " likeness " (*paṭimā*). When, on the other hand, probably to begin with in the first century A.D., the Buddha was represented in human form it is significant that in its most typical aspect the image is not really the likeness of a man, but reflects the old concept of the " Great Citizen " (*mahā-purisa*) or Person or Cosmic Man, and more directly repeats the established type of the image of a Yakkha—Agathos, Daimon or Tutelary Genius. This accords with the fact that the Buddha is himself " the Yakkha to whom sacrifice is due," with the doctrine of the " Yakkha's Purity," and with the whole background of the pre-Buddhist Sākyan, Licchavi and Vajjian cult of Yakkhas, whose customary service the Buddha himself had earnestly advised the Vajjians never to neglect. As a Bodhisatta he had once been mistaken for the spirit of the tree under which he was sitting ; and just as the Buddha was represented at the Jetavana and in early Buddhist art by a tree-shrine (*rukkha-cetiya*) so were the Yakkhas, at whose " temples " the Buddha was so fond of staying when on tour. All these considerations are only fully significant when we bear in mind that *the Yaksa* (Yakkha) of the Vedas and Upanishads had been originally a designation at once of Brahma as the principle of life in the Tree of Life and of the immortal Self that inhabits this human " city of Brahma " (*brahma-pura*) from which the Man as " citizen " takes his name of Purusa ; and that epithets " Wake " (*buddho*) and " Brahma-become " (*brahma-bhūto*) are recognized synonyms of Him who is also called the " Great Citizen " (*mahā-purisa*), and is at least once explicitly and often implicitly equated with the universal Self (*D*. iii. 84, *et passim*).

By this time the number of the disciples had grown enormously, and had come to consist of various bodies of Mendicants (*Bhikkhu*) or Exiles (*Pabbajita*), no longer always " wandering," but often resident in monasteries that had been presented to the community by wealthy lay adherents. Already in the Buddha's lifetime questions of discipline had arisen, and the Buddha's decisions on these points are the basis of the Rule (*vinaya*)—as regards residence, clothing, food, conduct, deportment, induction and expulsion—under which the Mendicants lived. In the community (*sangha*) as a whole were to be found a relatively small number of graduate (*asekho*) masters and a much larger number of undergraduate (*sekho*) disciples. This distinction is especially noteworthy in the case of the great disciple Ānanda, the Buddha's own first cousin, who became a mendicant at Kapilavatthu in the second year of the Buddha's predication and after twenty years was chosen to be the Buddha's personal attendant and confidant, messenger and representative and yet was unable to " graduate " until some time after the Master's decease.

Ānanda was responsible for the admission of women to the Mendicant Order. We are told that Mahā Pajāpatī, Suddhodana's second wife, and the Bodhisatta's foster-mother after Mahā Māyā's early dormition, begged for admission to the Order, but to her great sorrow was refused. She cut off her hair, assumed the orange robes of a Mendicant, and together with a following of other Sākya women again sought the Buddha ; all these women, wayworn and covered with dust, stood and waited at the door of his residence in Vesālī. Ānanda was deeply touched, and presented their case to the Master, who thrice repeated his refusal. Then Ānanda took up the problem

from another angle ; he asked, " Are women, if they abandon
the household life and live according to the doctrine and discipline
taught by the Truth-finder, *capable* of realizing the fruits of
' entering the stream,' becoming a ' once-returner,' or a ' non-
returner,' or the state of being Arahant ? " The Buddha could
not deny it ; and agreed that there should be an Order of
Bhikkhunīs, side by side with that of the Bhikkhus. But he
added that if women had not been admitted to the Order and
the practice of the Walk with Brahma, the True Law (*saddhamma*)
would have stood for a thousand years, whereas now it would
stand fast for only five hundred.

In his eightieth year the Buddha fell sick, and though he
recovered temporarily he knew that his end was near. He said
to Ānanda, " I am now old, my journey is near its end, I am
turning eighty years of age ; and just as a worn-out cart,
Ānanda, can be kept going only with the help of thongs, so,
methinks, the body of the Truth-finder can be kept going only
by medicaments." Ānanda wanted to know what instructions
the Buddha left to the Mendicants ; the Buddha replied that
if anyone thought that the community depended on him,
it was for *him* to give instructions,—" Why should *I* leave
any instructions regarding the community ? " The Truth-
finder had preached the Law in full, withholding nothing, and
all that was needed was to practise, contemplate and propagate
the Truth, in pity for the world and for the welfare of men and
Gods. The Mendicants were not to rely upon any external
support, but to make " the Self (*attā*) their refuge, the Eternal
Law their refuge "—and so, " I leave you, I depart, having
made the Self my refuge " (*D.* ii. 120).

It was at Kusinārā, in the Sāla-grove of the Mallas, that the
Buddha lay down to die, assuming the " lion's repose." A great
host of laymen, mendicants and gods of all ranks surrounded
the couch, over which Ānanda kept watch. The Buddha gave
him instructions regarding the cremation of the body and the
erection of a cairn (*thūpa, dhātu-gabbha*) to contain the bones
and ashes. At the sight of such cairns, erected for Buddhas,
other Arahants, or a King of kings, many people would be
made calm and happy, and that would lead to their resurrection
in a heaven hereafter. Ānanda wept at the thought of not yet
being a graduate. The Buddha assured him that he had done
well and would soon be " free from the fluxes," that is, become

an Arahant ; and he commended Ānanda to the company of
the Mendicants, comparing him to a King of kings.

"Corruptible are all things composite ; in sobriety work
out your goal" ; these were the Truth-finder's last words.
Entering at will into each of the four higher contemplative
"states," he emerged from the fourth, and was forthwith
wholly despirated.[1] The Truth-finder's death was announced
by Brahmā, who realized that the death of all beings whatsoever,
even that of the Great Teacher, is inevitable. The well-known
lines were repeated by Indra :

> Transient are all things composite ; theirs to originate and age,
> And having originated, to be again destroyed ; to have stilled them is beatitude.

Anuruddha, an Arahant, pronounced a brief eulogy in which
he pointed out that "there was no panting struggle for that
steadfast heart, when the Sage, the immovable, found peace."
Ānanda was profoundly moved ; only the younger Mendicants
wept and rolled on the ground in their grief, crying out that
"Too soon has the Eye in the World gone in." For this they
were blamed by the elder Mendicants, who reminded them that

> Corruptible are all composite things, how else ?

The body was cremated, and the relics, having been divided
into eight parts, were distributed to the clansmen, who erected
eight monuments to contain them.

Thus the Buddha, who for so long as he was visible to human
eyes had possessed but could not be identified with all or any
of the five factors of personality (S. iii. 112), "burst the vestment
of selfhood" (A. iv. 312 ; cf. Vin. i. 6). He had long since
been an Immortal (M. i. 172 ; Vin. i. 9 ; It. 46, 62), unborn,
unageing, undying (KhA. 180 ; DhA. i. 228). "The body ages,
but the True Law does not age" (S. i. 71). "The body dies,
the Name survives" (S. i. 43, cf. RV. vi. 18, 7 ; BU. iii. 2, 12).
"His Name is Truth" (A. iii. 346, iv. 289). "Truth is the
Eternal Law" (S. i. 169) ; and even now it can be said that
"he who sees the Law sees Him (S. iii. 120 ; Mil. 73) by whom
the Doors of Immortality were opened" (M. i. 167 ; Vin. i. 7).

Let us now ask what was that Law and Truth with which he
identified his essence.

---

[1] Parinibbāyati ; here in the sense "died," although not often used in this
physical context.

THE BUDDHIST DOCTRINE

Then only will you see it, when you cannot speak of it : for the knowledge of it is deep silence, and suppression of all the senses.

Hermes Trismegistus, *Lib.* X. 5

TO CONVEY AN ADEQUATE IDEA OF THE CONTENT OF EARLY Buddhist doctrine presents almost insuperable difficulties. The Buddha already describes the Eternal Law (*dhamma sanantana, akālika*)—which he had by no means excogitated by a process of ratiocination, but with which he identifies himself, and which had been taught by his predecessors in ages past as it would be taught by his successors in ages to come—as a matter profound and difficult of comprehension by otherwise-trained and other-minded hearers ; it is a doctrine for those whose wants are few, not for those whose wants are many. In his own lifetime the Buddha repeatedly found it necessary to correct the misinterpretations of his teaching—to explain, for example, in what precise sense his was and was not a doctrine of " excision " : *was*, in the sense of " cutting out " self-love and evil or sorrow ; and *was not*, in the sense of the annihilation of any reality. His was, indeed, a doctrine of self-naughting,— whoever would be free must have literally *denied* himself ; for what remains, the terms of logic—either-or—are inadequate ; but it would be altogether inappropriate to say of the despirated Arahant, liberated by his super-gnosis, that " he neither knows nor sees " (*D.* ii. 68).

If misunderstanding was possible in the Buddha's own time when, as he says, the Ancient Way that he reopens had been long neglected and a false doctrine had arisen, how much more is misinterpretation inevitable in our day of progress, self-expression and the endless pursuits of higher material standards of living ? It has been almost completely forgotten, except by professional theologians, that an ultimate reality can be correctly described only by a series of negations of all that it is not. In any case, as Miss Horner remarked as recently as 1938, " the study of early Buddhism is admittedly still in its infancy " (*Bk. of the Discipline*, 1, vi). If the reader thinks of Buddhism, quite rightly, as a way of " escape," he has still to ask himself from what, of what, and to what " there *is* in the world a way of escape " (*S.* i. 128).

The difficulties have been intensified by the misinterpretations of Buddhism that are still to be found even in the works of scholars. For example, one of the most notable scholars fails completely to distinguish the " becoming " of which the cessation coincides with the realization of immortality from the " making become " of our immortal part. Actually, " becoming " corresponds to what is now called " progress," regardless of the fact that change may be for better or for worse ; and we are reminded that now, as then, " there are Gods and men who delight in becoming, and when they hear of putting a stop to becoming, their minds do not respond " (*Vism.* 594). Another great scholar asserts that early Buddhism " denied a God, denied a Soul, denied Eternity," and it is almost universally claimed that the Buddha taught that there is no Self,—thus ignoring that what is actually denied is the reality of the mutable Ego or psycho-physical " individuality," and that what is said of the Self and of the Truth-finder (or Thus-come) and Perfect Man after death, is that none of the terms " becomes " or " does not become," " becomes and does not become," or " neither becomes nor does not become," apply to it or to Him (*S.* iv. 384 f., 401–402 ; *Ud.* 67, etc.). Again, it is still often asserted that Buddhism is a " pessimistic " doctrine, notwithstanding that its goal of freedom from all the mental suffering that man is heir to is one attainable here and now : in any case, over-looking that a doctrine can be judged only in terms of its truth or falsity, and not by whether we like it or not !

The Buddha is primarily concerned with the problem of evil as suffering or pain (*dukkha*) ; the problem, that is to say, of the corruptibility of all things born, composite and mutable, their liability to suffering, disease, inveteration, and death. That this liability is a fact,[1] that it has a cause, that its cause can be suppressed, and that there is a Way or Walk or Faring by which this cause can be suppressed—these are the " Four Ariyan Truths " that are the beginning of wisdom. " Both now and

---

[1] " The whole human race is so miserable and above all so blind that it is not conscious of its own miseries " (Comenius, *Labyrinth of the World and Paradise of the Heart*, C. XXVIII). It was precisely because of this blindness that the Buddha hesitated to preach the Dhamma to men whose eyes are filled with dust.

heretofore I teach just this, ill and the end of ill "[1] (*M. i.* 140). Accordingly, Buddhism can be and often is reduced to the simple formulae of "causal origination" (*paticca samuppāda*) : "this being so, that becomes ; this not being so, that does not become." From the beginningless operation of mediate causes there is no escaping any of their composite effects ; escape is possible only from the field in which the causal efficacy of past actions (*kamma*) operates, and only for that which was never an integral part of the field.

Buddhist doctrine is reducible to a statement of the law of causality because of the pertinence of this law to the problem of mutability and corruptibility ; if the cause of misery can be suppressed there will be no further need to bother with its symptoms. In the cycle or vortex of becoming (*bhava-cakka, saṁsāra*) the instability, inveteration, and death of whatever has had a beginning is inevitable ; life or becoming is a function of sensibility, sensibility of wanting (*taṇhā*, thirst), and wanting a function of ignorance (*avijjā = moha*, delusion). Ignorance, the ultimate origin of all suffering and bondage, all pathological states of subjection to pleasure and pain,[2] is of the true nature of things "as become" (*yathā-bhūtam*), and in particular of their inconstancy (*aniccam*). Everything becomes, everything flows like a river ; there is nothing of which it can be said that it *is* (*sabbe saṁkhārā aniccā*). All that becomes is mortal ; to have put a stop to becoming, no longer to be moved, is to be immortal. This intimately concerns ourselves ; the most dangerous aspect of ignorance—the "*original* sin"—is that which leads us to believe that we "ourselves" *are* this or that and that we can survive from moment to moment, day to day or life to life as an identity.

Buddhism, then, knows of no "reincarnation" in the popular and animistic sense of the word : though many are "still under the delusion that Buddhism teaches the transmigration of souls" (*SBE.* xxxvi. 142 ; *Dialogues,* ii. 43). Just as for Plato, St Augustine, and Meister Eckhart, so here, all change is a sequence of death and rebirth in continuity without identity, and there is no constant entity (*satto*) that can be thought of as passing over from one embodiment to another (*Mil.* 72) as a

---

[1] Taught as early as in the First Utterance.
[2] "Ignorance" is subjection to pleasure and pain . . . "yielding to oneself". (Plato, *Protagoras,* 356, 357).

man might leave one house or village and enter another (*Pv.* iv. 3). Indeed, like that of "self," the very notion of an "entity" as applied to anything existent is merely conventional (*S.* i. 135), and there is nothing of the sort to be found in the world (*Mil.* 268). That which perishes and again arises "not without otherness" is an individuality (*nāma-rūpa*) (*Mil.* 98) or discriminating consciousness (*viññāṇa*) that inherits the former's "works" (*M.* i. 390 ; *A.* iii. 73). If the Buddha says that there are, assuredly, personal agents (*A.* iii. 337–338), this does *not*, as Mrs Rhys Davids supposed, "wipe out the doctrine of *anatta* altogether" (*GS.* iii. xiii). The Buddhist point of view is exactly the same as the Brahmanical : "'I am not the doer of anything, it is the senses that move amongst their objects,' such is the view of the bridled man, a knower of the Suchness" (*BG.* v. 8–9, xviii. 16–17). The individual is, indeed, responsible for and will inherit the consequences of his actions for so long as he thinks of "himself" as the agent ; and no one is more reprehensible than the man who says "I am not the doer" while he is still actually involved in activity (*Ud.* 45 ; *Dh.* 306 ; *Sn.* 661), and argues that it does not matter what he does, be it good or evil (*D.* i. 53). But to think that I *am* or another *is* the doer, or that I or another will reap as I have sown is to miss the point (*Ud.* 70) : there is no "I" that acts or inherits (*S.* ii. 252) ; or to speak more strictly, the question of the real existence of a personal agent is one that cannot be answered by a simple "Yes" or "No," but only according to the Middle Way, in terms of causal origination (*S.* ii. 19–20). But all these composite "entities" that originate causally are the very things that are repeatedly analysed and found to be "not my Self" ; in this ultimate sense (*paramatthikena*) a man is not the agent. It is *only* when this has been realized and verified that a man can dare deny that his actions are his own ; until then there are things *he* ought and things *he* ought not to do (*Vin.* i. 233 ; *A.* i. 62 ; *D.* i. 115).

There is nothing in the doctrine of causality (*hetuvāda*) or in that of the causal effect of actions (*kamma*) that in any way necessarily implies a "reincarnation" of souls. The doctrine of causality is common to Buddhism and Christianity, and in both is effectively the statement of a belief in the orderly sequence of events. The "reincarnation" that the Buddhist would dispense with permanently is not a matter of any one eventful death and rebirth to be expected hereafter, but the whole vertiginous process of repeatedly dying and being born again that is equally the definition of temporal existence here as a "man" and of aeviternal existence there as a "God" (one amongst others). The accomplished Arahant knows better than to ask, "What was I in the past? What am I now? What shall I be hereafter?" (S. ii. 26–27). He can say "I" for everyday practical purposes without in any way intending what the notion of I or myself implies to an animist (D. i. 202 ; S. i. 14–15). Time implies motion, and motion change of place ; in other words duration involves mutation, or becoming. Hence it is not an immortality in time or any where, but apart from time and place, that the Buddhist envisages. Stated in the pragmatic terms of everyday discourse, of which the application is only to things that have a beginning, development and end (D. ii. 63), it can be said of the Ego, " Once it was and then was not, once was not and then it was," but in terms of truth, " It was not, will not be, nor can it now be found ; it neither is nor shall be ' mine ' " (Ud. 66 ; Th. i. 180). The Buddhist vortex or wheel of becoming is nothing but St James' ὁ τροχὸς τῆς γενέσεως ; the Ego is an unreality for the Buddhist, just as it had been for Plato and Plutarch, by the very fact of its mutability. The squirrel cage revolves, but "that's not me," and there *is* a way of escape from the round.

The evil for which the Buddha sought a remedy is that of the wretchedness involved in the corruptibility of all things born, composite and inconstant. Misery, mutability, un-Self-isness [1] (dukkha, anicca, anatta) are the characteristics of all composite things, all that is not-my-Self ; and of all these things the Ego, I, self (aham, attā) is the pertinent species, since it is with man's last end that we are concerned. It is axiomatic that all existences [2] (S. ii. 101, etc.) are maintained by food, solid and mental, as fire is fed by fuel ; and in this sense the world is on

---

[1] In all traditional philosophies, in which it is axiomatic that " there are two in us," it is unavoidable to distinguish " Self" from " self" or Ego, le moi from le soi, the savant from the connoisseur. In the present context Selflessness coincides with self-isness ; to have said " unselfishness " would have been to say the opposite of what is meant,—it is only of the Self that an ontological un-self-isness, and therefore an ethical un-selfishness can be predicated. For the present we are discussing only the Ego, or self; the problem of the Self in Buddhism will be dealt with later.

[2] " Existence," as distinguished from " being," esse from essentia, γένεσις from οὐσία.

fire and we are on fire. The fires of the Ego-consciousness, or self-isness, are those of appetite (*rāga = kāma, taṇhā, lobha*), resentment or irascibility (*dosa = kodha*), and delusion or ignorance (*moha = avijjā*). These fires can only be quenched by their opposites (*A.* iv. 445 ; *Dh.* 5, 223), by the practice of corresponding virtues and the acquisition of knowledge (*vijjā*), or, in other words, only cease to " draw," and so go out, or rather *in*, when their fuel is withheld. It is this " going out " that is called a " despiration " (*nibbāna*, Skr. *nirvāṇa*), and is naturally linked with the notion of a " cooling off " (compare the vernacular, Why so hot, my little man ?). Nirvana—to use the word in its more familiar form—is a Buddhist key-word, than which, perhaps, no other has been so much misunderstood.[1] Nirvana is a death, a being *finished* (both in the meaning of " ended " and of " perfected "). In its passive senses it has all the connotations of Greek τελέω, ἀποσβέννυμι, and those of φύχω. Nirvana is neither a place nor an effect, nor in time, nor attainable by any means ; but it is and it can be " seen." The " means " that are actually resorted to are not in themselves means to Nirvana, but means to the removal of all that obscures the " vision " of Nirvana : as when a lamp is brought into a dark room one sees what is already there.

We can now understand why the self (*attā*) must be tamed, conquered, curbed, rejected, and given its quietus. The Arahant or Perfect Man is one whose self has been tamed (*atta-danto*), whose self has been cast off (*atta-jaho*) ; his burden has been laid down (*ohita-bhāro*), what there was to be done has been done (*katam-karaṇīyam*). All of the epithets that are applied to the Buddha himself, who has no longer a personal name,[2] are applicable to him ; he is " released " (*vimutto*), he is " despirated " (*nibbuto*), there is no more becoming for him, he has earned his rest-from-labour (*yoga-k-khemam*), he is awake (*buddho*, an epithet applicable to any Arahant, not only to *the* Buddha), he is immovable (*anejo*), he is an " Ariyan," no longer a disciple (*sekho*) but a Master (*asekho*).

Selfishness (*mamattam*, " possessiveness " ; *maccheram*, " bad

---

[1] " Extinction " (as of a fire) is not illegitimate ; but " annihilation " is misleading. In India, the " going out " of a fire is always thought of as a " going home ".

[2] Even " Gotama " is not a personal, but only a family name ; Ānanda, too is a Gotamid.

behaviour," " law of the sharks ") is a moral evil, and therefore the taming of the self requires a moral discipline. But selfishness is supported by " Self-isness " (*asmi-māna, anattani attā ditthi*), and mere commandments will hardly suffice unless and until the erroneous view that " this is me " has been shattered. For the self is always self-assertive, and it is only when the true nature of the inconstant self has been realized that a man will set out in earnest to overcome his own worst enemy and make him a servant and ally. The first step is to acknowledge the predicament, the second to unmask the self whose sole liability it is, the third to act accordingly ; but this is not easy, and a man is not very willing to mortify himself until he has known these appetitive congeries for what they are, and until he has learnt to distinguish his Self and its true interest from the Ego, his self and its interests. The primary evil is ignorance ; and it is, in fact, by the truth that the self must be tamed (*S. i.* 169). Only " The truth shall make you free ! " The remedy for self-love (*atta-kāma*) is Self-love (*atta-kāma*) and it is precisely in this sense, in the words of St Thomas Aquinas, that " a man, out of charity, ought to love himself more than any other person, more than his neighbour (*Sum. Theol.* II.–ii. 26.4). In Buddhist terms " let no man worsen welfare of himself for other's weal however great ; if well he knows the Self's true interest, let him pursue that end " (*Dh.* 166). In other words, man's first duty is to work out his own salvation,—from himself.

The procedure, in often-repeated expositions of the " un-Self-isness " (*anattā*) of all phenomena, is analytical. The repudiation is of what would nowadays be described as " animism " : the psycho-physical, behaving mechanism is not a " Self," and is devoid (*suñña*) of any Self-like property. The Ego or self-consciousness or self-existence (*atta-sambhāva*) is a composite of five associated grounds (*dhātu*) or stems (*khandha*), viz. the visible body (*rūpa, kāya*), and invisible sensation (*vedana,* pleasant, unpleasant or neutral), recognition, or awareness (*saññā*), constructions or character (*samkhārā*) [1]

---

[1] *Samkhārā* (σύνκριτοι, σύνθετοι) here with reference to mental images, phantasms, notions, postulates, complexes, opinions, prejudices, convictions, ideologies, etc. In a more general sense *samkhāra* defines all things that can be referred to by name or sensibly perceived, all *nāma-rūpa,* all " things," ourselves included.

and discrimination, discretion, judgment, or valuation (*viññāṇa*),[1] in short, a composite of body and discriminating consciousness (*sa-viññāṇa-kāya*), the psycho-physical existent. The causal origination, variability, and mortality of all these factors is demonstrated ; they are not " ours," because we cannot say " let them, or let me, be thus or thus " (*S.* iii. 66–67) : on the contrary, " we " are what they " become,"—" a biological entity, impelled by inherited impulses."[2] The demonstration always concludes with the words : " That's not mine, I'm not that, that's not my Self." To have done with them for good and all, to have put away the notions " I am So-and-so," " I am the agent," " I am," will prove to be " for your advantage and your happiness " (*S.* iii. 34). The Buddha, or any Arahant, is a " Nobody " ; one cannot properly ask his name.

Otherwise stated, any thing or individuality is characterized by " name and shape " (*nāma-rūpa* = ὁ λόγος καὶ ἡ μορφή, Aristotle, *Met.* viii. 1.6) ; " name " referring to all the invisible, and " shape " or " body " (*rūpa* being interchangeable with *kāya*) to all the visible and sensible constituents of individuality. This is as much as to say that " time and space " are the primary forms of our understanding of things that become ; for while the shape or body of anything is evanescent, its name survives, and by its name we still hold on to it. It is by his " names," those of the " Law " and " Truth," that the Wake survives *in the world*, although, like the rivers when they reach the Sea, *his* liberation is from name and shape, and whoever has " gone home " is no longer in any category, no longer this or that, or here or there (*Sn.* 1074).

All this is nothing peculiarly Buddhist, but the burden of a world-wide philosophy, for which salvation is essentially from oneself. *Denegat seipsum ! Si quis . . . non odit animam suam, non potest meus discipulus esse !*

" The soul is the greatest of your enemies."[3] " Were it not for the shackle, who would say ' I am I ' ? "[4] " Self is the root, the tree, and branches of all the evils of our fallen state "[5] ;

---

[1] The five *khandhas* are nearly the same as the five " powers of the soul " as defined by Aristotle (*De an.* II, III) and St Th. Aquinas (*Sum. Theol.* i. 78. 1), viz. the vegetative (nutritive), sensitive, appetitive, motive, intellectual (diagnostic, critical).

[2] L. Paul, *The Annihilation of Man*, 1945, p. 156.

[3] Al-Ghazālī, *Al-Risālat al-Laduniyya*, Ch. II.   [4] Rūmī, *Mathnawī* i. 2449.

[5] W. Law, Hobhouse p. 219.

" it is impossible to lay hold twice of the essence of anything
mortal . . . at one and the same moment it arrives and is
dissolved " [1]—such citations could be multiplied indefinitely.
It is less often realized that many modern naturalists and psychologists have reached the same conclusions. " The naturalist
. . . maintains that the states and events called mental exist
only when certain organizations of physical things also occur
. . . [and] are not exhibited by those things unless they are so
organized. . . . The structured object is simply manifesting
the behaviour of its constituents . . . [it] is not an additional
thing which . . . controls . . . the behaviour of its organized
parts." The naturalist's and the Buddhist interpretation of the
behaviour of the " structured object " are so far identical :
but whereas the former identifies himself with the behaving
object,[2] the Buddhist insists that there is *no object* that can
properly be called " my Self." The psychologists, on the
other hand, prescinding from the Ego, still, like the Buddhist,
leave room for something other than the Ego and that can
experience an " infinite happiness." " When we see that all
is fluid . . . it will appear that individuality and falsity are
one and the same,"—the direct implication being, as in the
anatta doctrine, that " we " are other than our individuality.
" In the traditionally [*sc.* customarily] emphasized individuality
of each one of us, ' myself ' . . . we have *the very mother of
illusions* . . . [and] the tragedy of this delusion of individuality
is that it leads to isolation, fear, paranoid suspicion, and wholly
unnecessary hatreds ; " " any person would be *infinitely happier*
if he could accept the loss of his ' individual self ',"—as the
Buddha puts it, he does not worry about what is unreal. " In
the epoch of scientific rationalism, what was the psyche ? It
had become *synonymous with consciousness* . . . there was no
psyche outside the ego. . . . When the fate of Europe carried
it into a four-years' war of stupendous horror . . . no one
realized that European man was *possessed* by *something that
robbed him of his free choice* ; " but over and above this Ego

---

[1] *Timaeus* 28 A, *cf. Cratylus* 440 ; Plutarch, *Moralia* 392 B. For the Buddhist
doctrine of the " moment " (*khaṇa*) in which things originate, mature, and
cease, *cf. Vis.* i. 239, and the fuller development in the Mahāyāna.

[2] Such an identification reverts to the animistic proposition, " I think, therefore
I am," and involves the unintelligible concept of a single agent that can will
opposite things at one and the same time. The logical positivist ought to deny
the possibility of any " self-control,"—perhaps he does.

there is a Self " around which it revolves, very much as the earth rotates about the sun," although " in this relation there is nothing knowable in the intellectual sense, because *we can say nothing of the contents of the Self.*" [1]

What has Buddhism to say of the Self? " That's not my Self " (*na me so attā*) ; this, and the term " non-Self-isness " (*anattā*) predicated of the world and all " things " (*sabbe dhammā anattā*) [2] have formed the basis of the mistaken view that Buddhism " denies [not merely the self but also] the Self." But a moment's consideration of the logic of the words will show that they assume the reality of a Self that is not any one or all of the " things " that are denied of it. As St Thomas Aquinas says, " primary and simple things are defined by negations ; as, for instance, a point is defined as that which has no parts ; " and Dante remarks that there are " certain things which our intellect cannot behold . . . we cannot understand what they are except by denying things of them." This was the position of the older Indian philosophy in which Buddhism originated : whatever can be said of the Self is " Not so." To acknowledge that " nothing true can be said of God " is certainly not to deny his essence !

When the question is pressed, Is there a Self, the Buddha refuses to answer " Yes " or " No " ; to say " Yes " would involve the " eternalist " error, to say " No " the " annihilationist " error (*S.* iv. 400–401). And similarly, when the postmortem destiny of a Buddha, Arahant, or Very Man arises, he says that none of the terms " becomes " (*hoti*) or " does not become " or " neither becomes nor does not become " or " both becomes and does not become " apply. Any one of these propositions would involve an identification of the Buddha with some or all of the five factors of personality ; all becoming implies modality, but a Buddha is not in any mode. It should be emphasized that the question is always asked in terms of becoming, not in terms of being. The logic

---

[1] The naturalists and psychologists cited are Dewey, Hook and Nagel, Charles Peirce, H. S. Sullivan, E. E. Hadley, and C. G. Jung. It will be seen that the latter, who speaks of the " absolute necessity of a step beyond science," is a metaphysician in spite of himself. The citations are not made by way of proving the truth of the Buddhist analysis, but to help the reader to understand it ; the *proof* of the pudding will be in the eating. (The italics are mine).

[2] Identical with the Brahmanical " of those who are mortal, there is no Self ", (*anātmā hi martyah*, *ŚB.* ii. 2. 2. 3).

of language only applies to phenomenal things (*D.* ii. 63), and the Arahant is uncontaminated by any of these "things" : there are no word-ways for one whose self is no more ; one "gone home" is no longer in any category (*Sn.* 1074, 1076). Nevertheless it is also said that the Buddha "is" (*atthi*), though he cannot be seen "here or there," and denied that an Arahant "is not" after death. If, indeed, absolutely nothing remains when the self is no more, we could not but ask, Of what is an immortality predicated ? Any reduction of a reality to the nothingness of "the son of a barren woman" would be meaningless and unintelligible ; and, in fact, the Buddha in repudiating the "annihilationist" doctrines that were attributed to him by some contemporary heretics expressly denies that he ever taught the destruction of anything real (*sato sattassa* = ὄντως ὄν) (*M.* i. 137, 140). There *is*, he says, "an unborn, un-become, unmade (*akatam*),[1] incomposite (*asaṃkhataṃ*), [2] and were there not, there would be no escape from the born, the become, the made and the composite (world) " (*Ud.* 80) : "knower of what was never made (*akataññū*) art thou, O Brahman, having known the waning away of all composite things."

The Buddha expressly "holds nothing back," making no distinction of a within from a without, his is "not a closed fist " (*D.* ii. 100) ; but the Eternal Law, and Nirvana, are "incomposite," and for this transcendent Worth (*param'attha*) all words are inadequate—*all'alta fantasia qui mancò possa* (*Paradiso* xxxiii. 142)—in which the disciple must have Faith (*saddhā*) until he can experience it, until Faith is replaced by Knowledge ; "he whose mind has been fired by the desire of the Untold (*anakkhāta*), he is one freed from all loves, a swimmer against the current " (*Dh.* 218),—"the Buddhas do but tell the Way " (*Dh.* 276). If there is a salvation by faith (*Sn.* 1146), it is because "Faith is most conducive to knowledge " (*S.* iv. 298) : *Crede ut intelligas.* Faith implies authority : and the Buddha's authority (*mahāpadesa*), which rests upon his own immediate experience, is that of his words as spoken or as reported by competent Mendicants ; in the latter case not merely rightly

[1] The "unmade world " (Brahmaloka) of the Upanishads.

[2] "Incomposite," i.e. without origination, growth or mutation, *A.* i. 152 ; Nirvana, *Mil.* 270 ; Dhamma, *S.* iv. 359. On the other hand, even the highest Contemplative "states " are composite, and it is even from these exalted conditions that there is a "final escape ".

grasped, but checked for their consistency with the texts of the Canon and the Rule. In this initial dependence in what has not yet been " seen " there is nothing uniquely Buddhist or credulous. The Buddha's doctrine is always about what he claims to have personally seen and verified, and what he tells his disciples can be seen and verified by them if they will follow him in Brahma-faring. " The Buddhas do but tell the Way, it is for *you* to swelter at the task " (*Dh.* 276) ; the " End remains untold " (*Sn.* 1074) ; it has no sign (*S.* i. 188, *Sn.* 342), and is a gnosis that cannot be communicated (*A.* iii. 444) ; and those whose reliance is only on what can be told are still under the yoke of death (*S.* i. 11).

In the discussion of Faith it is too often overlooked that the greater part of our knowledge of " things," even of those by which our worldly actions are regulated, is " authoritative " ; most, indeed, even of our daily activities would come to an end if we did not believe the words of those who have seen what we have not yet seen, but might see if we would do what they have done, or go where they have been ; in the same way those of the Buddhist neophyte would come to an end if he did *not* " believe " in a goal not yet attained. Actually, he believes that the Buddha is telling him the truth, and acts accordingly (*D.* ii. 93). Only the Perfect Man is " faithless," in the sense that in his case knowledge of the Unmade has taken the place of Faith (*Dh.* 97), for which there is no more need.

For the Buddhist, Dhamma, the Lex Aeterna,[1] synonymous with the Truth (*S.* i. 169), is the ultimate authority and " King of kings " (*A.* i. 109, iii. 149). It is with this ultimate, timeless and temporal, transcendent and immanent authority that the Buddha identifies himself, that Self in which he has taken refuge : " he who sees the Dhamma sees me, and he who sees me sees the Dhamma " (*S.* iii. 120 ; *It.* 91 ; *Mil.* 73). One of the most impressive of the Buddhist books is called the *Dhamma-pada*, " Footprints of the Law " ; it is a chart and guide-book for those who " walk in the Way of the Law " (*dhammacariyaṃ caranti*), which is also the " Way of Brahma " or " Brahma-faring " (*brahmacariyaṃ*), and " that old road that was followed by the formerly All-awakened." The Buddhist words for

---

[1] " A Law above our minds, which is called the Truth," St Augustine, *De ver. relig.* xxx. *Cf.* St Thomas Aquinas, *Sum. Theol.* ii–i. 91. 2.

" Way " (*magga*) and for " seeking " (*gavesana*),[1] with the Self
as object (*Vin.* i. 23 ; *Vis.* 393), both imply the following of
tracks or footprints.[2] But these tracks end when the shore of
the Great Sea is reached ; until then the Mendicant is a disciple
(*sekho*), thereafter an expert (*asekho*),—" no longer under a
pedagogue " (*Gal.* iii. 25). The Way prescribed is one of self-
naughting, virtue and contemplation, walking alone with
Brahma ; but when the end of the " long road " has been reached,
whether here or hereafter, there remains only the " plunge "
into the Immortal, into Nirvana (*amat'ogadham, nibbān'ogadham*),
into that fathomless Ocean that is an image at once of Nirvana,
Dhamma, and the Buddha himself (*M.* i. 488, ; *S.* iv. 179, 180,
376, v. 47 ; *Mil.* 319, 346). This is an old simile, common to
the Upanishads and Buddhism : when the rivers reach the
Sea, their name and shape is lost, and one only speaks of " the
Sea." This last end is already prefigured in the adoption of
the monastic vocation ; like the rivers when they reach the
Sea, so men of whatever caste becoming Mendicants are no
longer called by their former names or lineage, but are simply
of the lineage of those who have sought and found the Truth
(*Vin.* ii. 239 ; *A.* iv. 202 ; *Ud.* 55).

" The dewdrop slips into the shining sea." Yes, but this is
not an exclusively Buddhist formula ; we find it in Rūmī,[3]
(Nicholson, *Dīwān*, xii. xv ; *Mathnawī, passim*), in Dante
(*sua voluntate . . . è quel mare tutto si move* [*Paradiso* iii. 84]), in
Meister Eckhart (*also sich wandelte der tropfe in daz mer*—" the
sea of God's unfathomable nature . . . plunge in, this is the
drowning "), Angelus Silesius (*Wenn du das Tröpflein wist im
grossen Meere nennen, Den wist du meine Seel' im grossen Gott
erkennen* [*Cher. Wandersmann* ii. 25]), and in China, where the
Tao is the ocean to which all things return (*Tao te Ching* xxxii).
Of all those who reach it it can only be said that their life is
hidden, enigmatic. The Buddha visibly present in the flesh
is even now " unattainable " (*anupalabhyamāno*) and " past

---

[1] *Cf.* the story of Gavesin, p. 41.

[2] As in Plato, ἰχνεύω, *passim*. Meister Eckhart's " soul following the spoor of
her quarry, Christ ".

[3] *Attham-gato* is a good example of the numerous etymological ambiguities
that are met with in Pali. Where *attham*=Skr. *astam*, the sense is that of " gone
home," but where *attham*=*artham*, that of " having attained one's purpose, or
goal." Such an ambiguity is far from inconvenient, since the " return home"
and the " attainment of the end " have a common reference.

finding out" (ananuvejjo) ; no one thus "gone home" can be referred to any category (sankhaṁ na upeti [Sn. 1074]). For "no one who sees me in any shape sees me" ; "name and aspect are none of mine" ; he only who sees the Eternal Law sees the Buddha, and that as effectively to-day as when he still wore the personality (persona, "mask," "disguise") that at death "he burst like a coat of mail" (A. iv. 312).

The equation between Dante's mare with the Buddhist "Sea," implied above, may seem to import a theistic sense into the supposedly "atheistic" Buddhist doctrines ; but it need only be pointed out that no real distinction can be drawn between the immutable Will of God and the Lex Aeterna, his Justice of Wisdom, that Nature which is also his Essence and to act against which would be to deny himself. The Law, Dhamma, had always been a nomen Dei, and is still in Buddhism synonymous with Brahma. If the Buddha identifies himself with the Eternal Law, this means that he cannot sin ; he is no longer "under the Law," but being himself the Law can only act accordingly, and we find amongst the interpretations of the epithet "Thus-come" or "Truth-finder" that "as he says, so he does." But for those who are still Wayfarers and learners, sin (adhamma) is precisely an offence against that Natural Law which represents the share of the Eternal Law that determines the individual's responsibilities and functions. In other words, the Eternal Law has its immanent correlative in every man's "own law" (sa-dhamma [Sn. 1020]), by which his natural inclinations and proper functions (attano kamma = τὰ ἑαυτοῦ πράττειν) are determined ; and it is only greed or ambition that leads to the disparagement of the nativity by which a man is normally "protected" (Sn. 314, 315). I mention this only because of currency of the erroneous opinion that the Buddha "attacked" the caste system. What he actually did was to distinguish the Brahman by mere birth from the true Brahman by gnosis, and to point out that the religious vocation is open to a man of any birth (A. iii. 214 ; S. i. 167) : there was nothing new in that. Caste is a social institution, and the Buddha was speaking mainly for those whose preoccupations are no longer social ; for the householder it is observed that his entelechy consists in the perfection of his work (A. iii. 363), and only those occupations that injure others are condemned. The duties of a Ruler are often enumerated. The Buddha himself was a

Royalty inasmuch as he laid down a Law, and was a Brahman by character (*Mil.* 225–227). Brahmans are only disparaged in so far as they do not live up to their ancient norm. In many contexts " Brahman " is synonymous with " Arahant."

It has been asserted that Buddhism knows only of the personal God Brahmā and nothing of the Godhead Brahma : this would have been strange indeed in India of the fifth century B.C., in one who had studied under Brahman masters, and in scriptural contexts that are so often reminiscent of the Brāhmanas and Upanishads. Actually, there can be no doubt that in the grammatically ambiguous expression *brahma-bhūto* which describes the condition of those who are wholly liberated, it is Brahma and not Brahmā that must be read ; it is Brahma that one who is " wholly awake " has " become." For (1) the comparatively limited knowledge of a Brahmā is repeatedly emphasized, (2) Brahmās are, accordingly, the Buddha's pupils, not he theirs (*S.* i. 141–145 ; *Mil.* 75–76), (3) the Buddha had already been, in previous births, a Brahmā and Mahā Brahmā (*A.* iv. 88–90), hence it would be meaningless, in the equation *brahma-bhūto* = *buddho* (*A.* v. 226 ; *D.* iii. 84 ; *It.* 57, etc.), to assume that *brahma* = Brahmā, and (4) the Buddha is explicitly " much more than a Mahā Brahmā (*DhA.* ii. 60). It is true that the Buddha is often addressed by Brahmans as Brahmā (*Sn.* 293, 479, 508), but here Brahmā is not the name of the God, but (as in *Skr.*) the designation of a true and learned Brahman,[1] and tantamount to Arahant (*Sn.* 518, 519). As for the " Gods " (*deva*), *e.g.* Indras, Brahmās and many other and lesser divinities or angels, not only are these at least as real as men, not only do the Buddha himself and other Arahants visit their worlds and converse with them, and not only is the Buddha the " teacher of Gods *and* men " (*S.* iii. 86), but in response to questions he explicitly ridicules the notion that " there is no other world " (as maintained by the " Nothing-morists," whom we should now call Positivists [*M.* i. 403]) and the preposterous view that " there are no Gods " (*M.* ii. 212). Finally, inasmuch as the same things are said of the Self and of the Buddha, *e.g.* that definitions of either in terms of either or are invalid, not

---

[1] In Vedic ritual, *the* Brahmā is the most learned of the four Brahman officiants, and their standard in all matters of doubt ; hence Brahmā, as from one Brahman to another, is the most respectful possible form of address.

only is " Buddha " explained as " one whose Self is awake " [1]
(*Vis.* 209 ; cf. *BU.* iv. 4.13), but there can hardly be any doubt
that the Commentator is right in asserting that in such contexts
the Truth-finder or Thus-come " is the Self" (*Ud.* 67 with
UdA. 340). That the Buddha is not only a transcendent
principle—Eternal Law and Truth—but also universally immanent as the " Man in this man " is implied by the epithet
" All-within " (Vessantara = Viśvāntara [*M.* i. 386 ; *It.* 32]
applied to him, and by the words, " Whoever would nurse
me, let him nurse the sick " (*Vin.* i. 302),—this last a striking
parallel to Christ's " inasmuch as ye have done it unto one of
the least of these my brethren ye have done it unto me."

In the whole of the Buddhist canonical literature it is nowhere
stated that " there is no Self," no reality distinguishable from the
empirical self that is repeatedly subjected to destructive analysis.
On the contrary, the Self is both explicitly and implicitly asserted ;
notably in the recurrent phrase according to which this, that or
the other " is not my Self." We cannot ignore the axiom, *Nil
agit in seipsum* : Plato's " when there are two opposite impulses
in a man at the same time about the same thing, we say that there
must be two in him " (*Rep.* 604 B). This will apply, for example,
when the conditions are described in which Self is the friend or
the foe of self (*S.* i. 57, 71–72 as in *B.G.* vi. 5–7), and whenever a
relation between two selves is asserted. The Buddhist is expected to " honour what is more than self" (*A.* i. 126), and this
" more " can only be the " Self that's Lord of self, and the goal
of self" (*Dh.* 380). It is of the Self and certainly not of himself
that the Buddha is speaking when he says, " I have taken refuge
in the Self" (*D.* ii. 120), and similarly when he asks others to
" seek for the Self" (*Vin.* i. 23 ; *Vis.* 393), and to " make the
Self your refuge and your lamp " (*D.* ii. 100, *S.* v. 163 ; *cf. S.* iii.
143). Distinction is also made of the " Great Self" (*mah'attā*,
" Mahātmā," " the magnanimous ") from the " little self"
(*app'ātumo*, " the pusillanimous "), and of the " Fair Self" from
the " Foul self," the former blaming the latter when wrong is
done (*A.* i. 57, 149, v. 88). In short, it is quite certain that
the Buddha neither " denied a God, denied a Soul, [nor] denied
Eternity."

---

[1] *Buddh'attā buddho, Vis.* 209, *cf. BU.* iv. 4. 13 *pratibuddho ātmā.* The " awakened
Self" will be the " Self made-become " (*bhāvit'attā, passim*), i.e. the " unborn
Self (*ajāta'attā*) that neither ages nor dies," *DhA.* i. 228, *cf. BG.* ii. 20.

In numerous contexts, the Buddha and other Arahants or
Perfect Men are described as " having made the Self become "
(bhāvit'atto) ; " made become," i.e. " as a mother fosters her only
son," for this causative form of the verb " become " (the want
of which in English is a serious inconvenience) means to
" foster," " care for," " cultivate," " serve " or " provide for,"—
like θεραπεύω. This " making become " of the Self is an indispensable part of the Buddhist pilgrim's progress, and certainly
no less so than is the corresponding negative task of putting a stop
to all " becoming."   To have completed either task is to have
completed the other, and to have reached the goal : and " so,"
as Wordsworth says, " build we up the being that we are."   But
the modern scholar must be careful to distinguish the " becoming " that is a mere metabolism, an undirected process of auto-
matic growth or " progress," from the " making become " that
is a selective cultivation.   It is only the empirical self, composite
of body and consciousness (viññāṇa) that " becomes."   Apart
from the bodily constitution, consciousness cannot arise ;   our
" former habitations," i.e. past lives, are composites of this sort,
but " not mine," " not my Self " (S. iii. 86) ; and of the Mendicant in whom the conditions that lead to the renewed becoming
of a consciousness have been suppressed it is said that he is one
whose Self is liberated, existent, altogether content, and that he
knows that for him there is no more birth, no more becoming
(S. iii. 55).

Merely to have reached the Brahma-worlds or to have become
a Brahmā there is not the last end ; to have become a Brahmā,
or even the Mahā Brahma of the aeon, is indeed a tremendous
achievement, but it is not the same as to have become Brahma,
or totally despirated Buddha and Arahant.   The distinction of
Brahmā from Brahma, expressed in Christian terms, is that of
God from Godhead, and it will help to make the matter clearer
in the Buddhist contexts if I quote analogous statements from
two of the greatest and most intellectual of the Christian
" mystics " :

" You must," says Meister Eckhart, " learn what God and
Godhead are.   God works, the Godhead does no work.   God
becomes and unbecomes (wirt und entwirt), and is an image of all
becoming (werdenne) ; but the Father's nature does not become
(unwerdentlich ist), and the Son is one with Him in this un-
becoming (entwerdenne).   The temporal becoming ends in the

eternal un-becoming " (Pfeiffer, 516 and 497). So "it is more necessary that the soul lose God than that she lose creatures" (Evans, i. 274), if she is to reach that state in which we shall be " as free as when we were not, free as the Godhead in its non-existence." "Why do they not speak about the Godhead? Because all that is there is one and the same, and there is nothing to be said. . . . When I go back into the ground, into the depths, into the well-spring of the Godhead, no one will ask me whence I came or whither I went" (Pfeiffer, 180–181). "Our essence is not annihilated there, for although we shall have there neither cognizance, nor love, nor beatitude, but there it becomes like unto a desert in which God alone reigns."[1] Accordingly, the unknown author of *The Book of Privy Counselling* and *The Cloud of Unknowing* makes a difference between those who are called to salvation and those who are called to perfection, and citing Mary's choice of "that best part, the which shall not be taken away from her" (*Book of Privy Counselling*, f. 105 a), remarks of the contemplative life that "if it begin here, it shall last without end," adding that in that other life "there shall be no need to use works of mercy, nor to weep for our wretchedness" (*Cloud of Unknowing*, Ch. 21).

Parallels such as these are sometimes even more conducive to an understanding of the content of Buddhism than are the direct citations from the Buddhist canon; for they enable the reader to proceed from a known to a lesser-known phraseology. It need hardly be said that for a European reader or scholar who proposes to study any Oriental religion seriously a considerable knowledge of Christian doctrine and thinking, and of its Greek background, is almost indispensable.

The two selves are in dramatic contrast whenever one reproaches the other. "Self upbraids the self (*attā pi attānam upavadati*) when what should not be done is done (*A.* i. 57–58): for example, when the Bodhisatta begs his food for the first time, he cannot stomach the unappetising scraps he receives, but "he blames *himself*," and *he* does not allow *himself* to weaken (*J.* i. 66). The Self knows what is truth and what is falsity, and

[1] Meister Eckhart's "non-existence," "well-spring," "desert" correspond to the Buddhist Sea (as discussed above) in which all differentiation is lost (*cf.* Nicolas of Cusa's definition of theosis as *ablatio omnis alteritatis et diversitatis*) and to Rūmī's "Sea" of Love or Non-existence,—the lover becoming there the Beloved (*Mathnawī* i. 504, 1109, ii. 688–690, 1103, iii. 4723, vi. 2771 *et passim*, with Nicholson's notes).

the Foul self cannot hide its evil deed from the Fair (*A.* i. 149).
The Self is, then, our conscience, inwit and synteresis ; the Socratic Daimon "who cares for nothing but the Truth" and
"always holds me back from what *I* want to do." It is a matter
of universal experience that, as Plato says, "there is a something
in the soul that bids men drink, and a something that forbids,
that hungers and thirsts, and another one that keeps account,"
and it is for us to decide "which shall rule, the better or the
worse." Self is the Agathos Daimon, whom it is for "me" to
obey.

This leads us to consider the doctrine of the "Daimon's
purity" (*yakkhassa suddhi*). Ignoring that there can be a multi-
plicity of Genii, just as in other traditions there can be a multi-
plicity of "spirits other than the Spirit," it must be premised
that *the* Daimon (*yakṣa*) had been originally and was still for the
Upanishads, Brahma—that Brahma, who is at once transcendent
and, as the "Self of the self," immanent. The Sakyas themselves
had been worshippers of a Yakkha Sakyavardhana, who can
probably be equated with this "ever-productive" Nature. In
Buddhism, the Buddha, who is so often described as "Brahma-
become" (*brahma-bhūta*), is also called a Yakkha, the Daimon
whose "purity" was mentioned above. The Buddha is "uncontaminated" (*anūpalitto*), wholly despirated, goal-attained
(*attha-gata*, as predicted by his given name of Siddhartha), pure
(*suddho*), immovable (*anejo*), and undesirous (*Sn.* 478, *cf. M.* i.
386, *buddhassa . . . āhuneyyassa yakkhassa*) : "such is the
Daimon's purity, he the Truth-finder has a right to the oblation,"
he is the *āhuneyya* Daimon, "to whom the sacrificial offering
should be made" (*S.* i. 141 ; *M.* i. 386 ; *Sn.* 478). Whereas all
existences are maintained by and delight in "food" (physical or
mental) (*D.* iii. 211), the question is asked, "What is that
Daimon's name, who takes no pleasure in food?" (*S.* i. 32 ;
cf. Sn. 508). How vividly this recalls the question, "Won't you
tell me who he is?" and Socrates' reply, "You would not know
him if I told you his name!" and the fact that in the Indian
and some other traditions, "Who?" is the most appropriate
name of the god who is "the Self of all existences," but has
neither come from anywhere or ever become anyone. This
"Self of all beings" is the Sun—not "the sun that all men see,
but the Sun whom few know with the mind" and whom the
Vedas describe as "uncontaminated" (*arepasa*, i.e. *anupalitto*).

This is only one of the many reasons for identifying the *brahma-bhūta* Buddha, who is also called " the Eye in the World " and " whose name is Truth," with this " Light of lights " and " Sun of men."

Our immediate concern is with the word " uncontaminated." Whether explicitly or implicitly, and equally in Buddhist and pre-Buddhist contexts (where also the Sun is " the one lotus of the sky ") the analogical reference is to the purity of the lotus, which is " not wetted by the water " on which it floats. In the same way, the Buddha is " uncontaminated by human affairs " (*Sn.* 456 ; *cf. S.* iv. 180) : uncontaminated by the world (*A.* iii. 347) and all things in it (*A.* iv. 71). What this implies will throw some light for us upon the nature of the goal that the Buddha and other Perfect Men had pursued and reached. It is too often assumed that the notion of a goal " beyond good and evil " is of modern origin. It appears, however, not only in Indian but also in Islamic and Christian contexts, and is intrinsic to the normal differentiation of the active from the contemplative life, virtue being *essential* to the former and only *dispositive* to the latter, of which the perfection is man's ultimate goal—that of the beatific contemplation of Truth. The notion recurs again and again in Buddhist contexts : that by which the Perfect Man is uncontaminated is not merely evil or vice, but also good or virtue. This is stated explicitly in many contexts, *e.g.* : " uncontaminated whether by virtue or by vice, self cast away, for such there's no more action needed here " (*Sn.* 790) ; " one who hath here escaped attachment whether to virtue or vice, one sorrowless, to whom no dust adheres, one pure, him I call a very Brahman " (*Dh.* 412), i.e. Arahant. But even more notably in the parable of the raft : " abandon right and a fortiori wrong ; one who has reached the farther shore has no more need of rafts " (*M.* i. 135), for which there are exact parallels in St Augustine's " let him no longer use the Law as a means of arrival when he has arrived " (*De spir. et lit.* 16) and Meister Eckhart's " having gotten to the other side I do not want a ship " ; and as the latter also says, " Behold the Soul divorced from every aught . . . leaving no trace of either vice or virtue."

" Purity " is not attainable by belief, audition, knowledge, morals or works, nor without them (*Sn.* 839) ; in other words, moral training is absolutely indispensable, but does not by itself involve perfection. Rules of conduct are laid down for householders and for Mendicants ; those for the latter are naturally more stringent, but in no way extreme ; self-torture is strongly deprecated. Those of the Mendicants who offended (and it is admitted that there were some who joined the order for quite unworthy reasons) could be cited and censured in public monastic assembly, or, in case of serious offences, unfrocked. On, the other hand Mendicants were not, and are not nowadays, bound by any irrevocable vows, and are free to return to the household life if they wish ; this is regarded simply as a failure or weakness and an occasion of reproach.

The practice of moral virtues whether by a householder or Mendicant disciple leads to rebirth in a lower or higher heaven, as the case may be. The former earns merit by moral conduct and above all by generosity ; in this connection it may be noted that the Buddha instructs a householder, who has been converted and has become a lay-adherent, not to abandon his former practice of supporting the members of a rival order of Mendicants, although from the Buddhist standpoint these were heretics. The Mendicant, who had no possessions apart from his robes, begging bowl, jug, and staff, could not in the same way be generous with his goods, but might be a teacher of others, and there is no gift more worthy than that of the Eternal Law ; he no longer recognized family ties, as bonds implying duties, nor might he concern himself with politics or participate in the pleasures, trials, or affairs of men living in the world, but he was not only expected to return love for hate if anyone abused him verbally or physically, and also to practise the Brahma-bidings or Divine " States " (*brahma-vihāra*) of Love, Pity, Tenderness, and Impartiality (*mettā, karuṇā, muditā, upekkhā*). The first of these consists in the deliberate radiation of well-wishing Love towards all living things whatever,—" with heart of Love he abides irradiating one, a second, third, and fourth quarter ; and so the whole wide world, above, below, athwart, and everywhere, he continues to irradiate with heart of Love abounding, measureless, guileless," and thinking, " May all be happy " (*Sn.* 143 f). Here the reference of " all " is by no means only to human beings, but absolutely universal. Impartiality, on the other hand, is a subjective state of patience or detachment, as of one who looks upon whatever pleasant or unpleasant things befall himself as one might look on at a play, present at but not involved in the hero's predicaments. The " heart's liberation " thus brought about tends to an ultimate rebirth in the Brahma-worlds and to companionship and coincidence with Brahmā ; inasmuch as the disposition of the Mendicant who develops these friendly and unacquisitive states of mind is the same as that of Brahmā. It will not be overlooked that the procedure so far is strictly ethical, and that it presupposes the virtue of Innocence (ahiṁsā, M. i. 44 ; S. i. 163 ; Sn. 309, 368, 515, etc.), a term that has become again very familiar in modern times as the principle of "non-violence" advocated by Gandhi as a rule of conduct under all circumstances,—"put up thy sword." The training of the will is logically prior to the training of the intellect.

But these ethical procedures, in which the notion of oneself and others is still involved, are only a part of the Mendicant's "Walking with God" (brahma—cariyaṁ = θεῷ συνοπαδεῖν) or "Walking with the Law" (dhamma-cariyaṁ), and not the end of the road ; there is "still more to be done." We are told that, like Mendicants who are not yet "absolutely freed" but flatter themselves that their work is done (A. v. 336 ; cf. M. i. 477), the Gods are often subject to the mistaken impression that their condition is unchangeable and everlasting, and that for them there is nothing more to be achieved (A. iv. 336, 355, 378 ; S. i. 142). Even a Brahmā, the highest of the Gods, imagines that there is no "further escape" (uttariṁ nissaraṇaṁ) from the glorious state that is already theirs (M. i. 326 ; A. iv. 76 ; S. i. 142). We find, accordingly, the Buddha reproaching Sāriputta for having instructed a Brahman questioner in no more than the way "to the lower Brahma-worlds where there is still more to be achieved" (M. ii. 195–196). It is always assumed that those who have not effected their Total Despiration (Parinirvana) here, if they have gone so far as to be "non-returners," can attain to their perfection and make their final escape from whatever may be their position in yonder world ; it is for that that the Buddha is the teacher not only of men but also of the Gods.

What, then, is the remaining task to be accomplished by some Mendicants and those who have attained to an aeviternal life in the Empyrean heavens but are not yet Arahants "whose work is done"? There is no further question of a higher status to be acquired by good works,—the fruit of works has already been earned ; it is a matter now entirely of the life of Contemplation (jhāna). Jhāna (Skr. dhyāna, Chinese ch'an, Japanese zen) corresponds almost exactly to the second term of the series "Con-

sideration, Contemplation, and Rapture " in Western practice ;
samādhi, literally " com-posure," or " synthesis," as of radii at
the centre of their circle,[1] corresponding to " Rapture " and
implying the consummation of Jhāna at any stage. Jhāna
implies the active and intentional realisation of states of being
other than that in which the contemplative is normally existent
at the time ; and its force is entirely betrayed by those scholars
who have called it " musing," or, still more ineptly, " reverie."
Contemplation is a strenuous mental discipline, demanding a
long training, and not a kind of day-dreaming ; " there is no
suggestion of trance, but rather of enhanced vitality " (PTS. Pali
Dictionary, s.v. jhāna). The expert can pass from one to another
of the hierarchy of " states " at will, and back again (D. ii. 71,
156) ; and this positive command and control of contemplative
" states " sharply distinguishes the Indian Yoga from all merely
passive and adventitious " mystic " experience. The contemplative " states " are a kind of ladder by which one can ascend
from lower to higher states of being or levels of reference ;
but the final goal of Liberation lies beyond them all. The first
four Jhānas are sometimes practised by laymen as well as by
Mendicants.

The Jhānas are typically four (available to laymen as well as to
Mendicants), or if taken together with the four Āruppa-Jhānas
(formless or altogether immaterial states) a set of eight stages of
liberation (vimokkha [D. ii. 69-71, 112, 156, et passim]). In the
first, making the mind " one-pointed," attention is directed to
some specific support of contemplation naturally suited to the
pupil's disposition and constitution, and often chosen for him by
the Master whose disciple he is. In the second Jhāna the practitioner still sees the external form, but is unaware of his own ;
the experience is ecstatic. In the third, the ecstasy passes, and
there remains only awareness of the endlessness of the power of
discrimination (viññāṇa). In the sixth the sense that " there is
nothing " (n'atthi kiñci) prevails. In the seventh there is no
further discrimination, and the condition is one neither with nor
without consciousness (saññā). In the eighth there is an arrest of

---

[1] In the architectural symbolism often employed the concentration of the
powers of the soul at their source effected in samādhi is illustrated by the synthesis
of the radiating rafters in the roofplate of a domed building ; and this (perforated)
roofplate itself is the " sundoor " by which one escapes from whatever conditioned
world is represented by the interior space or cavity (the Platonic " cave ") of the
building itself.

all consciousness and sensation (*D.* ii. 69–71, 112, 156). And once a Mendicant has mastered these eight degrees of liberation in sequence, in reverse sequence, and in both sequences successively, so that he can submerge himself in or emerge from any of them at will and for as long as he will ; and when also by the eradication of the fluxions he enters into that Freedom of the Will (*ceto-vimutti*) and into that Intellectual Freedom (*paññā-vimutti*) which he of himself has come to know and realize here and now, then such a Mendicant is said to be " Free in both ways " ; nor is there any other or higher Freedom in both ways than this (*D.* ii. 71 ; *cf. Sn.* 734, 753).

It must, however, be very clearly understood that the attainment of such a complete command of the hierarchy of the states of existence, or successive heavens, is not an end in itself, but a means to final Liberation from all " states " ; all are contingent, all originate and pass away, and no one who knows their true nature, who understands their pleasures and pains, and who knows the way of escape (*nissaraṇaṁ*) from them, would delight in them or wish to remain permanently in any of them, even the highest (*D.* ii. 79). Whatever one's position in the hierarchy of the worlds may be, there is always a still farther shore to be reached, and it is only for one completely liberated that there is nothing more to be done ; from the point of view of the *summum bonum* it is little better to have reached a heaven than to be still on earth ; the great work is still unaccomplished. To make this clear the Buddha propounds the great doctrine of the Middle Way,—*majjhena tathāgato dhammaṁ deseti.*

This very important doctrine, Platonic, Aristotelian, and Scholastic as much as it is Brahmanical and Buddhist, has as many applications as there are alternatives, of which the choice between this and some other world, thought of as contrasted " shores," is only one case ; the true " world-ender " (*lok'anta-gū*) is not attached to existence in this or any other world, however exalted; for all beings (*sattā*), men and Gods alike, are in Death's bonds (*S.* i. 97, 105). There are always two extremes (*antā*), and it is as against the extremist (*anta-g-gahika*) who attaches an absolute value to either that the Buddha propounds his Mean ; the true " Walking with God " (*brahmacariya*) is a Middle Way. Already as a Bodhisatta, having been reared in luxury, and thereafter having mortified his flesh to the very point of death, the Buddha had discovered that neither of these extremes would lead him to

the knowledge that he sought, and that he attained to by following the Middle Way (*Vin.* i. 10). In the same way, Purity cannot
be attained by virtue,—nor without it (*Sn.* 839) ; purity is not
only from vice but also from virtue. In the same way as regards
all "theories" (*diṭṭhi*), affirmations and denials : "is" (the
Eternalist error) and "is not" (the Annihilationist error) are
neither of them true descriptions of an ultimate reality (*S.* ii. 19–
20, 117),—just as for Boethius, faith is a "mean between contrary
heresies." This does not mean that the Middle Way has any
dimension ; in terms of space, the goal is neither here nor beyond
nor in-between (*Ud.* 8), and it is "not by paces" but within you
that World's End must be reached (*S.* i. 61–62 ; *A.* ii. 48–49 ;
S. iv. 94). In the same way—and this is perhaps the most interesting aspect of the atomic principle—as regards time. The
existence—origin and dissolution—of all things is momentary
(*khaṇika* [*Vis.* i. 230, 239 ; *Dpvs.* i. 16]) ; as it had been for
Heracleitus (*cf.* Plutarch, *Moralia*, 392 B,C.). This in-*stant*
(*khaṇa*), in which things arise, exist, and cease to be simultane-
ously, is the now without duration that separates past from future
and gives to both their meaning ; time, in which change super-
venes, is nothing but the unbroken succession of flow of such
moments, each of which—timeless in itself [1]—is our Middle Way
(*A.* iv. 137). Life, as we know it empirically, is the field of
transient action, and it is precisely such actions that have heritable
consequences. Immanent activities, on the other hand, remaining in the agent, do not involve the agent in external events and,
for the same reason, are inaccessible to observation. Several
Buddhist expressions (*e.g. ṭhit'atto* [*S.* iii. 55 ; *Sn.* 519, *cf.* 920], to
be contrasted with the transience, *aniccaṃ*, of all that is not-Self)
imply the immobility of the liberated Self. What this means is
that the transcendent, supra-logical Life of the liberated Self
is Self-contained. The moments themselves are one ; their
apparent succession is conventional.

The "moment" without duration is, then, our great opportunity,—"*now* the day of salvation,"—and we find the Buddha
praising those of the Mendicants who have "seized their

---

[1] It is true that "men feel that what cannot be put in terms of time is meaningless," but "the notion of a static, immutable being ought to be understood
rather as signifying a process so intensely vivacious . . . as to comprise beginning
and end at one stroke" (W. H. Sheldon in the *Modern Schoolman* xxi. 133).
"Plus la vie du moi s'identifie avec la vie du non-moi [i.e. le soi], plus on vit
intensément". (Abdul Hādī in *Le Voile d'Isis*, Jan. 1934).

moment," and blaming those who have let it pass them by (*S.* iv. 126 ; *Sn.* 333). The moments, indeed, pass us by ; but whoever seizes one of them escapes from their succession ; for the despirated Arahant time is no more. In every case the Buddha teaches the Mean by the principle of causality ; and whatever the two extremes may be, it is " appetite " or, literally, " thirst " (*taṇhā*) that " sews " one to renewed becoming, and it is only as a mentor of the Mean that one is uncontaminated by either extreme (*A.* iii. 399–401 ; *Sn.* 1042),—just as for Plato it is only by holding on to the golden thread of the Common Law that the human puppet can avoid the contrary and unregulated pulls that drag us to and fro to good or evil actions determined by our appetites (*Laws*, 644).

It is not without good reason that the Mendicant is called a Workman (*samaṇa*, literally " toiler," and exact semantic equivalent of " ascetic ") ; he can know no rest until he is one " who has done what there was to be done " (*katakaraṇīyo*). He must be one who is the master of his will or thought, not one who is at their mercy ; and the man whom the Buddha commends as an " illuminer " of the forest in which he lives alone, is the Mendicant who, when he returns from his round for alms, assumes his contemplative seat determined never to rise again until he has freed himself from the fluxes. For the winning of what has not yet been won, the reaching of what has not yet been reached, the verification of what has not yet been verified, the Mendicant who has left the world in faith and is still a disciple must exercise manhood or heroism (*viriyam* = ἀνδρεία, *virtus*), resolving, like the Bodhisatta himself : " Rather let skin, sinews, and bones alone remain, while flesh and blood dry up, than let there be any rest from the exercise of manhood until I shall have won what can be won by human endurance, manhood, and persistent advance " (*S.* ii. 28 ; *M.* i. 481 ; *A.* i. 50 ; *J.* i. 71). These are his intentions : " I shall become not of the stuff that any world is made of, I shall eradicate the notion of ' I ' and ' mine,' I shall become fully-possesst of the gnosis that cannot be imparted, I shall see clearly the cause and the causal origination of all things."

We have seen that the Bodhisatta's original and primary purpose (*attha*) was to effect the conquest of death, and that in fact he conquered Death on the night of the Great Awakening, and thereafter by his teaching of the Eternal Law " opened the gates of immortality " for others. It will be, then, a kind of test and proof of the efficacy of the Mendicant's Walking with Brahma in accordance with his teaching if we ask ourselves how the graduate Arahant looks on at the death of others, or looks forward to his own. As for the death of others, it is a part of his discipline, to be " mindful of death," and this mindfulness of death includes the reflection that all beings whatever, up to and including the Gods of the Brahma-world, are ultimately mortal ; and bearing this in mind, the graduate Mendicant remains unmoved even by the Buddha's own decease, for he is aware that decay and dissolution are inherent in all component things, and it is only the novices and the inferior deities who weep and wail when " the Eye in the world " is withdrawn. It had been an old story in India that immortality in the body is impossible ; the Arahant, then, is well aware that his own time will come. The untaught, average man, when the end is at hand, " mourns, pines, weeps and wails " ; but not so the Ariyan disciple in whom the fires of selfhood have been quenched—he knows that death is the inevitable end of all born beings, and taking this for granted, only considers, " How shall I best apply my strength to what's at hand ? " (*A.* iii. 56) until he dies. Having already died to whatever can die, he awaits the dissolution of the temporal vehicle with perfect composure and can say : " I hanker not for life, and am not impatient for death. I await the hour, like a servant expecting his wages ; I shall lay down this body of mine at last, foreknowing, recollected " (*Th.* i. 606, 1002). Or even if the Ariyan disciple, whether a Mendicant or still a householder, has not yet " done all that there was to be done," he is assured that having come into being elsewhere according to his deserts, it will still be possible for him to work out his perfection there. The words, " O grave, where is thy victory ? O death, where is thy sting ? " might well have been the Buddha's or those of any true Buddhist. For him, there will be no more becoming, no more sorrow ; or if there is, it will not be for long, for he has already gone far on that long road that leads to Nirvana, " and, indeed, he will soon have reached the goal."

EXTRACTS

FROM

THE BUDDHIST DOCTRINE

I. INTRODUCTORY

IN OLDEN TIMES, ĀNANDA, THERE WAS AT THIS PLACE A RICH and flourishing city thronged with many people ; and near the city, Ānanda, there dwelt the lord, Kassapa,[1] the perfected one, the wholly awakened. And Gavesin[2] was a lay-disciple of Kassapa, but he did not keep the moral habits.[3] Now, because of Gavesin, there were a great many lay-disciples who testified and who were stirred, but they did not keep the moral habits. Then it occurred to him : " I have well served these many lay-disciples, being the first to be stirred, but neither I nor they keep the moral habits. In this way there is exact similarity (between us), leaving no whit of a more. Come now, I'm for something more." So Gavesin went up to the others and said : " Know that from to-day I am one who keeps the moral habits." Then, Ānanda, these others thought to themselves : " If this master Gavesin becomes one who keeps the moral habits, then why not we, too ? "

Again . . . thought Gavesin : " In this way, too, there is exact similarity (between us), leaving no whit of a more. Come now, I'm for something more," and he said to them : " Know that from to-day I am a Brahma-farer, one living remote, abstaining from sex-life." And they thought : " Why not we, too ? "

Again . . . thought Gavesin : " In this way, too, there is exact similarity (between us), leaving no whit of a more. Come now, I'm for something more," and he said to them : " Know that from to-day I eat but one meal a day, abstaining from food at night and from eating at the wrong time."[4] And they thought : " Why not we, too ? "

And, Ānanda, Gavesin, reflecting on all that he had done and the others likewise, thought : " In this way there is indeed exact similarity (between us), leaving no whit of a more. Come now, I'm for something more." And he asked the lord Kassapa for the going forth[5] (into the monastic Order) in his presence,

[1] The Buddha preceding Gotama.
[2] This name means literally " one seeking cows." So Gavesin is the " seeker."
[3] Cf. section on the Moral Habits.
[4] Between noon and sunrise.   [5] *pabbajjā*, cf. Intr., p. 5, n. 1.

and for ordination ; and the others did likewise. All received the going forth and ordination, and soon afterwards Gavesin became a perfected one.[1] He then thought : " I indeed can obtain this unsurpassed bliss of freedom, at will, easily, without difficulty. Would that these other monks might also obtain it." And they, withdrawn, zealous, ardent, self-resolute, not long afterwards, with Gavesin at their head, in striving from higher things to higher, from strength to strength, came to realize unsurpassed freedom.

Wherefore, Ānanda, train yourselves in this way : From higher to higher, from strength to strength, we will strive, and we will come to realize unsurpassed freedom. Truly, Ānanda, this is how you must train yourselves.   *A.* iii. 215–218

> The Brahma-faring is well shown,
> It is here and now, it is intemporal.
>
> *Sn.* 567

By the Brahma-faring one becomes a Brahman.

Sn. 655

They in the world are " Brahmans " who are unfettered and awake.   *Ud.* 4

Monks, this Brahma-faring is not lived to cheat or cajole people. It is not concerned with getting gain, profit, or notoriety. It is not concerned with a flood of gossip nor with the idea of " let folk know me as so-and-so." No, monks, this Brahma-faring is lived for the goal of restraint, for the goal of abandoning, for the goal of dispassion, for the goal of making to cease.

> The lord taught the Brahma-faring—no matter of mere hearsay—
> Restraint is its goal, abandoning is its goal ;
> It leads to immergence in nirvana.
> This Way is followed by great Selves, great saints.
> Those who go along it as taught by the Wake,
> Doers of the teacher's bidding, will make an end of ill.
>
> *A.* ii. 26 ; *It.* p. 28

[A brahman, Sangārava, speaks thus to the lord :]

" Let me tell you, good Gotama, that brahmans offer sacrifice and get others to do so. Therefore, good Gotama, whoever

---

[1] *arahant, cf.* section on Arahants.

himself offers a sacrifice, or whoever gets others to do so—all these are following a course of merit benefiting many persons and which is due to sacrifice. But whoever, whether of this or that family, has gone forth from home into homelessness—he tames (but) one self,[1] calms (but) one self, makes (but) one self attain utter nirvana.[2] Thus he is following a course of merit which benefits one person and which is due to going forth."

"Well, brahman, I will ask you a question in reply. What do you think ? A Truth-finder [3] arises here in the world, a perfected one, a wholly awakened one, endowed with knowledge and right conduct, well-farer, knower of the worlds, incomparable, charioteer [4] of men to be tamed, teacher of *devas* and men, awakened one, lord. He speaks thus : 'Come, this is the Way, this is the course I have followed until, having realized by my own super-knowledge the matchless immergence in the Brahma-faring, I have made it known. Come you too, follow (them) likewise, so that you too, having realized by your own super-knowledge the matchless immergence in the Brahma-faring, may abide in it.' It is thus that the Teacher himself teaches *dhamma*, and others follow for the sake of suchness (truth). Moreover these number many hundreds, many thousands, many hundred thousands. So what do you think, brahman ? This being so, does the course of merit that is due to going forth benefit one person or many persons ?"

"Because this is so, good Gotama, the course of merit that is due to going forth benefits many persons."   *A.* i. 168–169

---

[1] "One self," as in *Dh.* 103, "Compared with one who conquers in battle a thousand thousand men, he is the best of conquerors in battle who conquers but one self" (himself). *Cf. D.* iii. 61 where monks visiting are described as taming, etc., "but one self," unlike the king who tames many. *Cf.* Sacrifice section, p. 135.
[2] *parinibbāpeti.*   [3] *tathāgata.*
[4] *J.* vi. 252, "the Self is the charioteer" ; *S.* i 33, "Dhamma is the charioteer" ; *Dh.* 151, "The chariots decay, not so the Dhamma" ; *S.* iii. 120, "He who sees the Dhamma sees me".

II. THE FOUNDER AND THE ARAHANTS

1. GOTAMA : AUTOBIOGRAPHICAL

ONCE UPON A TIME I, MONKS, WAS STAYING AT URUVELĀ, ON the bank of the river Nerañjarā, under the Goatherds' Banyan, just after I had become fully awakened. As I was meditating alone, I thought : Ill it is to live neither reverencing nor obeying. What recluse or brahman is there under whom I could live paying him honour and respect ? For the perfecting of the sum total of moral habits, of contemplation, of wisdom, of freedom not yet perfected, I would live under another recluse or brahman paying him honour and respect. But I do not see in the world with its *devas*, Māras, Brahmās, among the whole race—recluses, brahmans, *devas* or mankind—any other recluse or brahman more accomplished in these branches of study than myself, and under whom for that reason I could live paying him honour and respect.

Then I thought : This *dhamma* in which I have been fully awakened—suppose that I were to live under this *dhamma*, paying it honour and respect ? Thereupon, monks, Brahmā Sahampati, having vanished from the Brahma-world, appeared in front of me and said : " Even so, Exalted One, even so, wellfarer ! They who in time past were perfected ones, fully awakened ones, those Exalted Ones also dwelt only under *dhamma*, honouring and respecting it. Those Exalted Ones who shall come in the future, these will do the same. So let the Exalted One, lord, who is now a perfected one, a fully awakened one, also dwell only under *dhamma*, honouring and respecting it." And Brahmā Sahampati added this further :

> The Perfect Buddhas who have passed,
> The Perfect Buddhas yet to come,
> The Perfect Buddha who is now,
> And hath for many banished woe—
> All dwelt true *dhamma* honouring,
> Do dwell and shall dwell : 'tis their way.
> So he to whom the Self is dear,
> Who longeth for the Great Self—he
> Should homage to true *dhamma* pay,
> Remembering the Buddha-word.[1]

A. ii. 20–21 ; *cf. S.* i. 138–140

[1] Verse translation, as in *G.S.* ii. 21, except that, above, " true *dhamma* " is substituted for " their *dhamma* ".

44

When you are assembled, monks, there is this one of two (things) to be done : either there is talk on *dhamma* or there is the ariyan silence.[1]

These, monks, are the two quests : the ariyan [2] quest and the unariyan quest.[3] What is the unariyan quest ?

Take the case of someone who, liable to birth because of the self, seeks what is likewise liable to birth : wife and children, men and women slaves, sheep and goats, cocks and swine, elephants, cattle, horses and mares, gold and silver ; and who, liable to old age, to decay, dying, sorrow and to impurity, all because of the self, seeks what is likewise liable to these states (the same as those just mentioned, except that gold and silver are omitted from the cases of decay, dying, sorrow). This is the unariyan quest.

And what, monks, is the ariyan quest ? In this case someone, liable to birth because of the self, having seen the peril in what is likewise liable to birth, seeks the unborn, the uttermost security from bondage,[4] nirvana. Someone, liable to old age because of the self . . . seeks the unageing, the uttermost security from bondage, nirvana. Someone, liable to dying because of the self . . . seeks the undying, the uttermost security from bondage, nirvana. Someone, liable to sorrow because of the self . . . seeks the unsorrowing, the uttermost security from bondage, nirvana. Someone, liable to impurity because of the self, having seen the peril in what is likewise liable to impurity, seeks the stainless, the uttermost security from bondage, nirvana. This is the ariyan quest.

I, too, monks, before my full awakening, while I was still a *bodhisatta* and not fully awakened, because I was liable to birth because of the self, sought what was likewise liable to birth, and so on. It occurred to me : Why do I, liable to birth because of the self, seek what is likewise liable to birth, and so on ? Suppose that I (although) liable to birth because of the self, having seen the peril in what is likewise liable to birth, were to seek the unborn, the uttermost security from bondage, nirvana ? And sup-

---

[1] Cf. p. 53 ; and *Ud.* 31.

[2] Or noble, right (in the sense of belonging to *this* Dhamma and discipline)

[3] Two Quests mentioned in *A.* i. 93 : that for material things, and that for *dhamma.*

[4] *Yogakkhema*, usually immunity to the data of the six senses (mind being the sixth) ; literally " rest or cessation from application "—a " reward of labour," rather than practice of control of the senses.

pose that I, liable to old age, dying, sorrow and impurity because
of the self, having seen the peril in what is likewise subject to
these states, were to seek the unageing, the undying, the unsorrowing, the stainless, the uttermost security from bondage,
nirvana ?

So I went forth from home into the houseless state, a quester
for what is good, seeking for the incomparable path to peace.
I approached first Āḷāra Kālāma and then Uddaka Rāmaputta,
but of the *dhamma* and discipline of both I realized : This *dhamma*
does not conduce to disregarding or to dispassion or to cessation
or to tranquillity or to super-knowledge or to awakening or to
nirvana—only, under Āḷāra, as far as the plane of self-naughting,
and under Uddaka, as far as the plane of neither-perception-nor-
non-perception. So I, a quester for what is good, seeking for the
incomparable path to peace, walking on tour through Magadha,
in due course arrived at Uruvelā, the Camp township. There I
saw a delightful stretch of level ground, a lovely grove, and a
clear flowing river with a village for support nearby.[1] I thought :
What more for his striving can a young man need who is set on
striving ? So I sat down there thinking it a fit (place) for striving.
Then I, monks, liable to birth because of the self, having seen the
peril in what is likewise liable to birth, seeking the unborn, the
uttermost security from bondage, nirvana, won to the unborn,
the uttermost security from bondage, nirvana . . . seeking the
unageing . . . the undying . . . the unsorrowing . . . won
to the unageing, the undying, the unsorrowing. Then I, liable
to impurity because of the self, having seen the peril in what is
likewise liable to impurity, seeking the unstained, the uttermost
security from bondage, nirvana, won the stainless, the uttermost
security from bondage, nirvana. Knowledge and vision arose in
me : Unshakable is freedom for me, this is my last birth, there
is not now becoming again.   *M.* i. 161–167

Those who speak thus, Vaccha : " The recluse Gotama is
omniscient, all-seeing ; he pretends to all-embracing knowledge
and vision, and thinks : Whether I am walking or standing still,
whether I am asleep or awake, knowledge and vision are continu-
ally and perpetually at my disposal "—these do not speak correctly about me, but they misrepresent me with what is untrue
and not in accordance with fact.

[1] I.e. the village he would visit for alms.

If you said, Vaccha : " The recluse Gotama is a threefold-knowledge man "—explaining thus, you would speak correctly about me and would not misrepresent me with what is not in accordance with fact, and you would be explaining in accordance with *dhamma*, and there would be no occasion for a co-religionist holding a sectarian thesis to censure it. For I, Vaccha, remember manifold former abodes as far back as I please, that is to say from one birth backwards, in all their detail and features. Then I, Vaccha, see with the purified *deva*-vision, surpassing that of men, creatures deceasing (hence), and uprising (elsewhere). Then I, Vaccha, by the destruction of the fluxions,[1] having realized here and now by my own super-knowledge the freedom of heart and freedom of intellect which are fluxionless, abide in them.[2]   *M.* i. 482

Of the ultimate beginnings of things I have foreknowledge, Bhaggava ; I have foreknowledge both of that and of more than that. And having foreknowledge of that, I lay no stress on it. As I lay no stress on it, known subjectively to me is that calm which is such that, knowing it intuitively, the Truth-finder falls into no error.   *D.* iii. 28

> The Wheel by me set rolling (said the lord),
> The Wheel of *dhamma*, Sela, without peer,
> 'Tis Sāriputta who keeps that aroll.
> He is the heir born to the Man-thus-come.[3]
> All things meet to be known are known by me,
> Meet to be quickened quickened are by me,
> Relinquishéd by me relinquished are :
> Therefore am I awake, O brahmana !
> Dispel thou doubt in me, incline thy heart !
> Full rare and seldom are the Wakened seen.
> Of those rare men, seen seldom in the world,
> Lo ! I am one, physician without peer.
> Wholly awakened, brahmana, become
> As Brahm, beyond compare : all foes are quelled,
> Crushed Māra's hosts, and fearless I rejoice.[4]
>   *Sn.* 557–561

> My age is now full ripe, my life draws to its close,
> I leave you, I depart ; the Self I've made my refuge.
>   *D.* ii. 120

---

[1] *āsava.*
[2] These three " knowledges " given in greater detail, p. 223 ff.
[3] *Tathāgata*, elsewhere in this volume translated " Truth-finder ".
[4] E. M. Hare, *Woven Cadences.* More references to Sāriputta rolling the wheel of *dhamma* occur, p. 201 ff.

[The brahman Doṇa approaches the lord and asks :]

" Will your reverence become a *deva* ? "

" No, indeed, brahman, I will not become a *deva*."

" Will your reverence become a *gandharva* ? "

" No, indeed, brahman, I'll not become a *gandharva*."

" A *yakkha*, then ? "

" No, indeed, brahman, not a *yakkha*."

" Then will your reverence become a human being ? "

" No, indeed, brahman, I'll not become a human being."

" . . . Who then, pray, will your reverence become ? "

" Brahman, those fluxions whereby, if they were not abandoned, I should become a *deva*—those fluxions in me are abandoned, cut off at the root, made like a palm-tree stump, made non-existent, of a nature not to arise again in a future time. Those fluxions whereby, if they were not abandoned, I should become a *gandharva*, a *yakkha*, a human being—those fluxions in me are abandoned . . . not to arise again in a future time. Just as, brahman, a lotus, blue, red, or white, though born in the water, grown up in the water, when it reaches the surface stands there unsoiled by the water—just so, brahman, though born in the world, grown up in the world, having overcome the world, I abide unsoiled by the world. Take it that I am awake,[1] brahman.

> The fluxions whereby would be
> A *deva*-birth or airy sprite,
> Gandharva, or whereby myself
> Would reach the state of yakkhahood,
> Or go to birth in human womb—
> Those fluxions now by myself
> Are slain, destroyed, and rooted out.
>
> As a lotus, fair and lovely,
> By the water is not soiled,
> By the world am I not soiled ;
> Therefore, brahman, am I awake.[2]

A. ii. 38–39

When I had taught, roused, incited, and gladdened the assembly with talk on *dhamma*, I entered into the condition of fire [3] and

---

[1] *Buddha* here as in the preceding *Sn.* extract. Also, of course, meaning The Wake, or the Awakened One.

[2] Following F. L. Woodward, *G.S.* ii. 44–45, but rendering *āsava* as fluxions, and *buddha* as awake.

[3] *Tejadhātu samāpajjitvā. Tejas* is heat, fire, or fiery energy. The above extract appears to point to some legend of the Buddha as a pillar of fire.

rose above the ground to the height of seven palm-trees, and after having produced a flame to burn and smoke to the height of another seven palm-trees, I came down again at the Gabled Hall in the Great Wood. *D. iii. 27*

II. SOME PROPHECIES ATTRIBUTED TO GOTAMA

There was once a time, monks, when this Mount Vipula was given the name of Crooked, and the people here were called Rohitassas and the measure of their life-span was thirty thousand years. It took them three days to climb Mount Crooked and three days to descend. The Exalted One, Konāgamana, had arisen in the world at that time, and he had as his pair of chief disciples, Bhiyyosa and Uttara, a comely pair. But see, the name of this hill has vanished and these people have passed away and this Exalted One has attained utter nirvana. So impermanent are the constructions, so transient, so unreliable. There was once a time when this Mount Vipula was given the name of Fairside, and the people here were called Suppiyas, and the measure of their life-span was twenty thousand years. It took them two days to climb Mount Fairside and two days to descend. The Exalted One, Kassapa, had arisen in the world at that time, and he had as his pair of chief disciples, Tissa and Bhāradvāja, a comely pair. But see, the name of this hill has vanished and these people have passed away and this Exalted One has attained utter nirvana. So impermanent are the constructions, so transient, so unreliable.

And now to this Mount Vipula has come just the name Vipula, and to these people has come just the name Māgadhese; the measure of their life-span is small, little, fleeting, and he who lives long lives a hundred years or but a little more. The people of Magadha climb Mount Vipula in a short time and descend in a short time. And I have arisen in the world, the perfected, the wholly Awakened. And as my pair of chief disciples I have Sāriputta and Moggallāna, a comely pair.

There will come a time when the name of this hill will vanish and these people will pass away and I will attain utter nirvana. So impermanent, monks, are the constructions, so transient, so unreliable. As far as this, monks, it is enough to disregard, to be dispassionate towards, to be free from all the constructions. *S. ii. 191–193*

Once upon a time, monks, the Dasārahas had a kettle-drum called Summoner. As it began to split, the Dasārahas fixed in ever another peg, until the time came when the Summoner's original drumhead had vanished and only the framework of pegs remained. Even so, monks, will the monks come to be in the future. Those discourses spoken by the Truth-finder, deep, deep in meaning, other-worldly, dealing with emptiness—to these they will not listen as they are being spoken, they will not lend ear, they will not predispose their thoughts to profound knowledge, and they will not hold that these are teachings that should be learnt and mastered.

But, monks, those discourses which are made by poets, which are poetry, which are a manifold of words and phrases, alien,[1] the utterances of disciples—to these they will listen as they are being spoken and will hold that these are the teachings that should be learnt and mastered. Thus it is that the discourses spoken by the Truth-finder, deep, deep in meaning, other-worldly, dealing with emptiness, will come to vanish.

S. ii. 266–267

At the time, monks, when human beings live to the age of eighty thousand years, there will arise in the world the perfected one, the wholly Awakened, the lord named Metteyya,[2] endowed with knowledge and right conduct, well-farer, knower of the worlds, incomparable, charioteer of men to be tamed, teacher of *devas* and men, the Wake, the lord—just as I have now arisen as the perfected one, the wholly Awakened, endowed with knowledge and right conduct, well-farer, knower of the worlds, incomparable, charioteer of men to be tamed, teacher of *devas* and men, the Wake, the lord. He, by his own super-knowledge, will realize and make known this world with its *devas*, its Māras, its Brahmās, creation with recluses and brahmans, with *devas* and men, even as I now, of my own super-knowledge, realize them and make them known. He will teach *dhamma*, he will proclaim the Brahma-faring, lovely at the beginning, lovely in the middle, lovely at the ending, with its goal and its meaning, completely fulfilled, utterly pure, even as I do now. He will lead an Order of monks numbering several thousands even as I now lead an Order of monks numbering several hundreds.

D. iii. 76

[1] Or external to the Buddha's teaching.   [2] Meaning " Friendliness ."

" Now, who are these, Ānanda, who are building a fortified town at Pāṭaligāma ? "

" Sunidha and Vassakāra, lord, chief ministers in Magadha, are building a fortified town at Pāṭaligāma for repelling the Vajjis."

" As though, Ānanda, having consulted together with the *devas* of the Thirty-Three, even so, Ānanda, do Sunidha and Vassakāra, chief ministers in Magadha, build a fortified town at Pāṭaligāma for repelling the Vajjis. Now I, Ānanda, getting up at the end of this night towards dawn, saw with the *deva*-sight, purified and surpassing that of men, many *devatās* occupying sites at Pāṭaligāma. Now, in whatever region powerful *devatās* occupy sites, they bend the minds of powerful kings and the kings' chief ministers to build dwellings there ; in whatever region *devatās* of middling (power) occupy sites, they bend the minds of kings of middling (power) and the kings' chief ministers to build dwellings there ; in whatever region *devatās* of lowly (power) occupy sites, they bend the minds of kings of lowly (power) and the kings' chief ministers to build dwellings there. Ānanda, as far as the ariyan region (extends), as far as there is trading, this will be a leading town, Pāṭaliputta,[1] (where there was) the breaking of the seed-boxes. But, Ānanda, there will be three dangers to Pāṭaliputta, from fire or from water or from internal dissension."   *Vin.* i. 228 ; *Ud.* 88 ; *D.* ii. 87

III. THE ARAHANT [2]

I call him man-of-calm ; not heeding lusts,[3]
Without a knot, he hath the foul mire crossed.

No sons, kine, fields, nor property are his ;
Naught to assume or to reject he finds.

Gone envy, greed, the sage speaks not of " high,"
" Low," " equal," [4] seeking not time's web, weaves none.

Who here hath naught, nor grieves o'er loss, nor goes
To views, he truly man-of-calm is called.[5]
                         Sn. 857–858, 860–861

[1] The modern Patna. According to Waddell (*E.R.E.*, art : Patna) the *pāṭali*-tree is the trumpet-flower tree (*bignonia suaveolens*). There is a tradition that the village, Pāṭaligāma, was so-called because shoots of the *pāṭali*-tree sprouted out of the ground on the day that the village was founded—this fact being referred to in the phrase " the breaking of the seed-boxes ".
[2] Man of worth, perfected one.
[3] *kāma*, elsewhere translated " pleasures of the senses ".
[4] *Cf.* below, p. 88.   [5] E. M. Hare, *Woven Cadences.*

Anyone, monks, in whom passion is not abandoned, in whom hatred is not abandoned, in whom delusion is not abandoned, is called one bound by Māra, Māra's snare is fastened on him, and he is to be done to in accordance with the wishes of the Evil One. Anyone, monks, in whom passion is abandoned, in whom hatred is abandoned, in whom delusion is abandoned, is called one not bound by Māra, Māra's snare is loosed from him, and he is not to be done to in accordance with the wishes of the Evil One.

Who passion and hate and ignorance have left,
Him they call one who has made the self become,
Who is Brahma-become, truth-finder,
An awakened one, who's passed by fear and dread,
One who has abandoned everything.

It. p. 56–57

Whose bourn no *devas*, men, nor *gandharvas*
Can tell—the man-of-worth from fluxions purged—
This one do I a brahman [1] call.

Sn. 644 ; *Dh.* 420

There is no tracing the course of those monks who are men-of-worth, in whom the fluxions are destroyed, who have greatly lived, done what was to be done, shed their burden, won their own goal, completely destroyed the fetters of becoming, and are freed with right profound knowledge. *M.* i. 141

Lo, Upasīva (he replied),
As flame flung on by force of wind
Flees to its end, reaches what none
Can sum ; the silent sage, released
From name-and-form, goes to the goal,
Reaches the state that none can sum.

Know, Upasīva (then he said),
There is no measuring of man
Won to the goal, whereby they'ld say
His measure's so : that's not for him.
When all conditions are removed,
All ways of telling are removed.[2]

Sn. 1074, 1076

Happy indeed the men-of-worth, in them no craving's seen,
The "I" conceit is rooted up ; delusion's net is burst.
Lust-free they have attained ; translucent is the heart of them.
These, unspotted in the world, fluxionless, have Brahm become . . .

---

[1] *Cf.* p. 88, n. 1.   [2] E. M. Hare, *Woven Cadences.*

Worthy of praise the very men, sons of the Wake true-born . . .
That essence of the Brahma-life,[1] that they have made their own . . .
Roar they their lion's roar—supreme in the world are the Wake.[2]

S. iii. 83–84

A person who is neither a tormentor of self nor a tormentor of others is, in this very life, stilled, attained to nirvana,[3] become cool, he is one who experiences bliss, he lives with a self that has become Brahma.[4]   *A.* ii. 206

Learn this from rivers' flow
In mountain cleft and chasm :
Loud gush the rivulets,
The great stream silent moves.

Loud booms the empty thing,
The full is ever calm :
Like pot half-full the fool,
Like full pool is the sage.

When the recluse speaks much,
'Tis of and on the goal :
Knowing, of *dhamma* tells,
Knowing, he speaketh much.

Who knows and curbed-of-self,
Tho' knowing, speaks not much :
That sage still wisdom worths,
That sage still wisdom wins.[5]

Sn. 720–723

---

[1] *Cf.* p. 209.   [2] *Cf.* translation in *K.S.* iii. 69–70.
[3] *nibbuta.* The root is the same as that in *nibbāna* (Skrt. *nirvāṇa*), the cool, waning, despiration (*not* heaven, *not* annihilation of anything but the corruptions), and therefore somewhat tautological with the next, *sītibhūta.*
[4] *Cf.* This Self . . . this Brahma, *BU.* ii. 5. 11.
[5] E. M. Hare, *Woven Cadences. See* reference to the "ariyan silence," **p.** 45.

III. TRAINING

1. TRAINING AND PROGRESS

Arise (from sloth), sit (meditating) ;
What good are dreams to you ?
What sleep is there for th' afflicted,
Pierced, wounded by a barb ?

Arise (from sloth), sit (meditating) ;
Train swiftly for tranquillity.
Let not death's king find you proud,
Nor dupe you to subjection.

The purposes by which
Devas and men stay tied—
Cross over this entanglement,
Nor let the " moment " [1] pass ;
The " moment " missed they grieve,
Consigned to Niraya Hell.

Slothfulness is dust . . .
Being prone to it is dust :
By diligence, by knowledge,
Draw out the barb of self.

Sn. 331–334

Well then, 'tis yours to swelter,[2]
Dhotaka (the lord replied) ;
If here you're prudent, mindful,
Hearing its renown from here—
Train for nirvana of the self.

Sn. 1062

Alertly, Upasīva, seek
The state of man-of-naught (he said),
And aided by the thought " naught is,"
Thou'lt cross the flood ; and day and night,
Lust-rid, doubts gone, see craving end.

Ay, Upasīva (then he said),
Who passion for all pleasures ends,
Helped by the state of man-of-naught,
Rid of all else, in yondermost
Release of sense released, he would
Stay poised untrammelled in that state.[3]

Sn. 1070, 1072

---

[1] The " moment " is the Eternal Now.   [2] *Cf. Dh.* 276, p. 181.
[3] E. M. Hare, *Woven Cadences.*

Faith is the seed, austerity the rain,
      Wisdom my yoke and plough ;
My pole is modesty, mind is the strap,
      And I have mindfulness
For share and goad. Warded in act and word,
      In eating temperate,
With truth I clear the weeds [1] ; and full of bliss
      Is my deliverance.
To a security from moil doth draw
      Vigour, my team in yoke :
And on it goes, nor turns it back ; it goes
      Where is no suffering.
And thuswise is this ploughing ploughed, and thence
      There comes the deathless fruit ;
And whoso hath this ploughing ploughed, set free
      Is he from every ill.[2]

Sn. 77–80 ; *S.* i. 172

I, monks, praise not standing still, far less waning in states that
are good. I, monks, praise growth in states that are good, not
standing still, not waning. And how is there waning, not standing still, not growth ?

Take the case of a monk who is a striver in faith, in moral
habit, in the heard, in giving up, in wisdom, in ready speech.
Suppose these good states neither stand still nor grow in him.
This, monks, I call waning in states that are good, not standing
still, not growth.

And how is there standing still in states that are good, not
waning, not growth ?

Take the case of a monk who is a striver in the states already
referred to. Suppose these states neither wane nor grow in him.
This I call standing still in states that are good, not waning, not
growth. Thus there is standing still in states that are good, not
waning, not growth.

And how is there growth in states that are good, not standing
still, not waning ?

Take the case of a monk who is a striver in faith, in moral
habit, in the heard, in giving up, in wisdom, in ready speech.
Suppose these states neither stand still nor wane in him. This,
monks, I call growth in states that are good, not standing still,
not waning. Thus, monks, there is growth in states that are
good, not standing still, not waning.   *A.* v. 96

---

[1] Or " Truth is the harvest that I reap ".
[2] E. M. Hare. *Woven Cadences.*

I do not say, brahman, that everything is to be cultivated, nor do I say that not everything is to be cultivated. If, as a result of what is cultivated, faith grows, moral habit grows, learning grows, giving up grows, wisdom grows, *that*, I say, is to be cultivated. *M.* ii. 180

Monks, growing in five (ways of) growing, a woman ariyan disciple grows in the ariyan growth and becomes one who takes hold of the essence, who takes hold of the better. What five? She grows in faith, she grows in moral habit, she grows by what she has heard, she grows by what she gives up, she grows in wisdom.

> Who here in faith, in moral habit grows,
> In wisdom, in giving up and in the heard,
> Such as she, a disciple of moral habit,
> Here wins what is the essence of the self.

S. iv. 250 ; *A.* iii. 80

So long as monks become full of faith, growth may be expected for monks, not decline. So long as monks become conscientious, become afraid of blame, become great listeners, become of stirred-up energy, become mindful, become wise, growth may be expected for monks, not decline.

A. iv. 23

So long as monks make become perception of impermanence, growth may be expected for monks, not decline. So long as monks make become perception of what is not the Self, growth may be expected for monks, not decline. So long as monks make become perception of the unlovely, perception of peril, of ejection, of dispassion, so long as monks make become perception of arrest, growth may be expected for monks, not decline.

A. iv. 24

Prince, there are five factors for striving. What are they? Herein a monk is full of faith, he has faith in the awakening of the Truth-finder, thinking : " Indeed this lord is a perfected one, a wholly awakened one, endowed with knowledge and right conduct, well-farer, knower of the worlds, incomparable, charioteer of men to be tamed, teacher of *devas* and men, awakened one, lord." He is without disease, he is without illness, endowed with a good digestion that is neither too cool nor too warm, but medium, innuring to striving. He is not dishonest or deceitful, but manifests himself as he really is to the teacher or an intelligent fellow in the Brahma-faring. He fares along putting forth energy for the ejection of bad states and for the setting up of good states, he is staunch, strong in effort, persevering in regard to states that are good. He comes to be wise, endowed with wisdom that is ariyan and discriminating as to arising and ending and that leads to the total destruction of ill. These, prince, are the five factors for striving. Endowed with these five factors for striving, a monk, taking the Truth-finder as his guide, having realized here and now by his own super-knowledge that supreme goal of the Brahma-faring for the sake of which young men of family rightly go forth from home into homelessness, may fare along towards it. *M. ii. 95, 128*

The Truth-finder, monks . . . turns the Brahma-wheel,[1] saying : " Such is material shape, such its arising, such its passing away ; such is feeling . . . such is perception . . . such are the constructions . . . such is consciousness, such is its arising, such its passing away. Thus, if ' this ' is, ' that ' comes to be ; from the arising of this, that arises ; if this is not, that does not come to be ; from the stopping of this, that is stopped. That is to say, the constructions are conditioned by ignorance, consciousness by the constructions, individuality by consciousness, the six (sense) spheres by individuality, contact by the six spheres, feeling by contact, craving by feeling, grasping by craving, becoming by grasping, birth by becoming ; conditioned by birth, old age and dying, grief, lamentation, ill, sorrow, and despair come into being. Such is the uprising of this entire mass of ill. But from the utter fading away and stopping of ignorance the constructions stop, and so stops each of the rest. Such is the stopping of this entire mass of ill." [2]

Thus, monks, *dhamma* being well declared by me, made manifest, disclosed, brought to light, stripped of swathings, it is enough for the young man of family who has gone forth through faith to stir up energy and think : " Gladly would I be reduced to skin and sinew and bones and let my body's flesh and blood dry up if there came to be a vortex of energy so that that which is not

[1] *Brahma-cakka* also at *M.* i. 69 and *A.* v. 32–36.
[2] *Cf.* section on Causality below.

yet won might be won by human strength, by human energy, by human striving."

Sadly, monks, lives the man of sloth, involved in evil wrong states of mind, and great is the goal itself that he fails to win.[1] But he of stirred-up energy lives happily, aloof from evil wrong states of mind, and great is the goal itself that he makes perfect. Not through what is low comes the attainment of the highest, but through what is high comes the attainment of the highest. This Brahma-faring is worthy of praise. The Teacher has come (to you) face to face. Wherefore stir up energy for the attainment of the unattained, for the mastery of the unmastered, for the realization of the unrealized. Thus will this, your going forth, become not barren but a fruitful and growing thing.[2]

S. ii. 27–29

Two things, monks, have I realized : to be discontented in good states and not to shrink back in the struggle.[3] Without shrinking back, monks, I struggle on thus : " Gladly would I be reduced to skin and sinew and bones and let my body's flesh and blood dry up if there came to be a vortex of energy so that that which is not yet won might be won by human strength, by human energy, by human striving." By my earnest diligence, monks, I won awakening, I won the uttermost security from bondage.

And you, too, monks, struggle on without shrinking back, saying to yourselves : Gladly would I be reduced to skin and sinew and bones . . . so that that which is not yet won might be won by human strength, by human energy, by human striving. Then you, too, monks, having by your own super-knowledge attained here and now that goal of the Brahma-faring for the sake of which young men of family rightly go forth from home into homelessness, will soon abide in it.

Wherefore I say unto you, monks, this is how you must train yourselves : We will not shrink back, but will struggle on, with this thought : Let me be reduced to skin and sinew and bones

---

[1] *Cf. A.* i. 150, p. 72.
[2] *Cf. M.* i. 272, p. 63.
[3] At *Buddhist Psychological Ethics*, 2nd edn., p. 333, 334, both these phrases are elaborated, the latter to mean " the thorough and persevering and unresting performance, the absence of stagnation, the unfaltering volition, the unflinching endurance, the assiduous pursuit, exercise and repetition which attend the cultivation of good states ".

and let my body's flesh and blood dry up if there came to be a vortex of energy so that that which is not yet won might be won by human strength, by human energy, by human striving. This is how you must train yourselves. *A. i. 50*

"Now you, Kesi, are a teacher of horses to be tamed. In what way do you, Kesi, train a horse to be tamed ? "

" By gentleness, lord, also by harshness, also both by gentleness and harshness."

" If a horse responds to none of these methods, what do you do to him ? "

" I destroy him, lord. The reason ? Lest he bring discredit on my teacher's family. But the lord is the matchless teacher of men to be tamed. How does the lord train men to be tamed ? "

" By gentleness, Kesi, also by harshness, also both by gentleness and harshness. This is the way by gentleness : thus is good conduct by body, thus its fruit ; thus is good conduct by speech, thus its fruit ; thus is good conduct by thought, thus its fruit ; thus are *devas*, thus are men.

This is the way by harshness : thus is bad conduct by body, thus its fruit ; thus is bad conduct by speech, thus its fruit ; thus is bad conduct by thought, thus its fruit ; thus is Hell, thus is rebirth as an animal, thus is the realm of the departed.[1]

" This is the way by gentleness and harshness : thus is good conduct by body, thus its fruit ; thus is bad conduct by body, thus its fruit . . . thus is good conduct by thought, thus its fruit ; thus is bad conduct by thought, thus its fruit ; thus are *devas*, thus are men ; thus is Hell, thus is rebirth as an animal, thus is the realm of the departed."

" But if a man to be tamed responds to none of these methods, what does the lord do to him ? "

" I destroy him, Kesi."

" But onslaught on creatures is not pleasing to the lord.[2] So how can the lord say, ' I destroy him, Kesi ' ? "

" It is true that onslaught on creatures is not pleasing to a Truth-finder. But if a man to be tamed responds to none of these methods, a Truth-finder deems that he is not to be spoken to, not to be instructed, and the learned in the Brahma-faring deem the same. This is destruction in the discipline for an ariyan—

---

[1] *peta*, perhaps " ghosts," usually near a dead body.
[2] *Cf.* section on the Moral Habits.

both when a Truth-finder and the learned in the Brahma-faring
deem that he is not to be spoken to, is not to be instructed."

A. ii. 112–113

I, monks, do not say that attainment of profound knowledge
comes straightaway ; nevertheless it comes by a gradual training,
a gradual (doing of) what is to be done, a gradual course.[1] In
this connection, one having faith draws near, he comes close,
he lends ear, he hears *dhamma* and learns it by heart, examines
the import of the things so learnt, is in an ecstasy of delight
over them ; strong desire rises in him, he is emboldened, he
weighs it all, he strives ; being self-resolute, by means of body
he realizes the highest truth itself, and penetrating it by means
of wisdom, sees it.

I will propound a fourfold exposition to you and you shall
understand it from me. Even a teacher who sets store on material
things, who makes them his heritage and lives in association with
them—why, even he is not met by higgling and haggling
stipulations that his followers will or will not do certain things
according as they like them or not. So, what has this to do with
the Truth-finder who lives apart from material things ? To the
disciple who has faith in and is in unison with the Teacher's
instruction, it comes to be a principle that : " The Teacher is the
lord, a disciple am I ; the lord knows, I do not know." To such
a one the Teacher's instruction comes to be a furthering of
growth, giving strength. To such a one it comes to be a principle that : " Gladly would I be reduced to skin and sinew and
bones and let my body's flesh and blood dry up if there came to
be a vortex of energy so that that which is not yet won might be
won by human strength, by human energy, by human striving."

M. i. 479–481

And again, you, Mahānāma, should recollect the *devatās* thus :
" There are the *devas* who are the Four Great Regents, there are
the *devas* of the Thirty-Three, there are the *devas* of Yama, there
are the *devas* of Delight, there are the *devas* who delight in
creation, there are the *devas* who have power over the creation of
others, there are the *devas* of Brahmā's retinue, there are the *devas*
Beyond That. In me, too, there exists a faith like unto that faith
endowed with which these *devatās*, having deceased hence, have

[1] Cf. Vin. ii. 238, p. 195.

arisen there. In me, too, there exists moral habit . . . learning
. . . giving up . . . wisdom like unto the moral habit . . .
learning . . . giving up . . . wisdom endowed with which
these *devatās*, having deceased hence, have arisen there." At any
time, Mahānāma, when an ariyan disciple recollects his own or
the faith and moral habit and learning and giving up and wisdom
of those *devatās*, his mind at that time becomes obsessed with
neither passion, hatred, nor delusion. His mind at that time becomes straight, fixed upon the *devatās*. When his mind is straight,
the ariyan disciple gains enthusiasm for the goal, he gains enthusiasm for *dhamma*, he gains the delight that is connected with
dhamma ; joy is born in one who has delight, the body of one
who has joy is calmed, one whose body is calmed feels ease, the
mind of one who is at ease is contemplative.[1] This one,
Mahānāma, is called an ariyan disciple who, having won to even-
ness, fares on amid folk who go unevenly ; who, free from
malice, fares on amid folk who are malicious ; who, having
reached the stream of *dhamma*,[2] makes become recollection of the
devatās.   *A. v.* 331–332

A number of *devatās* of even mind approached me here,
Sāriputta, and when they had greeted me they stood at a respectful distance and spoke to me thus : " Lord, this Sāriputta is in
the Eastern Monastery in the palace of Migāra's mother ; he is
teaching the monks about the man who has subjective fetters
and objective fetters. The company is delighted. It were well,
lord, if the lord were to go to Sāriputta out of compassion for
him." Then, Sāriputta, these *devatās* having come to be ten (in
number), having come to be twenty, thirty, forty, fifty, sixty,
stood in as little space as is occupied by the point of a gimlet and
did not harm one another. It may be, Sāriputta, that you may
think : " Was not the mind of these *devatās* made to become of
such a kind there [3] that they, having come to be ten (in number),
having come to be twenty, thirty, forty, fifty, sixty, stand in as
little space as is occupied by the point of a gimlet and do not harm

[1] *Cf.* p. 74.
[2] One floats downstream on the *dhamma-sota* (the stream of *dhamma*) to the
" sea "—which is thus used in a good sense ; but the " sea " is also the goal of
the stream of sensation, Māra's stream, *Mārassa sota*, and is therefore also used
in a bad sense. Similarly with " pool," as e.g. *S.* i. 169 (p. 133) in a good sense,
and *It.* p. 113–115 (p. 192) in a bad sense.
[3] I.e. in another world.

one another ?" But this, Sāriputta, is not to be regarded thus. It is just *here*, Sāriputta, that the mind of these *devatās* was made to become of such a kind that they, having come to be ten (in number), having come to be twenty, thirty, forty, fifty, sixty, stand in as little space as is occupied by the point of a gimlet and do not harm one another.

Therefore, Sāriputta, you must train yourselves thus : We will become calm in the sense-organs, calm in thoughts. Thus indeed must you train yourselves, Sāriputta. For if your sense-organs are calm, so will acts of body become calm, calm the acts of speech, calm the acts of mind ; and one may think : " We will offer an offering—calm itself—to our fellow Brahma-farers." It is thus, Sāriputta, that you must train yourselves. Lost indeed, Sāriputta, are the wanderers belonging to other sects who do not hear this disquisition on *dhamma*.   *A. i. 65*

I do not say that for each and every monk there is something to be done through diligence in the field of the six senses. But, on the other hand, I do not say that for each and every monk there is not something to be done through diligence in the field of the six senses. For those who are perfected, who have done what was to be done, who are freed with complete profound knowledge—for these I say there is nothing to be done through diligence in the field of the six senses. It has (already) been done by these, through diligence, and they cannot become those to be indolent. But those who are learners and are diligently striving after the uttermost security from bondage—of these I say that there is something to be done through diligence in the field of the six senses. This is because there are for each of the six sense-organs data that are delightful or repulsive, but these, although impinging on the mind again and again, need not lay hold of it and persist. For unflinching energy comes to be put forth, mindfulness is set up unconfused, the body is tranquil, not per-turbed, the mind contemplative and one-pointed. It is because I, seeing this fruit of diligence, say in respect of such learners that there is something to be done through diligence in the field of the six senses.   *S. iv. 124–125 ; cf. M. i. 477*

" Recluses "—so they call you " recluses." Well, see to it that you make this become a true word and your profession become genuine ; see to it that your religious life becomes not barren but of great fruit.[1] Train yourselves to become this and then that. Nor rest content thinking that what is done is enough and that there is nothing further to be done. I declare to you, I protest to you : Let there be no falling back in your aim while there is something further to be done. And what is there further to be done ? First, to become conscientious and scrupulous ; thereafter, successively, to become pure in deed, speech, thought and mode of living ; to become guarded as to the senses ; to become moderate in eating ; to become intent on diligence ; to become mindful and circumspect ; to become possessed of the sixfold super-knowledge. Each of these is, successively, something further to be done, and while there is something further to be done let there be no falling back in your aim. But when they are all accomplished, the recluse can finally say : Lived is the Brahma-faring, done is what was to be done. *M.* i. 271 ff.

Again you, Nandiya, should recollect the *devatās*, thinking : " Those *devatās* who, passing beyond the companionship of *devas* who subsist on material food, have uprisen in a certain mind-made body—these do not perceive that there is something (further) to be done by the self or an increase (to be added) to what has been done." Nandiya, these *devatās* are like a monk who is not completely freed and who does not perceive that there is something (further) to be done by the self and an increase (to be added) to what has been done. *A.* v. 336 ; *cf. A.* iii. 378

When name and shape (noumenon and phenomenon) have been completely understood, then I say that there is nothing further to be done. *S.* ii. 100 ; *cf. S.* iv. 124

[Sāriputta is asked, What is the way to attain fellowship with Brahmā ? and instructs his brahman questioner in the practice of the Brahma-vihāras. The Buddha comments :]

Why did you establish this brahman only in the lower Brahma-world, where there is still something (further) to be done ? *M.* ii. 195–196

Name and shape combined with consciousness are to be found only where there may be birth or age or dying, or falling from

[1] *Cf. S.* ii. 29, p. 58.

or arising (in other worlds), only where there is signification, interpretation and cognition, only where there is motion involving cognisability as such or such.[1]   *D. ii. 63*

[The standard description of the Arahant, or perfected one :]

He knows, " Birth is done with, the Brahma-life has been lived, done is what was to be done, for me there is no more being such and such."   *Vin. i. 14 et passim*

Even as, monks, in this Rose-apple Land [2] trifling in number are the pleasant parks, the pleasant groves, the pleasant grounds and lakes, while more numerous are the steep precipitous places, unfordable rivers, dense thickets of stakes and thorns, and inaccessible mountains—just so few in number are those beings that are reborn among men : more numerous are the beings reborn among others than men. Just so few in number are those beings that are possessed of the ariyan eye of wisdom : more numerous are those sunk in ignorance and bewilderment. Just so few in number are those beings who, on hearing *dhamma*, learn it by heart ; who examine the aim of the doctrines that they have learnt ; who, understanding the aim and understanding *dhamma*, live in accordance with it ; who are stirred by stirring topics ; who, being stirred, strive systematically ; who, making resolution their object, win concentration, one-pointedness of mind : more numerous are they that do not. Just so few in number are those beings who are winners of the flavour of the aim, the flavour of *dhamma*, the flavour of freedom : more numerous are they that are not.

Wherefore I say unto you, monks, thus must you train yourselves : We will become winners of the flavour of the aim, of the flavour of *dhamma*, of the flavour of freedom. That is how you must train yourselves.   *A. i. 35–36*

Monks, this Brahma-faring is lived for the advantage of the training, for the further wisdom, for the essence of freedom, for mastery in mindfulness.

And how, monks, does there come to be the advantage of the

---

[1] That is to say, logical definitions are applicable only to things in time : not to the unborn, unageing, undying.

[2] Jambudīpa : one of the four " great islands," of which the southernmost includes India.

training ? Herein, monks, the training in the higher practice laid down by me for disciples is for pleasing those who are not (yet) pleased and for increasing (the faith) of those who are pleased. Because I have laid this down, a disciple becomes one who does (the training) in full, perfectly, consistently, spotlessly ; undertaking them, he trains himself in the rules of training. And again, monks, the training that is fundamental to the Brahma-faring, laid down by me for disciples, is for the total destruction of ill in every way.

And how, monks, does there come to be the further wisdom ? Herein, monks, the rules taught by me for disciples are for the total destruction of ill in every way. Because I have taught this, these rules come to be well scrutinized with wisdom by a disciple. Thus there comes to be the further wisdom.

And how, monks, does there come to be the essence of freedom ? Herein, monks, the rules taught by me to disciples are for the total destruction of ill in every way. Because I have taught this, these rules come to be associated by the disciple with freedom. Thus there comes to be the essence of freedom.

And how, monks, does there come to be mastery in mindfulness ? By the thought : " I will complete any training in the higher practice that is incomplete, or I shall, through wisdom here and there, take care of any training in the higher practice that is complete "—so is subjective mindfulness well set up. By the thought : " I will complete any training that is fundamental to the Brahma-faring and that is incomplete, or I shall, through wisdom here and there, take care of any training that is fundamental to the Brahma-faring and that is complete "—so is subjective mindfulness well set up. By the thought : " I shall scrutinize well any rule not well scrutinized, or I shall, through wisdom here and there, take care of any rule that is well scrutinized "—so is subjective mindfulness well set up. By the thought : " I shall apprehend through freedom any rule not apprehended, or I shall, through wisdom here and there, take care of any rule that is apprehended "—so is subjective mindfulness well set up. Thus there comes to be mastery in mindfulness. *A.* ii. 243–244

Monks, there are these five fears for the future from contemplating which the earnest, ardent, resolute monk, a forest-dweller, should live so as to attain the unattained, to master the un-mastered, to realize the unrealized. What five ?

Take the case of a monk, a forest-dweller, who reflects thus : " I am now quite alone in the forest, and while I am living alone in the forest a snake might bite me or a scorpion or a centipede ; and because I might pass away, that would be a stumbling-block to me. Come now, I will put forth energy to attain the un-attained, to master the unmastered, to realize the unrealized." This is the first fear.

Again, a monk, a forest-dweller, might reflect : " I may stumble and fall ; the food I have eaten may make me ill ; bile may convulse me ; phlegm choke me ; stabbing wind within shake me ; and because I might pass away, that would be a stumbling-block to me. Come now, I will put forth energy . . . to realize the unrealized." This is the second fear.

Again, he reflects : " While I am alone in the forest, I may meet with wild animals : with a lion, tiger, leopard, bear, hyena— they might deprive me of life, and because I might pass away, that would be a stumbling-block to me. Come now, I will put forth energy . . . to realize the unrealized." This is the third fear.

Again, he reflects : " While I am alone in the forest, I may meet with thieves. They might deprive me of life, and because I might pass away, that would be a stumbling-block to me. Come now, I will put forth energy . . . to realize the unreal-ized." This is the fourth fear.

Again, monks, a monk, a forest-dweller, reflects thus : " I am now quite alone in the forest, and there are fierce non-human beings in the forest—they might deprive me of life, and because I might pass away, that would be a stumbling-block to me. Come now, I will put forth energy to attain the unattained, to master the unmastered, to realize the unrealized." This, monks, is the fifth fear for the future from contemplating which the earnest, ardent, resolute monk, a forest-dweller, should live so as to attain the unattained, to master the unmastered, to realize the unrealized. *A. iii. 100–102*

Contemplation of dying, monks, when made become, when made much of, comes to be of great fruit, of great advantage, there is immergence in the Deathless, consummation in the Deathless. And how is this ? Take the case of a monk who, when day declines and night sets in, reflects thus : " Many indeed are the chances of dying for me. A snake or scorpion or centipede might bite me ; if I should pass away in consequence, this would be a stumbling-block for me.[1] I might stumble and fall ; the food I have eaten might make me ill ; bile might convulse me ; phlegm choke me ; stabbing wind within shake me ; or non-human beings might attack me ; if I should pass away in consequence, this would be a stumbling-block for me."

Monks, that monk must reflect thus : " Are there any evil and wrong states within me that have not been put away and that would be a stumbling-block for me if I were to pass away to-night ? " If, monks, on consideration he were to realize that there were such states, then in order to put away those same evil and wrong states an intense desire, an effort, endeavour, exertion, struggle, mindfulness and attentiveness is to be made by him. Monks, if his turban or hair were on fire he would make an intense desire, effort, endeavour, exertion, struggle, mindfulness and attentiveness to extinguish that fire. Even so, an intense desire, an effort, endeavour, exertion, struggle, mindfulness and attentiveness is to be made by him so as to give up every evil and wrong state.

But if that monk, on consideration, realize that there are no such states within him that have not been put away and that would be a stumbling-block for him if he were to pass away to-night—then let that monk live verily in delight and gladness, training himself day and night in states that are good. Monks, contemplation of dying, when so made become, when so made much of, comes to be of great fruit, of great advantage, there is immergence in the Deathless, consummation in the Deathless.

A. iv. 320–321 ; cf. A. iii. 306

[The Buddha quotes and endorses the doctrine of Araka, an ancient teacher who lived when the span of man's life was sixty thousand years ; *a fortiori* the doctrine applies to the present, when the span of life is only a hundred years :]

Brief is man's life, a trifle, fleeting, with many an ill. Like as a dewdrop on the tip of a blade of grass, when the sun rises, forthwith dries up and lasts not long ; like as a bubble that appears on the water when God rains ; like as the mark made by a stick on water that forthwith vanishes and lasts not long ; like as a torrent flowing from a distant mountain and carrying all before

[1] Comy. says (to his progress) in the Way.

it, never for a moment, instant, or second at rest, moving, eddy-ing, flowing ; and like as a cow about to be slaughtered, whose every step on her way to the shambles brings her nearer to death, such is man's life, a trifle, fleeting, with many an ill. Awaken ye to the doctrine, exert skill, lead the Brahma-faring, for " there is no immortality of anything born."

Such, I reckon, is (even now) man's life of a hundred years, with their seasons, months, days and nights, meal-times and intervals. Monks, all that a teacher should do for his disciples, seeking their good, in tender compassion, that have I done for you. At the root of these trees, there are your " empty houses." Contemplate ; be not of those who turn back afterwards. This is our teaching to you.   *A.* iv. 136–139 ; *D.* ii. 246 f.

Monks, these five subjects should be contemplated often by a woman or a man or by a house-dweller or one who has gone forth (from home into homelessness). What five ?

I am liable to old age ; I have not outstripped old age—this ought to be contemplated often by a woman or a man or by a house-dweller or one who has gone forth.

I am liable to disease ; I have not outstripped disease. . . .

I am liable to dying ; I have not outstripped dying. . . .

Among all that is near and dear to me there is variableness, there is separation. . . .

I am the result of my own deeds, heir to deeds, having deeds for matrix, deeds for kin ; to me the deeds come home again ; whatever deed I do, whether good or evil, I shall become its heir [1]—this ought to be contemplated often by a woman or a man or by a house-dweller or one who has gone forth.

Monks, to what end should the thought : I am liable to old age ; I have not outstripped old age, be contemplated often by a woman or a man or by a house-dweller or one who has gone forth ?

Monks, in the youth of beings there is pride in youth ; drunk with that pride they go about doing evil through body, doing evil through speech, doing evil through thought. Whoever contemplates this subject often, whatever is the pride of youth in youth, it is either given up altogether or it becomes reduced. Monks, it is to this end that this subject should be contemplated often by a woman. . . .

[1] See section on Deeds and " Transmigration ".

Monks, to what end should the thought : I am liable to disease ; I have not outstripped disease ; be contemplated often ? . . .[1]

Monks, in the health of beings there is pride in health ; drunk with that pride they go about doing evil through body, doing evil through speech, doing evil through thought. Whoever contemplates this subject often, whatever is the pride of health in health, it is either given up altogether or it becomes reduced. Monks, it is to this end . . .

Monks, to what end should the thought : I am liable to dying ; I have not outstripped dying, be contemplated often ? . . .

Monks, in the life of beings there is pride in life ; drunk with that pride they go about doing evil through body, speech, and thought. Whoever contemplates this subject often, whatever is the pride of life in life, it is either given up altogether or it becomes reduced. Monks, it is to this end . . .

Monks, to what end should the thought : Among all that is near and dear to me there is variableness, there is separation, be contemplated often ? . . .

There is, monks, among beings a passionate desire for those (people and things) that are dear ; drunk with that passion they go about doing evil through body, speech, and thought. Whoever contemplates this subject often, whatever the passionate desire for those that are dear, it is either given up altogether or it becomes reduced. Monks, it is to this end . . .

Monks, to what end should the thought : I am the result of my own deeds, heir to deeds, having deeds for matrix, deeds for kin ; to me the deeds come home again ; whatever deed I do, whether good or evil, I shall become its heir, be contemplated often by a woman or a man ? . . .

There is, monks, among beings a doing of evil through body, a doing of evil through speech, a doing of evil through thought. Whoever contemplates this subject often, either the doing of evil is given up altogether or it becomes reduced. Monks, it is to this end that the thought : I am the result of my own deeds, heir to deeds . . . whatever deed I do, whether good or evil, I shall become its heir, should be contemplated often by a woman or a man or by a house-dweller or one who has gone forth.

Monks, the ariyan disciple reflects thus : I am not the only one who is liable to old age, who has not outstripped old age ; for wheresoever there is the coming, the going, the deceasing, the

---

[1] The text repeats in full here and similarly elsewhere.

arising of beings, all beings are liable to old age, they have not outstripped old age. I am not the only one liable to disease . . . liable to dying. . . . I am not the only one for whom, among all that is near and dear, there is variableness and separation. . . . I am not the only one who is the result of his own deeds. . . . While he contemplates this subject often the Way comes into being. That Way he follows, makes become and develops ; and in so doing the fetters [1] are got rid of, the tendencies [2] are removed.

> Having these things : disease, old age and death—
> As they, so men : repulsive is the thought to average man.
> Not meet that I myself should be repelled
> At creatures having these, seeing that I
> Do lead my life no otherwise than they.

> While living thus, I having come to know
> *Dhamma* which has no substrate,
> I who was wont to vaunt in health, youth, life,
> O'ercame all pride, and from security beheld
> Renunciation. Striving for nirvana,
> Strength came to me. Ne'er can I now become
> Addict of sense desires. I will become
> One turning back no more,
> A further-farer in the Brahma-faring.

A. iii. 71–75. (The verses are also found at A. i. 147, with some different readings)

Monks, there are these three types of mastery.[3] What are the three ? Mastery of self, mastery of the worlds, mastery of *dhamma*.

What is mastery of self ? If a monk should think : " I, fallen

---

[1] The ten fetters are given at D. iii. 234 as wrong view as to what goes with body, doubt, belief in the efficacy of rites and customs, desire for sense pleasures, malevolence, desire for (rebirth in the sphere of) form, of non-form, pride, excitement, ignorance.

[2] Seven kinds are given at D. iii. 254 : that of passion for sense desires, of enmity, of wrong view, of doubt, of pride, of passion for becoming (rebirth), of ignorance.

[3] *ādhipateyya*, kingship, dominion. The rite of ordination of the stream-winner, which corresponds to the brahmanical initiation, and to Christian baptism in its original significance, follows out the pattern of a royal installation, especially as regards the " aspersion " (*abhiseka*), by which is conferred a " lordship both human and divine," S. v. 390 ; cf. D. ii. 152 where the Buddha instructs Ānanda to perform the *antevāsābhiseka* for Subhadda. The formula survives in the Mahāyāna (cf. R. Tajima, *Mahāvairocana Sūtra*, 1936, p. 12). The Buddha (like Christ) is both Brahman and Kṣatriya, Priest and King, *Miln.* 225–227.

on birth, old age and dying, sorrow and lamentation, am fallen on ill ; but perhaps some ending of all this mass of ill may be discerned. But if I, gone forth from home into homelessness, have left behind that kind of sense-desire, and should look about for sense-desires that are worse than those, that would be unseemly in me." But if he then thinks : " Stirred up for me shall unsluggish energy become ; called up unmuddled mindfulness ; calmed and serene my body, not turbulent ; concentrated my mind and one-pointed "—he, having obtained mastery of self, abandons wrong, makes right become, abandons what is blameworthy, makes what is blameless become ; he guards the pure Self. This, monks, is called mastery of self.[1]

And what, monks, is mastery of the worlds ? In this case, if a monk should think : " I, fallen on birth . . . (*as above*) . . . But if I, gone forth from home into homelessness, should think of sense-desires, should have malicious thoughts or thoughts of harming—why, surely, in this great company of men in the world there are recluses and brahmans, and there are *devas* too, of supernormal powers, clairvoyant and knowing the thoughts of others. Even from afar they can see me, and they know my mind with theirs. They would also know this of me : This clansman here, although he went forth from home into homelessness out of faith, yet lives mixed up with evil and wrong things." But if he then thinks : " Stirred up for me shall unsluggish energy become, called up unmuddled mindfulness ; calmed and serene my body, not turbulent ; concentrated my mind and one-pointed "—he, having obtained mastery of the worlds, abandons wrong, makes right become, abandons what is blameworthy, makes what is blameless become ; he guards the pure Self. This, monks, is called mastery of the worlds.

And what, monks, is mastery of *dhamma* ? In this case, if a monk should think : " I, fallen on birth, old age and dying, sorrow and lamentation, am fallen on ill ; but perhaps some ending of all this mass of ill may be discerned. Well taught is *dhamma* by the lord ; it is here and now, it is intemporal, a come-and-see thing, leading onwards, known to the wise subjectively. I have fellows in the Brahma-faring who go along knowing and seeing. If I, who have gone forth in this *dhamma* and discipline which are well taught, should be lethargic and indolent, that would not be suitable in me." But if he then thinks : " Stirred

---

[1] The Platonic alternative : to be subject to oneself, or master of oneself.

up for me shall unsluggish energy become, called up unmuddled
mindfulness ; calmed and serene my body, not turbulent ;
concentrated my mind and one-pointed "—he, having obtained
mastery of *dhamma*, abandons wrong, makes right become,
abandons what is blameworthy, makes what is blameless become ;
he guards the pure Self. This, monks, is called mastery of
dhamma. These, monks, are the three masteries.

> There is not in the world an evil deed that does lie hid.
> The Self, O man, knows what of thee is true or false.
> Ah, sir, the lovely Self, the witness, thou dost despise
> Who in the self hideth the self that is evil.
> *Devas* and Truth-finders see the fool walking unevenly 1 in the world ;
> Wherefore let the " master of himself " walk recollectedly,
> The " master of the worlds " heedfully, contemplative,
> The " master of Dhamma," *dhamma*-farer, fails not (of the goal).²

A. i. 147–150

This, monks, is reckoned to be lamentation in the discipline
for an ariyan, namely singing. In the discipline for an ariyan this
is reckoned as causing madness, namely dancing. In the discipline for an ariyan this is reckoned as childishness, namely im-
moderate laughter that displays the teeth. Wherefore, monks,
there is bridge-breaking ³ in singing, bridge-breaking in dancing.
Enough for you, if you are pleased righteously, to smile just to
show your pleasure.   *A.* i. 261

II. FAITH

> Faith is the wealth here best for man ;
> *Dhamma* pursued brings happiness ;
> And truth is sweet beyond compare ;
> Life wisely lived they say is best.

---

[1] " Even is the ariyan Way, ariyans are even in things uneven," *S.* i. 48.

[2] *Cf.* " great is the goal that he fails to win," p. 58 ; and " He fails of the goa
who chooses the pleasant, attains it who takes the best," *Kaṭha Up.* ii. 1.

[3] *Cf.* the stock passage at e.g. *Vin.* i. 59, 158, 250, iii. 6, 88 which is not however
attributed to Gotama : " Now, Truth-finders (sometimes) ask knowing, and
knowing (sometimes) do not ask ; they ask, knowing the right time (to ask),
and they do not ask, knowing the right time (when not to ask). Truth-finders
ask about what belongs to the goal, not about what does not belong to the goal ;
there is bridge-breaking for Truth-finders in whatever does not belong to the
goal," i.e. in such interminable problems as whether a Truth-finder is or is not,
or both is and is not, or neither is nor is not after dying. For a discussion of
crossing the tenuous Bridge, " with its hazards and great rewards . . . a feat
for heroes, or precisely for the Solar Hero," see Doña L. Coomaraswamy, *The
Perilous Bridge of Welfare, HJAS,* vol. 8, No. 2, August 1944, p. 196.

By faith the flood is crossed ;
By earnestness the sea ;
By vigour ill is passed ;
By wisdom cleansed is he.

With faith that men-of-worth
By *dhamma* cool [1] attain,
He earnest, fain to hear,
With wit shall wisdom gain. [2]

Sn. 182, 184, 186

As Vakkalin, Āḷavi-Gotama,
And eke Bhādravudha by faith did win
Release ; so e'en by faith thou too shalt win
Release ; and thou, O Pingiya, shalt go
To the beyond across the realm of death. [3]

Sn. 1146

Monks, there is no stepping-in of wrong so long as faith is set
on right things ; but if faith comes to have vanished, disbelief,
setting in, stays ; then there is a stepping-in of wrong. There is
no stepping-in of wrong so long as conscientiousness . . . fear
of blame . . . energy . . . wisdom is set on right things ; but
if wisdom comes to have vanished, lack of wisdom, setting in,
stays ; then there is a stepping-in of wrong.   *A.* iii. 5

Almost all beings, monks, find delight in pleasures of the
senses ; and of the young man of family who has laid aside the
sickle and pingo and gone forth from home into homelessness,
it is right to say : Through faith has the young man of family
gone forth. And why ? Pleasures of the senses, monks, are
acquired in youth, yes, those of all kinds. Moreover, monks,
low pleasures and the middling sort and those that are high, are
all just reckoned pleasures of the senses.

Monks, suppose a foolish baby boy, sprawling on his back,
were, owing to the carelessness of his nurse, to put a piece of stick
or stone into his mouth ; with what utmost haste she would at
once attend to the matter and remove it. And if she could not
get at it at once she would clasp him round the head with her left
hand, and with her right, crooking her finger, fetch it out, even
though she drew blood. And why ? Monks, such a thing is a
danger to the child ; it is not harmless, I say. Moreover, monks,

---

[1] *nibbāna.*   [2] E. M. Hare, *Woven Cadences.*
[3] E. M. Hare, *Woven Cadences.*

such an act ought to be done by the nurse out of love, seeking the child's good, out of pity and compassion. But when that boy is older and sensible, then she no longer looks after him, knowing : " The boy is now self-warded, he has done with remissness."

In just the same way, monks, so long as right things are not done by a monk through faith, conscientiousness, fear of blame, energy and wisdom, that monk must be watched over by me ; but when right things are so done, then I no longer look after him, knowing : The monk is now self-warded, he has done with remissness.[1]   *A.* iii. 5

III. THE MORAL HABITS

Ānanda, good moral habits have no-bad-conscience as their goal and good result ; no-bad-conscience has delight as its goal and good result ; delight has joy ; joy has calm ; calm has ease ; ease has contemplation [2] ; contemplation has knowledge and vision of what has really come to be ; knowledge and vision of what has really come to be has dispassion due to disregard (of empirical knowledge) ; dispassion due to disregard (of empirical knowledge) has knowledge and vision of freedom as its goal and good result. Thus, Ānanda, good moral habits gradually go on up to the highest.   *A.* v. 2

It is in respect only of trifling matters, monks, only of insignificant matters, only of moral habits, that an ordinary person would speak when speaking praise of the Truth-finder. When he is so doing, he would speak in the following ways :

" Abandoning onslaught on creatures, abstaining from it, the recluse Gotama lives as one who has laid aside the cudgel and sword ; he is scrupulous, kindly, friendly and compassionate towards all breathing things and creatures.

" Abandoning the taking of what is not given, abstaining from it, the recluse Gotama lives as one who takes (only) what is given, who waits for it to be given ; not by stealing he lives with Self become pure.[3]

" Abandoning unchastity, the recluse Gotama is chaste, keep-

---

[1] Translation almost exactly as at *G.S.* iii. 4.
[2] *Cf.* above, p. 61.
[3] *Cf.* " with a Self become Brahma," *A.* ii. 211.

ing remote (from unchastity), abstaining from dealings with women.

Abandoning lying speech, the recluse Gotama abstains from lying speech, he is a truth-speaker, a bondsman to truth, trustworthy, dependable, no deceiver of the world.

"Abandoning slanderous speech, the recluse Gotama abstains from it ; having heard something here, he is not one to repeat it elsewhere for (causing) variance among those (people), or having heard something elsewhere, he is not one to repeat it here for (causing) variance among these (people). In this way he is a reconciler of those who are at variance, one who combines those who are friends. Concord is his pleasure, his delight, his joy, concord is the motive of his speech.

"Abandoning harsh speech, the recluse Gotama abstains from it. Whatever speech is gentle, pleasing to the ear, affectionate, going to the heart, urbane, pleasant and agreeable to the many-folk—such speech does he utter.

"Abandoning frivolous chatter, the recluse Gotama abstains from it ; he is a speaker at a right time, a speaker of fact, a speaker on the goal, a speaker on *dhamma*, a speaker on discipline ; he speaks words that are worth treasuring, with similes at the right times, words that are discriminating, connected with the goal."

It is in these ways, monks, that an ordinary man would speak when speaking praise of the Truth-finder.   *D. i.* 3–5

> Who falls on breathing things, and utters lies,
> takes what folk give him not, and goes to wife
> of other man,
>
>   the man who's given o'er
> to drinking heady liquors : even here,
> in (this) world, he's digging at the root of self.[1]

Dh. 246–247

Monks, onslaught on creatures, when pursued, made become, made much of, brings one to hell, to an animal's womb, to the realm of the departed. The very trifling result of onslaught on creatures is that it brings short life to a man.

Monks, stealing, when pursued . . . brings one to hell. . . . The very trifling result is the loss of a man's wealth.

[1] Much as Mrs Rhys Davids' translation in *Min. Anth.* i.

Monks, fleshly lusts, when pursued . . . bring one to hell. . . .
The very trifling result is a man's rivalry and hatred.

Monks, lying, when pursued . . . brings one to hell. . . .
The very trifling result is the slandering and false-speaking of a
man.

Monks, back-biting, when pursued . . . brings one to hell.
. . . The very trifling result is the breaking-up of a man's
friendships.

Monks, harsh speech, when pursued . . . brings one to hell.
. . . The very trifling result is an unpleasing noise for a man.

Monks, frivolous chatter, when pursued . . . brings one to
hell. . . . The very trifling result is unacceptable speech for a
man.

Monks, drinking strong drink, when pursued, made become,
made much of, brings one to hell, to an animal's womb, to the
realm of the departed. The very trifling result of drinking strong
drink is madness for a man.   *A. iv.* 247

IV. WHAT OUGHT NOT AND WHAT OUGHT TO BE DONE

Ānanda, I say expressly that wrong conduct of body, speech,
and thought is something that ought not to be done. From
doing this which ought not to be done, this peril is to be expected : Surely the Self upbraids the self [1] ; the wise, having
ascertained (his wrong-doing), blame him ; an evil report of
him goes abroad ; he passes away bewildered ; on the breaking-
up of the body after dying he arises in the Waste, the Bad
Bourn, the Downfall, Niraya Hell.

Ānanda, I say expressly that right conduct of body, speech and
thought is something that ought to be done. From doing this
which ought to be done, this advantage is to be expected :
Surely the Self does not upbraid the self ; the wise, having ascertained (his right-doing), commend him ; a lovely report of him
goes abroad ; he passes away not bewildered ; on the breaking-
up of the body after dying he arises in the Good Bourn, the
heaven world.

[1] *Cf. A.* v. 88. For example, when the Buddha cannot stomach the scraps of
food that are given to him, then " Self upbraids self," *J.* i. 66. In all these cases
" Self " corresponds to the Socratic Daimon (Buddhist *Yakkha*) and our
" conscience ".

Abandon what is wrong. It is possible to abandon it. Were it not possible to abandon what is wrong, I would not say : Abandon it. But because it is possible, therefore I say : Abandon what is wrong.

Make what is right become. It is possible to make what is right become. Were it not possible to make what is right become, I would not say : Make what is right become. But because it is possible, therefore I say : Make what is right become.

A. i. 57–58

Rāhula, when you come to want to do any deed of body, speech, or thought, you should reflect : Does it conduce to the harm of self, to the harm of others, to the harm of both ? Is it wrong, productive of ill, ill in result ? If you know that it does conduce to the harm of self or to the harm of others or to the harm of both and that it is wrong, then, Rāhula, a deed such as this should not, as far as you are able, be done by you. You should hold back from it ; you should confess it and disclose it so as to come to restraint in the future. But should you know, upon reflection, that a deed of body, speech, or thought that you come to want to do does not conduce to the harm of self or to the harm of others or to the harm of both and that it is right, productive of good, good in result, then, Rāhula, a deed such as this is to be done by you. As a result you may go along in joy and delight training yourself day and night in states that are right.   *M. i. 415–417*

V. MEDITATION AND CONTEMPLATION

Monks, by getting rid of six things, one can become one to enter on and abide in the first (stage of) meditation.[1] What are the six ? Desire for sense-pleasures, ill-will, sloth and torpor, flurry and worry, doubt, and his peril among sense-pleasures becomes clearly seen by right wisdom as it really is.

Monks, by getting rid of (a further) set of six things, one can become one to enter on and abide in the first (stage of) meditation. What are the six ? Pre-occupation with sense-pleasures, with ill-will, with harming ; awareness of sense-pleasures, of ill-will, of harming.   *A. iii. 428*

[1] *jhāna.*

There are, monks, these four (stages in) meditation. What are the four ?

Herein, monks, a monk, aloof from the pleasures of the senses, aloof from wrong states of mind, enters on and abides in the first (stage in) meditation which has analysis and investigation, is born of aloofness, and is rapture and happiness.

By allaying analysis and investigation, with inner faith, the mind concentrated and one-pointed, he enters on and abides in the second (stage in) meditation which is without analysis, without investigation, is born of contemplation, and is rapture and happiness.

By the fading of rapture, he abides indifferent and mindful and thoughtful and experiences ease of body, so that, entering on the third (stage in) meditation, he abides in it, one of whom the ariyans say : "He is indifferent, mindful, an abider in ease."

By getting rid of happiness and by getting rid of suffering, by the going down of his former joys and sorrows, he enters on and abides in the fourth (stage in) meditation which is without suffering, without happiness, the utter purity of mindfulness which is indifference.

These, monks, are the four (stages in) meditation.

Monks, just as the river Ganges tends, slides and gravitates towards the East, even so, monks, does a monk who is making the four (stages in) meditation become, who is making much of them, tend, slide and gravitate towards nirvana.   S. v. 307–308

These four (stages in) meditation are known as right contemplation.[1]   S. v. 10

At a time, monks, when a monk, aloof from the pleasures of the senses, attains the first (stage in) meditation, at that time it occurs to that monk : "Now I, by going to the refuge for the fearful, dwell at present by means of Self and have nothing to do with Māra." And it also occurs to Māra, the Evil One : "Now the monk, by going to the refuge for the fearful, dwells at present by means of Self and has nothing to do with me." And it is the same, monks, when a monk attains the second, third, and fourth (stages in) meditation.

At a time, monks, when a monk, by passing entirely beyond the perception of form, by quelling perceptions of repulsion, by

[1] samādhi.

paying no attention to the divers perceptions, thinks : " Space is unending," he attains the sphere of infinite space. Monks, this monk is called one who has made Māra blind,[1] trackless, and who, having destroyed Māra's vision, goes invisible to the Evil One.

At the time, monks, when a monk, by passing entirely beyond the sphere of infinite space, thinks : " Consciousness is unending," he attains the sphere of infinite consciousness. Passing entirely beyond this, if he thinks : " There is nothing whatever," he attains the sphere of self-naughting.[2] Passing entirely beyond this, he attains the sphere of neither-perception-nor-nonperception. Having passed entirely beyond this, he attains the stopping of perception, knowing, and feeling, and because he has seen with wisdom, the fluxions are utterly destroyed. Monks, this monk is called one who has made Māra blind, trackless, and who, having destroyed Māra's vision, goes invisible to the Evil One, and has crossed over the entanglement in the world.

A. iv. 433–4 ; *cf. M*. i. 159–160

[Once when a monk entered his cell and sat silent and did not help the other monks at the time of making the robes, the lord asked him the reason for his conduct. " I do my own work, lord," he replied. Then the lord, knowing that monk's mind by his own, said to the monks :]

Do you not, monks, be vexed with this monk. He is one who obtains at will, without difficulty, and without trouble, the four (stages in) meditation which are abidings in happiness here and now and belong to the mind. He, having realised here and now by his own super-knowledge that incomparable consummation of the Brahma-faring, which is the goal for the sake of which young men of family rightly go forth from home into homelessness, abides in it.

> Nor him given to laxity, nor him of little strength,
> May reach nirvana, the freedom from all ill,
> But this young monk, this best of men,
> His last body bears, having worsted Māra and his train.

S. ii. 278

I will teach you *dhamma*, brahmans ; listen and pay careful

[1] Reading *andha* with *M*. instead of *anta* with *A*.
[2] Or nothingness.

attention, and I will speak. Imagine four men standing at the
four quarters (of the globe), each endowed with supreme pace
and speed and with supreme length of stride—as a skilled archer,
trained, dexterous, a marksman, may shoot an arrow through a
palm-tree's shadow with ease ; let them be endowed with speed
such as this. And with a length of stride such as this : as the
western sea from the eastern sea. Then suppose a man standing
at the eastern quarter (of the globe) were to speak thus : " By
walking I'll reach the end of the world." Though man's life-span
were a hundred years and he lived for a hundred years and walked
for a hundred years—save when eating, drinking, chewing,
munching, answering nature's calls and dispelling fatigue by
sleep—he would die or ever he reached the end of the world.
And suppose a man at the western quarter . . . at the northern
quarter . . . at the southern quarter were to say likewise . . .
though each walked for a hundred years—save when eating and
so forth—they would die or ever they reached the end of the
world. And why ? Not, brahmans, do I say that by such
journeys the world's end may be apprehended, seen, reached ;
yet, I declare, brahmans, that without reaching the end of the
world there is no ending of suffering.[1]

Brahmans, these five strands of sense-pleasures are called
" world " in the discipline for an ariyan. What five ? Shapes
cognizable by the eye, longed for, alluring, pleasurable, lovely,
bound up with sense-pleasures, causing excitement ; sounds
cognized by the ear, smells cognized by the nose, tastes cognized
by the tongue, things touched cognized by the body, longed for,
alluring, pleasurable, lovely, bound up with sense-pleasures,
causing excitement.

Now consider a monk, brahmans, who, aloof from pleasures
of the senses, has attained and dwells in the first (stage in) meditation. He is said to have come to the world's end and to abide at
the world's end. Some speak of him thus : " He is still world-
bound, he still has not gone out from the world." I, too, say
thus : This one is still world-bound, he still has not gone out
from the world.

Then consider a monk, brahmans, who enters on and abides
in the second, third, the fourth (stages in) meditation, the sphere
of infinite space, the sphere of infinite consciousness, of nothingness, of neither-perception-nor-non-perception. In each case he

[1] Cf. below, p. 159.

is said to have gone to the world's end and to abide at the world's end. Some speak thus of him, as before. I, too, say thus : This one is still world-bound, he still has not gone out from the world.

But again, brahmans, a monk, passing entirely beyond the sphere of neither-perception-nor-non-perception, enters on and abides in the stopping of perception, knowing and feeling, and of one who has seen by wisdom, the fluxions come to be utterly destroyed. Brahmans, this monk is called one who, having come to the world's end, abides at the world's end, he has crossed over the entanglement in the world.[1]   *A. iv. 429–432*

There are, monks, these five binding fetters of the higher kind. What are the five ? Lust for the corporeal, lust for the incorporeal, pride, excitement, ignorance. These are the five. It is for fully knowing, for utterly knowing, for utterly destroying, for getting rid of these five binding fetters of the higher kind that the ariyan eightfold Way is made to become . . . that the four (stages in) meditation are made to become.   *S. v. 61, 309*

There are, monks, these four types of meditators. What are the four ?

There is the meditator who, in contemplation, is skilled in contemplation, but who is not skilled in the attainment of contemplation.

There is the meditator who is skilled in the attainment of contemplation, but who, in contemplation, is not skilled in contemplation.

There is the meditator who, in contemplation, is not skilled in contemplation and who is not skilled in the attainment of contemplation.

There is the meditator who, in contemplation, is skilled in contemplation and who is skilled in the attainment of contemplation.

Herein, monks, whatever is the meditator who, in contemplation, is skilled in contemplation and who is also skilled in the attainment of contemplation, he is, of these four types of meditators, the foremost, the best, the head, the supreme, the most excellent. As from a cow comes milk, from milk curds, from curds butter, from butter ghee, from ghee the cream of the ghee

---

[1] Almost exactly as at E. M. Hare, *G.S.* iv. 288–291.

—and this is reckoned the best—even so, monks, the meditator who, in contemplation, is skilled in contemplation and who is also skilled in the attainment of contemplation, is of these four types of meditators reckoned the foremost, the best, the head, the supreme, the most excellent.[1]   *S.* iii. 263–264

Monks, being prudent and thoughtful, make become immeasurable contemplation. Monks, if immeasurable contemplation is made become by the prudent and thoughtful, to each one there accrue five (kinds of) knowledge.[2]   What are the five ?

This contemplation is ease for the present as well as resulting in ease in the future—this knowledge accrues to each one.

This contemplation is noble, disinterested—this knowledge accrues to each one.

This contemplation is practised by those who are not base men —this knowledge . . .

This contemplation is peaceful, excellent, it is for gaining tranquillity, for reaching one-pointed concentration, it is not of the habit of painful self-denial—this knowledge . . .

This contemplation is one which I, mindful, enter upon ; mindful, emerge from—this knowledge accrues to each one.

Monks, being prudent and thoughtful, make become immeasurable contemplation. Monks, if immeasurable contemplation is made become by the prudent and thoughtful, to each one there accrue these five (kinds of) knowledge.   *A.* iii. 24

Monks, I will teach you the making become of the ariyan right contemplation that is five-limbed. Listen carefully, pay attention, and I will speak. What are the five ?

Monks, take the case of a monk who, aloof from pleasures of the senses, aloof from wrong states of mind, enters on and abides in the first (stage in) meditation which has analysis and investigation and is the zest and ease that are born of aloofness. He drenches, permeates, fills, pervades this body itself with the zest and ease that are born of aloofness, so that there is not any part of

---

[1] At *S.* iii. 264–265 a meditator skilled in contemplation and skilled in the retention of contemplation ; and skilled in the emergence from contemplation are treated as above.

[2] Or " there arise individually five (kinds of) knowledge ".

this entire body that is not pervaded by the zest and ease that are born of aloofness.

Monks, as a skilled shampooer or his apprentice, having scattered bath-powder in a bronze vessel, might gradually pour in water so that the shampooing-ball, taking up the moisture, soaking up the moisture, is pervaded inside and out with moisture, although not dripping with it—even so, monks, does a monk drench, permeate, fill and pervade this body itself with the zest and ease that are born of aloofness. This, monks, is the first (way of) making become the five-limbed ariyan right contemplation.

Again, monks, a monk by the allaying of analysis and investigation, being inwardly calmed, the mind become concentrated on one point, without analysis, without investigation, enters on and abides in the second (stage in) meditation that is the zest and ease that are born of contemplation. He drenches, permeates, fills, pervades this body itself . . . not pervaded by the zest and ease that are born of contemplation.

Monks, as a pool of water having a spring of water, but no inlet for water either on the east side or on the west, or on the north or on the south, and where the (rain-) *deva* does not pour down showers from time to time, yet because cool waters have welled up in that pool of water, that pool of water would be drenched, permeated, filled, pervaded with the cool water, so that no part of the entire pool of water would not be pervaded by the cool water—even so, monks, does a monk drench, permeate, fill and pervade this body itself with the zest and ease that are born of contemplation so that there is not any part of this entire body that is not pervaded by the zest and ease that are born of contemplation.

And again, monks, a monk, by the fading of zest abides indifferent and mindful and circumspect, and he experiences that ease of body by reason of which the noble ones say of him that he is indifferent, mindful, an abider in ease ; and he enters on and abides in the third (stage in) meditation. He drenches, permeates, fills, pervades this body itself with an ease that lacks zest, so that there is not any part of this entire body that is not pervaded by ease that lacks zest.

Monks, as in a pond of red lotuses, in a pond of blue lotuses, in a pond of white lotuses, some lotuses in each pond are born in the water, grow up in the water, never rising above the water, but flourishing beneath it, are drenched, permeated, filled, pervaded from root to tip by the cool water so that there is no part of all the red, blue, and white lotuses that is not pervaded by the cool water—even so, monks, does a monk drench, permeate, fill, pervade this body itself with the ease that lacks zest so that there is not any part of that entire body that is not pervaded by the ease that lacks zest.

And again, monks, a monk by getting rid of ease, by getting rid of ill, and by the going down of his former joys and sorrows, enters on and abides in the fourth (stage in) meditation which, being without ease, without ill, is the utter purity of mindfulness that is indifference. As he, having permeated this body itself with a mind that is purified and cleansed, comes to be sitting down there is no part of his entire body that is not permeated by a mind that is purified and cleansed.

As in the case of a man who should be sitting down, having clothed himself including his head with a white cloth, there would be no part of his entire body not pervaded by the white cloth—even so, monks, does a monk, having permeated this body itself with a mind that is purified and cleansed, as he comes to be sitting down there is no part of his entire body that is not permeated by a mind that is purified and cleansed.

And again, monks, a feature for consideration comes to be rightly taken up by a monk, rightly attended to, rightly reflected upon, rightly penetrated by wisdom. It is as if, monks, some one should consider someone else—as one standing might consider one sitting, as one sitting might consider one lying down—even so, monks, does a feature for consideration come to rightly be . . . penetrated by wisdom. This, monks, is the fifth way of making become the five-limbed ariyan right contemplation.

Monks, when a monk has made become and has made much of the five-limbed ariyan right contemplation, he bends his mind for the realization by super-knowledge of whatever state it is that is to be realized by super-knowledge, so that in every case he attains to being a witness in whatever faculty it may be. . . .

(Thus) if he desires : " May I, from being one, become many ; from being many, become one . . ." [1] in every case he attains to being a witness in whatever faculty it may be.

If he desires : " May I, by the condition of *deva*-hearing which

[1] As on p. 107, Marvels section.

is purified and surpasses that of men, hear both kinds of sounds—
those of *devas* and those of men, and those which are distant and
those which are near," in every case he attains to being a witness
in whatever faculty it may be.

If he desires : " May I by mind know of other beings, of other
men, the minds which are passionate as such, the minds devoid of
passion as such, the minds full of hatred as such, the minds devoid
of hatred as such, the minds full of stupidity as such, the minds
devoid of stupidity as such, the congested minds as such, the
minds devoid of congestion as such, the diffuse minds as such, the
minds devoid of diffuseness as such, the liberal minds as such, the
illiberal minds as such, the inferior minds as such, the not
inferior minds as such, the contemplative minds as such, the
uncontemplative minds as such, the freed minds as such, the
unfreed minds as such," in every case he attains to being a
witness in whatever faculty it may be.

If he desires : " May I remember my manifold former abodes,
that is to say : One birth . . . I, deceasing thence rose up again
here," [1] in every case he attains to being a witness in whatever
faculty it may be.

If he desires : " May I see beings with *deva*-sight which is
purified and surpasses that of men . . . these, at the breaking-up
of the body arise in the Happy Bourn, the heaven-world,"
in every case he attains to being a witness in whatever faculty it
may be.

If he desires : " May I, through the destruction of the fluxions,
having realized here and now by my own super-knowledge the
freedom of mind, freedom of wisdom which are fluxionless—
may I abide in them," in every case he attains to being a witness
in whatever faculty it may be. *A*. iii. 25–29

VI. GO NOT BY HEARSAY

Now look you, Kālāmas.[2] Do not be misled by report or
tradition or hearsay. Do not be misled by proficiency in the
Collections,[3] nor by mere logic and inference, nor after consider-

---

[1] As on p. 223.
[2] At *A*. ii. 191 this advice is given to Bhaddiya.
[3] *Piṭaka*, the " baskets " of Sayings on Dhamma (Suttapiṭaka), on Discipline
(Vinayapiṭaka), on More-Dhamma (Abhidhammapiṭaka).

ing reasons, nor after reflection on some view and approval of it, nor because it fits becoming, nor because the recluse (who holds it) is your teacher. But when you know for yourselves : These things are not good, these things are faulty, these things are censured by the intelligent, these things, when performed and undertaken, conduce to loss and sorrow—then do you reject them.   *A. i. 189 ; ii. 191*

Monks, I will teach you these four great authorities. Listen and pay careful attention, and I will speak. And what, monks, are the four great authorities ?

In this case, monks, a monk might say : " Face to face with the lord, your reverence, did I hear it ; face to face with him did I receive it. This is *dhamma*, this is discipline, this is the Teacher's instruction." Now, that monk's words are neither to be welcomed nor scorned, but are to be closely scrutinized, laid beside the Discourses and compared with the Discipline. If they do not tally and agree, you must come to this conclusion : Surely this is not the word of this lord, perfected one, fully awakened one ; and it was wrongly taken by that monk. So reject it, monks. But if that monk's words tally and agree with the Discourses and the Discipline, then you must come to this conclusion : Surely this is the word of this lord . . . it was rightly taken by that monk. Bear this in mind as the first great authority.

Then again a monk might say : " In such and such a dwelling-place resides an Order (of monks) together with an elder monk, a leader. Face to face with that Order I heard it. . . ." . . . it was rightly taken by that Order. Bear this in mind as the second great authority.

Yet again a monk might say : " In such and such a dwelling-place resides a number of elder monks who have heard much, to whom the tradition has been handed down, experts in *dhamma*, experts in discipline, experts in the summaries. Face to face with those elder monks did I hear it. . . ." . . . you must conclude that this was the word of this lord and was rightly taken by those elders. Bear this in mind as the third great authority.

Then again a monk might say : " In such and such a dwelling-place resides a single elder monk who has heard much, to whom the tradition has been handed down, an expert in *dhamma*, an expert in discipline, an expert in the summaries. Face to face with that elder did I hear it. . . ." . . . But if that elder monk's words tally and agree with the Discourses and the Discipline, then you must come to this conclusion : Surely this is the word of this lord, perfected one, fully awakened one, and it was rightly taken by that elder monk. Bear this in mind, monks, as the fourth great authority.   *A.* ii. 167–170 ; *D.* ii. 123–126

IV. RELATIONS WITH OTHERS

1. Right Views and Heresies

INDEED THE TRUTH IS ONE, THERE IS NOT ANOTHER. *Sn.* 884

That freedom (of the knowledge of the destruction of all ill), based on truth, comes to be unshakable. That is falsehood which is by nature false. That is truth which is not by nature false, which is nirvana. This, monks, is the highest truth of the ariyans, that is to say what is not by nature false, nirvana.
M. iii. 245

Nirvana is not of the nature of falsehood—this the ariyans know as truth. *Sn.* 758

Wanderers, these four brahman truths have been made known by me after I had realized them through my own superknowledge. What are the four ?

In this case, wanderers, a brahman [1] speaks thus : " No living thing is to be harmed." So saying, a brahman speaks truth, not falsehood. Thereby he does not think " recluse " or " brahman " or " I am better or equal or inferior." [2] Moreover by fully comprehending this truth he comes to be one going along with mercy and compassion towards creatures.

Again, wanderers, a brahman speaks thus : " All pleasures of the senses are impermanent, ill, liable to change." So saying, a brahman speaks truth, not falsehood. Thereby he does not think " recluse . . . inferior." Moreover by fully comprehending this truth he comes to be one going along towards disregarding, towards being dispassionate in respect of, towards arresting pleasures of the senses.

Again, wanderers, a brahman speaks thus : " All becomings

---

[1] Early Buddhism retained the word " brahman " and gave it the meaning of " the best." The Comy. (*AA.* iii. 161) here explains it by *khiṇāsava*, one whose fluxions are destroyed, which is tantamount to *arahant*, man-of-worth, one perfected.
[2] *Cf.* p. 51 n. 4.

are impermanent, ill, liable to change." So saying, a brahman speaks truth, not falsehood. Thereby he does not think "recluse . . . inferior." Moreover by fully comprehending this truth he comes to be one going along towards disregarding, towards being dispassionate in respect of, towards arresting becomings.

Again, wanderers, a brahman speaks thus : " I am naught of anyone anywhere, nor is there anywhere aught of mine." So saying, a brahman speaks truth, not falsehood. Thereby he does not think " recluse " or " brahman " or " I am better or equal or inferior." Moreover by fully comprehending this truth he comes to be one going along to the practice of self-naughting.

These, wanderers, are the four brahman truths that have been made known by me after I had realized them through my own super-knowledge.   *A*. ii. 176–177

Monks, there are these six matters which are to be kept in mind, which cause affection, which cause respect, and which conduce to harmony, to absence of contention, to concord, and to unity. What are the six ?

If a monk's acts of body are done through love towards his fellows in the Brahma-faring, both openly and in private [1]—this is a matter to be kept in mind . . . and which conduces to . . . unity.

Again, if a monk's acts of speech are done through love. . . . Again, if his acts of thought are done through love towards his fellows in the Brahma-faring, both openly and in private—this too is a matter . . . which conduces to . . . unity.

Again, those legitimate acquisitions, acquired legitimately, even though they be but what has been put into the begging bowl, if a monk becomes one who shares such acquisitions, who enjoys them both openly and in private with his fellows in the Brahma-faring who are of moral habit—this too is a matter . . . which conduces to . . . unity.

And again, those moral habits which are without flaws, without defects, unspotted, without blemish, freeing, praised by the intelligent, untarnished, conducive to contemplation—if a monk fares endowed with moral habits such as these in regard to his

---

[1] *MA*. ii. 395, both in front of them and in front of others.

fellows in the Brahma-faring both openly and in private—this too is a matter . . . which conduces to . . . unity.

And again, whatever is a (right) view, ariyan, saving, and which leads the holder of it to the total destruction of ill—if a monk fares endowed with views such as these in regard to his fellows in the Brahma-faring both openly and in private—this too is a matter to be kept in mind, which causes affection, which causes respect, and which conduces to harmony, to absence of contention, to concord and to unity.

These, monks, are the six matters that are to be kept in mind . . . and which conduce to . . . unity. Of these six matters which are to be kept in mind, this is the chief, this is the roof-plate, this is the dome—that is to say, whatever view is ariyan, saving, and which leads the holder of it to the total destruction of ill. Monks, as in the case of a house with a finial, this is the chief, this is the roof-plate, this is the dome—that is to say, the finial—so of these six matters which are to be kept in mind, this is the chief, this is the roof-plate, this is the dome—that is to say, whatever view is ariyan, saving, and which leads the holder of it to the total destruction of ill.

M. i. 322 ; *cf. A.* iii. 289, *D.* iii. 245

What, householder, are the three forms of faring by *dhamma,* of faring evenly by means of the mind ? This is a case where a person comes to be uncovetous, not coveting the property of another, and thinking : " O might that which is another's be mine." He comes to be benevolently minded, his purposes are not malevolent, and he thinks : " May these beings, free from enmity, free from oppression, safe, at ease, take care of the self." Right view comes to be, an unperverted vision, to the effect : " There are alms, there is sacrifice, there is oblation, there is fruit and result of deeds well done and ill done, there is this world, there is the world beyond, there is mother, there is father, there are beings of spontaneous generation, there are in the world recluses and brahmans who walk and fare evenly and who, having realized this world and the world beyond by their own super-knowledge, declare them."   *M.* i. 288 ; *cf. A.* v. 267

Through not directly envisaging the arising and cessation of consciousness, and the way that leads to the suppression of consciousness, that is the reason of the endless variety of views [1] that spring up in the world—such views as that "the world is everlasting" or "not everlasting," "the body is the life" or "other than the life," "a Truth-finder becomes after dying," or "does not become," or "both becomes and does not become," or "neither becomes nor does not become."

S. iii. 262–263

I, monks, do not dispute with the world, but the world disputes with me. No one who professes *dhamma*, monks, disputes with the world. Whatever the learned in the world agree upon as "It is not," I too, monks, say of that, "It is not." Whatever the learned in the world agree upon as "It is," I, too, monks, say of that, "It is."

And what, monks, is agreed upon by the learned in the world as "It is not," and of which I say, "It is not"? That material shape is permanent, stable, eternal, not liable to change—the learned in the world agree that it is not, and I, too, say of it, "It is not." So with feeling, perception, the constructions, consciousness.

And what, monks, is agreed upon by the learned in the world as "It is," and of which I say, "It is"? That material shape is impermanent, suffering, liable to change—the learned in the world agree that it is, and I too say of it, "It is." So with feeling . . . consciousness.

There is, monks, a world-condition in the world which a Truth-finder thoroughly understands, thoroughly grasps, and which, when he has thoroughly understood and grasped it, he proclaims, teaches, lays down, establishes, opens up, analyses and makes clear. Such a world-condition is material shape, such is feeling, such is perception, such are the constructions, such is consciousness. Whoever, on having this thus proclaimed to him, taught, laid down, established, opened up, analysed and made clear, does not know, does not see, him, monks, an ignorant ordinary man, blind, visionless, unknowing, unseeing, do I set at naught.

Monks, as a blue, red, or white lotus, though born in the water, grown up in the water, when it reaches the surface stands there unsoiled by the water, even so, monks, does a Truth-finder,

[1] The views of "philosophers," or rather, "sophists," to none of which the Buddha adheres. With respect to all alternatives, he teaches a Middle Way.

though grown up in the world,[1] having overcome the world, live unsoiled by the world.   *S.* iii. 138–140

There is, Sīha,[2] a way [3] in which one speaking truly of me could say : " The recluse Gotama asserts what ought not to be done, he teaches a doctrine of what ought not to be done and in this he leads disciples." There is, Sīha, a way in which one speaking truly of me could say : " The recluse Gotama asserts what ought to be done, he teaches a doctrine of what ought to be done and in this he leads disciples. . . . The recluse Gotama asserts annihilation, he teaches a doctrine of annihilation and in this he leads disciples. . . . The recluse Gotama is one who detests, he teaches a doctrine of detestation and in this he leads disciples. . . . The recluse Gotama is one who diverts,[4] he teaches a doctrine of diverting and in this he leads disciples. . . . The recluse Gotama is a ' burner up,' he teaches a doctrine of ' burning up ' and in this he leads disciples. . . . The recluse Gotama is not destined to another kind of becoming, he teaches a doctrine of no other kind of becoming and in this he leads disciples." There is, Sīha, a way in which one speaking truly of me could say : " The recluse Gotama is confident, he teaches a doctrine of confidence and in this he leads disciples."

And what, Sīha, is the way in which one speaking truly of me could say : " The recluse Gotama is one who asserts what ought not to be done, he teaches a doctrine of what ought not to be done and in this he leads disciples ? " Indeed I, Sīha, assert of bad conduct in body, speech and thought that it ought not to be done ; I assert of manifold evil and wrong states (of mind) that they ought not to be done. This is the way, Sīha, in which one speaking truly of me could say : " The recluse Gotama asserts what ought not to be done, he teaches a doctrine of what ought not to be done and in this he leads disciples."

And what, Sīha, is the way in which one . . . could say : " The recluse Gotama asserts what ought to be done . . . trains

---

[1] " Born in the world " not in the text here as in extract from *A.* ii. 38–39, p. 48.

[2] The Licchavi general. The whole passage is a refutation of the false accusation that the Buddha teaches there is " no ought to be done " (*na-kiriya*) ; what he actually teaches is that there is an " ought not to be done " (*akiriya*) and an " ought to be done." (*kiriya*).

[3] *Pariyāya*, way, sense, form of words, paraphrase.

[4] *Venayika*, one who " leads " and " misleads." The Buddha is a diverter, averter, subverter or perverter, or leader off, of wrong states. The verb, translated above as " leads," is *vineti*.

disciples ?" Indeed I, Sīha, assert of good conduct in body, speech and thought that it ought to be done ; I assert of manifold right states (of mind) that they ought to be done. This is the way. . . .

And what, Sīha, is the way in which one . . . could say : "The recluse Gotama is one who detests, he teaches a doctrine of detestation and in this he leads disciples ?" Indeed I, Sīha, detest bad conduct in body, speech and thought. I teach a doctrine of detesting to enter upon manifold evil wrong states (of mind). This is the way. . . .

And what, Sīha, is the way in which one . . . could say : "The recluse Gotama is one who diverts, he teaches a doctrine of diverting and in this he leads disciples ?" Indeed I, Sīha, teach a doctrine of diverting passion, hatred, delusion ; I teach a doctrine of diverting manifold evil wrong states (of mind). This is the way. . . .

And what, Sīha, is the way in which one . . . could say : "The recluse Gotama is a ' burner up,' he teaches a doctrine of ' burning up' and in this he leads disciples ?" Indeed I, Sīha, speak of evil wrong states that are searing : bad conduct in body, speech and thought. He for whom, Sīha, evil wrong states that are searing are destroyed, cut off like a palm-tree at the stump, so utterly done away with that they can come to no future existence —him I call a "burner up". For a Truth-finder, Sīha, evil wrong states that are searing are destroyed, cut off like a palm-tree at the stump, so utterly done away with that they can come to no future existence. This is the way. . . .

And what, Sīha, is the way in which one . . . could say : "The recluse Gotama is not one who is destined for another kind of becoming, he teaches a doctrine of no other kind of becoming and in this he leads disciples" ? He for whom, Sīha, future conception in a womb, becoming again and coming forth are destroyed, cut off like a palm-tree at the stump, so utterly done away with that they can come to no future existence —him I call one not destined to another kind of becoming. For a Truth-finder, Sīha, future conception in a womb, becoming again and coming forth are destroyed, cut off like a palm-tree at the stump, so utterly done away with that they can come to no future existence. This is the way. . . .

And what is the way, Sīha, in which one speaking truly of me could say : "The recluse Gotama is one who is confident, he

teaches a doctrine of confidence and in this he leads disciples " ?
Indeed I, Sīha, am confident with the highest confidence,[1] I teach
a doctrine of confidence and in this I lead disciples. This is the
way, Sīha, in which one speaking truly of me could say : " The
recluse Gotama is confident, he teaches a doctrine of confidence
and in this he leads disciples."

Vin. i. 234–236 ; cf. Vin. iii. 2, A. iv. 174

[A brahman tells Gotama that in former days a brahman youth,
Soṇakāyana, had said to him :]

" The recluse Gotama lays down an ought-not-to-be-done in
regard to all deeds. But, in laying this down, he speaks of the
annihilation of the world, for this truth about deeds is that the
world persists through deeds."
" But I, brahman, do not even know the brahman youth,
Soṇakāyana, by sight. Whence then such a talk (by me) ? "

A. ii. 232

As, brahman householders, you have no favouite teacher, you
should undertake and practise this faultless *dhamma*. What is it ?
There are, householders, some recluses and brahmans who
speak in this way and hold these views : " There are no alms,
sacrifices or oblations, there is no fruit of deeds well done or ill
done, there is not this world, there is not the world beyond, there
is not mother or father, there are not beings of spontaneous
generation, there are not in the world recluses and brahmans who
walk and fare evenly and who, having realized this world and the
world beyond by their own super-knowledge, declare them."
But others speak in direct opposition to them and declare that
there are such things. Of those who hold the former set of views,
this is to be expected : having rejected the three good conditions
—right conduct in body, speech and thought—they undertake
and practise the three bad conditions—wrong conduct in body,
speech, and thought. These recluses and brahmans do not see
the peril, grossness, and corruption in the wrong conditions, nor

---

[1] *DA.* iii. 835 explains confidence by joy, happiness. *AA.* iv. 98 says " with
the highest confidence in the four ways and the four fruits." And *cf. D.* iii. 39
where wanderers are recorded to ask Gotama the name of the doctrine in which
he trains disciples and in which they, trained and attained to confidence, acknowledge a desire for the Brahma-faring.

the advantage in renouncing them for the good conditions, and which is allied to cleansing.

But, as there is indeed a world beyond, if one thinks : " There is no world beyond," and this is his view, this is a wrong view of his. As there is indeed a world beyond, if he resolves : " There is no world beyond," this is a wrong resolve of his. As there is indeed a world beyond, if he utters the speech saying : " There is not a world beyond," this is a wrong speech of his. As there is . . . if he says : " There is no world beyond," he contradicts those perfected ones who know the world beyond. As there is . . . if he convinces others that there is no world beyond, that convincing of his is not of the right *dhamma*, and by that convincing which is not of the right *dhamma* he exalts himself and disparages others. It is as though his former right conduct were destroyed and wrong conduct set up instead. And this wrong view, resolve, speech, contradiction of the ariyans, this convincing that is not of the right *dhamma*, this exaltation of himself, disparagement of others—these various evil wrong states come into being because of wrong view.

Take the case where an intelligent man reflects thus : " If there is not a world beyond, then this worthy individual at the breaking-up of the body will make the self his surety ; but if there is a world beyond, then he, at the breaking-up of the body after dying, will arise in the Downfall, the Bad Bourn, the Abyss, Hell. If it be said that there is not a world beyond and this is a true tenet of these recluses and brahmans, then that individual is here and now condemned by the intelligent who say the individual is of wrong moral habit, of wrong view, and a denier." If there is indeed a world beyond, then this individual is a loser on both counts : inasmuch as he is condemned here and now by the intelligent, and inasmuch as on the breaking-up of the body after dying he will arise in the Downfall, the Bad Bourn, the Abyss, Hell. Thus the faultless *dhamma* is badly taken up and badly practised by him, he has touched one side (only), he neglects the occasion for what is good.

But of those recluses and brahmans who speak thus : " There are alms, sacrifices and oblations, there is fruit of deeds well done and ill done, there is this world, there is a world beyond, there is mother and father, there is spontaneous generation, there are recluses and brahmans who walk and fare evenly and who, having realized this world and the world beyond by their own super-knowledge, declare them," this is to be expected : having rejected the three bad conditions—wrong conduct in body, speech, and thought—they undertake and practise the three good conditions—right conduct in body, speech, and thought. What is the reason ? These recluses and brahmans see the peril, grossness, and corruption in the bad conditions, and the advantage in renouncing them for the good conditions, and which is allied to cleansing.

As there is indeed a world beyond, if he thinks : " There is a world beyond," and this is his view, this is a right view of his . . . right resolve . . . right speech. . . . As there is indeed a world beyond, if he says, " There is a world beyond," he does not contradict those perfected ones who know the world beyond. As there is indeed a world beyond, if he convinces others that there is a world beyond, that convincing of his is of the right *dhamma*, and by that convincing which is of the right *dhamma* he neither exalts himself nor disparages others. It is as though his former wrong conduct were destroyed and right conduct set up instead. And this right view, resolve, speech, non-contradiction of the ariyans, this convincing which is of the right *dhamma*, non-exaltation of himself, non-disparagement of others—these various good conditions come into being because of right view.

Take the case where an intelligent man reflects thus : " If there is a world beyond, then this worthy individual at the breaking-up of the body after dying will arise in a Good Bourn, a heaven world. If it be said that there is a world beyond and this tenet of these recluses and brahmans is the truth, then this individual is here and now extolled by the intelligent who say he is of good moral habit, of right view, and an asserter of what is." If there is indeed a world beyond, then this individual is a winner on both counts : inasmuch as he is extolled by the intelligent here and now, and inasmuch as at the breaking-up of the body after dying, he will arise in a Good Bourn, a heaven world. Thus this faultless *dhamma* is well taken up and well practised by him, he has touched both sides, he neglects the occasion for what is bad.

There are some recluses and brahmans who speak in this way and hold these views : " Evil is not done by the doer, there is no result of evil or of merit." And some hold the opposite views. Of the former the same is to be expected as of those who hold " There is not a world beyond." For as there is indeed an ought-

to-be-done, if anyone think, "There is not an ought-to-be-done,"
and this is his view, this is a wrong view of his . . . wrong
resolve . . . wrong speech . . . a contradiction of those perfected ones who affirm that there is an ought-to-be-done. As
there is indeed an ought-to-be-done, if he convinces others that
there is not an ought-to-be-done, that convincing of his is not of
the right *dhamma*, and by that convincing which is not of the
right *dhamma* he exalts himself and disparages others. It is as
though his former right conduct were destroyed and wrong
conduct set up instead. And this wrong view, resolve, speech,
contradiction of the ariyans, this convincing that is not of the
right *dhamma*, this exaltation of himself, disparagement of others
—these various evil wrong states come into being because of
wrong view.

(*Continue as in the case of* " a world beyond," *reading* " an ought-
to-be-done.") Take the case where an intelligent man reflects
thus : " If there is an ought-to-be-done, then this worthy
individual at the breaking-up of the body after dying will arise
in a Good Bourne, a heaven world. If it be said that there is an
ought-to-be-done and this tenet of these recluses and brahmans
is the truth, then this individual is here and now extolled by the
intelligent who say he is of good moral habit, of right view, an
asserter of there is an ought-to-be-done." If there is indeed an
ought-to-be-done, then this individual is a winner on both
counts : inasmuch as he is extolled by the intelligent here and
now, and inasmuch as at the breaking-up of the body after dying
he will arise in a Good Bourn, a heaven world. Thus this faultless *dhamma* is well taken up and well practised by him, he has
touched both sides, he neglects the occasion for what is bad.

There are some recluses and brahmans who speak in this way
and hold these views : " There is no cause, no reason for the
depravity or purity of beings ; beings will be depraved or pure
without cause, without reason. There is no strength, no energy,
no human steadfastness, no human endeavour ; all beings, all
breathing things, all creatures, all living things are without
power, without strength, without energy, ripened into their
becoming by the force of necessity, encountering pleasure or
pain among (one of) the six classes of beings. Other recluses and
brahmans hold directly opposite views.

As there is indeed cause, if he thinks, " There is not cause," and
this is his view, this is a wrong view of his . . . (*continue as in the*

case of " There is no world beyond ") . . . Take the case of an intelligent man who reflects thus : " If there is not cause, then this worthy individual at the breaking-up of the body will make of self a surety ; if there is cause so will this worthy individual at the breaking-up of the body after dying arise in the Downfall, the Bad Bourn, the Abyss, Hell. If it be said that there is no cause and this tenet of these recluses and brahmans is the truth, then this individual is here and now condemned by the intelligent who say he is of wrong moral habit, of wrong view, an asserter of no cause." . . . Take the case of an intelligent man who reflects thus : " If there is cause, so will this worthy individual at the breaking-up of the body after dying arise in a Good Bourn, a heaven world. If it be said that there is cause and this is a true tenet of these recluses and brahmans, then this individual is here and now extolled by the intelligent who say he is of right moral habit, of right view, an asserter of cause." As there is indeed cause so is this individual a winner on both counts : inasmuch as he is extolled by the intelligent here and now, and inasmuch as at the breaking-up of the body after dying he will arise in a Good Bourn, a heaven world. Thus this faultless *dhamma* is well taken up and well practised by him, he has touched both sides, he neglects the occasion for what is bad.   *M. i.* 401–410

Monks, those wanderers, recluses and brahmans belonging to various sects (whom you have told me about), hold various views, are tolerant of various things, favour various things and are inclined to rely on various views. Some of them say this and hold this view : " The world is eternal, this is the truth, anything else is foolish." Others say that the world is not eternal, this is the truth and anything else is foolish. Some say that the world is an ending thing. . . . Others that it is an unending thing. . . . Some say that the living principle is the body. . . . Others that living principle is one thing and the body another. . . . Some say that the self [1] becomes after dying. . . . Others that it does not. . . . Others that it both becomes and does not become. . . . Others that it neither becomes nor does not become, and that this is the truth, everything else is foolish. So they, by nature wrangling, quarrelsome, disputatious, wounding one another with the weapons of the tongue, maintain : " This is *dhamma*,

[1] *Tathāgata*, translated by Truth-finder elsewhere in this volume. But the Comy. explains it here by *attā*, self ; and *MA.* iii. 141 by *satta*, creature.

this is not *dhamma*, this is not, this is." Monks, wanderers belonging to other sects are blind, unseeing, they do not know what is the goal and what is not the goal, they do not know what is *dhamma* and what is not *dhamma*. So they quarrel and dispute about what is and what is not the goal, about what is and what is not *dhamma*.

Formerly, monks, there was a certain rajah in this same Sāvatthī. He told a certain man to assemble in one place all the people of Sāvatthī who were born blind, and to show them an elephant. The man did so and said to the blind people : This is an elephant. And he presented the head of the elephant to some of the blind, its ear to others, its tusk to others, its trunk to others, and to others its body or foot or back or tail or the tuft on its tail, and to them all he said that that was the elephant.

Then the rajah went to the blind people and asked them to tell him what kind of thing the elephant was. Those who had had the head said the elephant was like a pot. Those who had had an ear said it was like a winnowing-basket. The tusk was like a ploughshare, the trunk like a plough, the body like a granary, the foot like a pillar, the back like a mortar, the tail like a pestle, the tuft on the tail like a besom. Then they began to quarrel, shouting, " Yes, it is ! No, it isn't ! An elephant isn't like that ! Yes, it is like that ! " and they came to fisticuffs. The rajah was delighted.

Even so, monks, wanderers belonging to other sects are blind and unseeing, they do not know what is the goal and what is not the goal, they do not know what is *dhamma* and what is not *dhamma*. So they wrangle, quarrel, and dispute about what is and what is not the goal, about what is and what is not *dhamma*.   *Ud.* 66–69

[The monk Mālunkyaputta argues to himself that if Gotama will tell him whether the views (*put forward in the Ud. 66–69 passage quoted immediately above*) are true, he will lead the Brahma-faring under the lord. But if Gotama will not tell him, then he will disavow the training and return to the low life " in the world." He approaches Gotama on the subject, and Gotama says :]

The leading of the Brahma-faring could not depend on the view that the world is eternal. Nor could it depend on the view that the world is not eternal. Although there is the view that the world is eternal and the view that it is not eternal, there *is* [1] birth, there is ageing, there is dying, there are grief, lamentation, sorrow and despair ; I lay down the destroying of these here and now. And I say the same in regard to each one of the other views.

Therefore understand as not taught what is not taught by me ; understand as taught what is taught by me. These views are not taught by me. For they are not connected with the goal, they are not fundamental to the Brahma-faring, they do not conduce to disregarding, to dispassion, to stopping, to tranquillity, to super-knowledge, to awakening, to nirvana.

But, what is taught by me ? That this is ill, this is the arising of ill, this is the stopping of ill, this is the course leading to the stopping of ill. And why is this taught by me ? This, Mālunkya-putta, is connected with the goal, this is fundamental to the Brahma-faring, this conduces to disregarding, to dispassion, to stopping, to tranquillity, to super-knowledge, to awakening, to nirvana. Therefore it is taught by me.   *M. i. 426 ff.*

[The wanderer Vacchagotta asks Gotama if he holds any of the views (*put forward in Ud. 66–69, previously quoted*). Gotama replies in the negative ; so Vacchagotta asks him what is the peril he sees in these views that makes him scout them all. Gotama replies :]

Each of these views is a thicket, a wilderness, a tangle, a bondage and fetter of views, attended by ill, distress, perturbation, fever, and does not conduce to disregarding, to dispassion, to stopping, to tranquillity, to super-knowledge, to awakening, to nirvana. I, Vaccha, seeing this as a peril, therefore scout all views. Views are discarded by a Truth-finder. For this has been seen by the Truth-finder : This is material shape, this is its arising, this its ceasing ; this is feeling . . . perception . . . the constructions . . . consciousness, this its arising, this its ceasing. Therefore I say it is by destroying, stilling, stopping, renouncing and abandoning all imaginings, all supposings, all thoughts of " I am the doer," " Mine is the doer," all latent " I am," that a Truth-finder is freed with no residuum (for rebirth remaining).   *M. i. 483–486*

Monks, you would like to possess something that was permanent, stable, eternal, not liable to change, that would stand

---

[1] *atth'eva*, emphatic.

fast like unto the eternal. But can you see any such possession?
Neither do I.

You would like to have a grip of the notion of self, such that
there would not arise grief, sorrow, suffering, lamentation, and
despair. But can you see any such grip? Neither do I.

You would like a foundation for views such that there would
not arise grief, sorrow, suffering, lamentation, and despair.
But can you see any such foundation? Neither do I.

Monks, if there were a self, would there be something of the
nature of a self in me? And if there were something of the
nature of a self would there be a self in me? But if both self
and anything of the nature of a self, even when actually present,
are incomprehensible, is not this basis for view mere absolute
folly : This one the world, this one the self whom I shall afterwards become—permanent, stable, eternal, not liable to change,
that would stand fast like unto the eternal?

Then, if material shape is impermanent, and if that which is
impermanent is suffering, you cannot regard that which is
impermanent, suffering and liable to change as : This is mine,
I am this, this is my Self. It is the same with feeling, perception,
the constructions, consciousness. From this it results that all
material shapes, feelings, perceptions, constructions, and all
consciousness, whether past, future or present, subjective or
objective, gross or subtle, mean or excellent, near or far, must
all be seen as : This is not mine, I am not this, this is not my
Self.

So seeing all these things, the instructed disciple of the ariyans
disregards material shapes, and the rest ; by disregarding he is
passionless ; through passionlessness he is freed ; in freedom,
the knowledge comes to be : I am freed, and he has foreknowledge : Destroyed is birth, lived is the Brahma-faring, done
is what was to be done, there is no more of being such or such.

M. i. 137–139 ; *cf. S.* iii. 68

Such a monk becomes one who is freed in heart, freed by
wisdom. He is said to have lifted the barrier, filled the moat,
pulled up the pillar, withdrawn the bolts, an ariyan, with flag
laid low, with burden dropped, without fetters.

And how, monks, has the monk lifted the barrier? Herein
is ignorance got rid of by the monk, cut down to the roots,
made as a palm-tree stump that can come to no future existence.

And how has the monk filled the moat ? Herein coming-to-
be again, birth and faring on are got rid of by the monk, cut
down to the roots. . . .

And how has the monk pulled up the pillar ? Herein craving
is got rid of by the monk, cut down to the roots. . . .

And how has the monk withdrawn the bolts ? Herein the
five fetters binding to the lower (shore) are got rid of by the
monk, cut down to the roots. . . .

And how, monks, is the monk an ariyan, with flag laid low,
with burden dropped, without fetters ? Herein, monks, the
latent bias " I am " is got rid of by the monk, cut down to the
roots, made as a palm-tree stump that can come to no future
existence.   *M*. i. 139–140 ; *A*. iii. 84

When a monk's heart is thus freed, not Indra or Brahmā or
Pajāpati with their *devas* succeed in a search for that discriminative
consciousness which is attached to a Truth-finder. And why ?
I, monks, say that here and now a Truth-finder is untraceable.
Although this is what I affirm and what I preach, yet some
recluses and brahmans charge me erroneously, vainly, falsely,
and as is contrary to fact with being a diverter, of laying down
the cutting off, the destruction and extirpation of the existent
entity. As this, monks, is just what I do *not* teach, therefore
these worthy recluses and brahmans charge me erroneously,
vainly, falsely, and with what is contrary to fact. Formerly,
monks, as well as now, I lay down just ill and the stopping of ill.
If therein others denounce and abuse a Truth-finder, there does
not come to be for him resentment or annoyance. If others
revere and honour him, there does not come to be for him
pleasure and satisfaction. It must be the same with you. As
to this, it should be thus for you : This that is well understood
is that such deeds were formerly done by us there. *M*. i. 140

Therefore what is not yours, monks, put it away. Putting it
away will come to be for a long time for your welfare and
ease. And what is not yours ? Material shape, monks, is not
yours, nor are feeling, perception, the constructions or consciousness. Put away each of them. The putting away of each of
them will come to be for your welfare and ease. It is as if a
man should gather, burn or do what he pleases with the grass,
sticks, branches, and foliage in this Jeta Grove—pray, would

you say that this man is gathering, burning *us*, doing what he pleases with *us* ? You would not, and why not ?

Because, lord, this is not our self, nor of the nature of self.

Even so, monks, material shape is not yours, nor are feeling, perception, the constructions or consciousness. These are not yours. Put them away. The putting away of each of them will come to be for a long time for your welfare and ease.

M. i. 140–141 ; *S.* iii. 33–34

Monks, these three sectarian folds, although strictly questioned, investigated and discussed by the wise, persist in the traditional (view) of an ought-not-to-be-done. What are the three ?

There are, monks, some recluses and brahmans who speak like this and hold this view : " Whatever a man experiences of pleasure or pain or neither, all this is due to something previously done." If they approach me, I ask them if it is true that they have this view, and if they say it is, I speak thus : " Well, then, the venerable ones will become those to make onslaught on creatures, to take what is not given, to lead what is not the Brahma-faring, they will become liars, slanderers, abusive, babblers, covetous, malicious, they will become of wrong view because of something done previously." Monks, to those who fall back on something done previously as the essential reason, there comes to be no desire or exertion connected with the idea that this is to be done or this is not to be done. Thus, if what is to be done and what is not to be done, though actually existing, are incomprehensible, the term recluse cannot be legitimately applied to yourselves, since you dwell muddled in mindfulness, unguarded.

There are, monks, some recluses and brahmans who speak like this and hold this view : " Whatever a man experiences of pleasure or pain or neither, all this is due to creation by an Overlord." If they approach me, . . . I speak thus : " Well, then, the venerable ones will become those to make onslaught on creatures . . . they will become of wrong view because of creation by an Overlord." Monks, to those who fall back on creations by an Overlord as the essential reason, there comes to be no desire or exertion connected with the idea that this is to be done or this is not to be done. Thus, if what is to be done and what is not to be done, although actually existing, are incomprehensible, the term recluse cannot be legitimately applied to yourselves, since you dwell muddled in mindfulness, unguarded.

There are, monks, some recluses and brahmans who speak like this and hold this view : " Whatever a man experiences of pleasure or pain or neither, all this is uncaused, unconditioned." If they approach me, . . . I speak thus : " Well, then, the venerable ones will become those to make onslaught on creatures . . . they will become of wrong view, uncaused, unconditioned." Monks, to those who fall back on no cause, no condition as the essential reason, there comes to be no desire or exertion connected with the idea that this is to be done or this is not to be done. Thus, if what is to be done and what is not to be done, although actually existing, are incomprehensible, the term recluse cannot be legitimately applied to yourselves, since you dwell muddled in mindfulness, unguarded.

A. i. 173-175

The world, Kaccāyana, is for the most part attached to two (propositions) : existence as well as non-existence. If anyone sees, through right wisdom, the arising of the world as it really comes to be—whatever is not existent in the world, that does not come to be. If anyone sees, through right wisdom, the stopping of the world as it really comes to be—whatever is existent in the world, that does not come to be.

Grasping after systems, imprisoned by dogmas for the most part is this world, Kaccāyana. But he who does not go in for this system-grasping, for this mental standpoint, for this dogmatic bias, who does not take it up, does not take his stand upon it, thinking : " It is not my self ; it is just ill uprising that uprises, ill being stopped that is stopped "—he neither doubts nor is perplexed ; by not depending on others, knowledge herein comes to be his own. To this extent, Kaccāyana, there comes to be right view.

" Everything exists " : this, Kaccāyana, is one dead-end. " Everything exists not " : this, Kaccāyana, is the other dead-end. Not approaching either of these dead-ends, the Truthfinder teaches *dhamma* by the mean : conditioned by ignorance are the constructions ; conditioned by the constructions is consciousness (and so on through the " chain of causation " [1]). Thus there comes to be the uprising of this entire mass of ill.

[1] *Cf.* section on Causality.

But from the utter fading away and stopping of ignorance, there is the stopping of the constructions ; from the stopping of the constructions there is the stopping of consciousness ; and so on. Thus there comes to be the stopping of this entire mass of ill.   *S.* ii. 17

" Now, good Gotama, is suffering wrought by oneself ? "
" Indeed not, Kassapa."
" But is suffering wrought by another ? "
" Indeed not, Kassapa."
" Is suffering wrought by oneself and by another ? "
" Indeed not, Kassapa."
" But has the suffering, wrought neither by oneself nor by another, originated by chance ? "
" Indeed not, Kassapa."
" Is it, good Gotama, that there is not suffering ? "
" It is not, Kassapa, that there is not suffering ; for, Kassapa, there is suffering."
" Well, then, the good Gotama does not know suffering, does not see it."
" It is not that I, Kassapa, do not know suffering, do not see it ; for I, Kassapa, know suffering, I see it."
" But, good Gotama, to all my questions you have replied : ' Indeed not, Kassapa.' You have said that there is suffering and that you know it and see it. Lord, let the lord explain to me about suffering : lord, let the lord teach me about suffering."
" He who does (a deed), it is he who experiences (its result) : this which you, Kassapa, spoke of at the beginning as ' suffering wrought by oneself '—this leads on up to the Eternalist theory. But to say, ' One does, another experiences '—if one is harassed by feeling, and thinks, ' Suffering is wrought by another '— this leads on up to the Annihilationist theory.
" Not approaching either of these dead-ends, the Truth-finder teaches you, Kassapa, *dhamma* by the mean : Conditioned by ignorance are the constructions . . .[1] Thus there comes to be the stopping of this entire mass of ill."   *S.* ii. 19–20.

" Now, lord, what is ageing and dying, and whose is this ageing and dying ? "

[1] *Cf.* " causal chain," p. 144.

"Not a fit question," the lord said. "Whatever monk should say this or whatever monk should say : ' Ageing and dying are one thing, but another's is this ageing and dying,' both these (questions) have the same meaning, just the form is different. If a monk has the view that the life-principle and the body are the same, there does not come to be a living of the Brahma-faring. Nor does this come to be if a monk has the view that the life-principle is one thing and the body another. Not approaching either of these dead-ends, the Truth-finder teaches you *dhamma* by the mean : Conditioned by birth are ageing and dying."

[The monks then asked the lord about each of the factors in the " causal chain," and to each question he answered as above, ending by mentioning the appropriate factor in the causal chain.]

" It is indeed, monks, by the utter fading away and stopping of ignorance that distortions, disagreements, scufflings, whatever they may be, that all such props come to be given up, cut off at the root, made like the stump of a palm-tree, so utterly done away with as not liable to come to any future existence."

S. ii. 60–62

Baka the Brahmā is indeed under an illusion if he should say that the impermanent is the same as the permanent, that the evanescent is the same as the everlasting, that the non-eternal is the same as the eternal, that the not-whole is the same as the whole, and that what is liable to pass on is the same as what is not liable to pass on ; and if he should say in regard to what is born and ages and dies and passes on and uprises : " But this is not born, does not age, does not die, does not pass on, does not up-rise " ; and if—there being another further escape—he should say : " There is not another further escape."

M. i. 326 ; S. i. 142

Whatever recluses and brahmans say that by becoming there is release from becoming, all these, I say, are unreleased from becoming. But whatever recluses and brahmans say that by de-becoming[1] there is an escape from becoming, all these, I say, have not gone out from becoming.   Ud. 33

_____
[1] *vibhava.*

Just now, brahman, people are ablaze with unlawful lusts, overwhelmed by depraved longings, obsessed by wrong doctrines. This being so, they seize sharp knives and take one another's lives. Thus many men come by their end. Again, on these who are thus ablaze, overwhelmed and obsessed, the rain does not pour down steadily. It is hard to get a meal. The crops are poor, afflicted with mildew, and stunted. Thus many men come by their end. Again, against those who are thus ablaze, overwhelmed, and obsessed, the Yakkhas let loose non-human things. Thereby many men come to their end. This is the reason, this the cause of the apparent loss and decrease of human beings. This is why villages are not villages, little towns are not little towns, towns are not towns, and the country districts are depopulated. *A. i.* 160

II. MARVELS

There are these three marvels. What are the three ? The marvel of psychic power, the marvel of thought reading, the marvel of teaching. And what is the marvel of psychic power ?

In this case, a monk enjoys various kinds of psychic power in divers ways. From being one he becomes many, from being many he becomes one ; manifest or invisible he goes unhindered through a wall, through a rampart, through a mountain as if through air ; he plunges into the earth and shoots up again as if in water ; he walks upon the water without parting it as if on solid ground ; he travels through the air, sitting cross-legged, like a bird on the wing. Even this moon and sun, although of such mighty power and majesty—he handles and strokes them with his hand. Even as far as the Brahma-world he has power in regard to his body. This is called the marvel of psychic power.

And what is the marvel of thought reading ? In this case a certain one can declare by means of a sign : " Thus is your mind. Such-and-such is your mind. Thus is your thought." And however much he may tell, it is exactly so and not otherwise. Here again, perhaps a certain one does not tell these things by means of a sign, but does so by hearing a voice from men or from non-human beings or from *devas*—and says : " Thus is your mind. Such-and-such is your mind. Thus is your thought." And however much he may tell, it is exactly so and not otherwise.

Here again, perhaps a certain one does not tell these things by means of a sign or on hearing a voice from men or non-human beings or *devas*, but does so (judging) from some sound he has heard, an utterance intelligently made by one who is reasoning intelligently. So hearing, he declares : " Thus is your mind. Such-and-such is your mind. Thus is your thought." And however much he may tell, it is exactly so and not otherwise. Then again, in this case, suppose a certain one does not tell by any of these ways . . . yet perhaps when he has attained contemplation, void of reflection and intelligence, he foreknows, fully grasping thought with his thought, that : " According as the mental workings of this man so-and-so are directed, he will apply his reasoning of mind to this and that object immediately." And however much he may tell, it is exactly so and not otherwise. This is called the marvel of thought-reading.

And what is the marvel of teaching ? In this case a certain one teaches thus : " Reason thus and not thus. Apply your mind thus and not thus. Abandon this state, acquire that state, and abide in it." This is called the marvel of teaching. So these are the three marvels.   *A.* i. 170 ; *cf. D.* i. 212

[But the first two marvels might be challenged thus :]

One of little faith, not believing, might say to one of faith, believing : " There is, good sir, a charm called Gandhārī. It is because of this that he exercises various kinds of psychic power in divers ways : from being one, becoming many and so on." It is because I see this peril in the marvel of psychic power that I am distressed by it, that I abhor it, that I loathe it. Similarly, in regard to the marvel of thought reading, one of little faith, not believing, might say to one of faith, believing : " There is, good sir, a charm called the Jewel : it is because of this that he tells the thoughts of other beings, of other men, and says : ' Thus is your mind. Such-and-such is your mind. Thus is your thought.' It is because I see this peril in the marvel of thought reading, that I am distressed by it, that I abhor it, that I loathe it.   *D.* i. 213

Indeed, Ānanda, I do understand how to reach the Brahma-world by psychic power both in this mind-made body and in this body of the four great elements. Truth-finders are marvellous and possessed of marvellous powers, they are wonderful and possessed of wonderful powers. At a time when a Truth-finder contemplates body in mind and mind in body, and in the body enters into and abides in the conscious-ness of ease and buoyancy, at that time his body becomes more buoyant, softer, more workable and more radiant. It is just like an iron ball, which, when it has been heated all day long, becomes lighter, softer, more workable and more radiant. Now, Ānanda, whenever a Truth-finder contemplates body in mind and mind in body, and in the body enters into and abides in the consciousness of ease and buoyancy, it is at that time that the body of the Truth-finder with but little effort rises up from the ground into the air ; he enjoys various kinds of psychic power in divers ways : from being one he becomes many ; from being many he becomes one ; manifest or invisible he goes unhindered through a wall, through a rampart, through a mountain as if through air ; he plunges into the earth and shoots up again as if in water ; he walks upon the water without parting it as if on solid ground ; he travels through the air, sitting cross-legged, like a bird on the wing. Even this moon and sun, although of such mighty power and majesty—he handles and strokes them with his hand. Even as far as the Brahma-world he has power with his body. And, Ānanda, just as a tuft of cotton seed or a ball of thistledown, lightly wafted on the wind, with but little effort rises up from the ground into the air, even so at a time when a Truth-finder contemplates body in mind and mind in body, and in the body enters into and abides in the consciousness of ease and buoyancy, it is at that time that the body of the Truth-finder with but little effort rises up from the ground into the air, and he enjoys the various kinds of psychic powers in their divers ways. *S.* v. 282

[A great merchant of Rājagaha once had a sandalwood bowl tied up at the top of a bamboo pole ; and he said : " Let whatever recluse or brahman who is one perfected and of psychic power get down this bowl, and to him it is given." After the leaders of six of the great heretical sects had tried and failed, the monk Piṇḍola the Bhāradvāja succeeded. The populace of Rājagaha greeted the news of his feat with clamorous applause. For, having risen above the ground and taken hold of the bowl, he had circled three times round Rājagaha, and on the request of the great merchant came to rest exactly at his dwelling. The lord, hearing the great noise made by the people, asked Ānanda the cause of it. He replied :]

"Lord, the venerable Piṇḍola the Bhāradvāja has fetched down the bowl belonging to the great merchant. That is why the people are making a great noise, a loud noise." The lord thereupon rebuked the venerable Piṇḍola, saying :

"It is not suitable, Bhāradvāja, it is not becoming, it is not fitting, it is not worthy of a recluse, it is not allowable, it is not to be done. How can you, on account of a miserable wooden bowl, exhibit a condition of further-men, a wonder of psychic power to householders ? Even as a woman exhibits a loin-cloth for the sake of a miserable stamped *māsaka*, even so was exhibited by you to householders, for the sake of a miserable wooden bowl, a condition of further-men, a wonder of psychic power."

Having rebuked him, the lord addressed the monks, saying : "Monks, a condition of further-men, a wonder of psychic power is not to be exhibited to householders. Whoever should exhibit them, there is an offence of wrong doing. Break, monks, this wooden bowl ; having reduced it to fragments, give them to the monks as perfume for ointment." *Vin.* ii. 111

III. AMITY AND MALICE

Monks, when the freedom of heart that is love is pursued, made become, made much of, made a vehicle and a basis, exercised, augmented, and thoroughly set going, eight advantages are to be expected. What are the eight ?

Happy one sleeps, happy one awakes, one sees no bad dreams, one is dear to human beings, one is dear to non-human beings, *devas* guard one, neither fire nor poison nor sword affects one, and though not penetrating further, one reaches the Brahma-world.

> Who makes unbounded love to become,
> Mindful, he sees th' attachments all destroyed,
> The fetters wear away. If, pure in heart,
> One being he does love, good follows thence.
> The ariyan, with heart compassionate
> For all mankind, abounding merit makes.

Those royal sages, having overcome
The teeming earth, make ample sacrifice ;
But, like the starry host beside the moon,
The sacrifices called The Horse, The Man,
The " Throwing of the Peg," the " Drinking Rite,"
The " House Unbarred " [1]—are not a sixteenth part
The worth of a heart with love enriched.
Who kills not, nor aught causes to be killed,
Who robs not, nor makes others rob, for all
Within his heart hath share, he hateth none.[2]

A. iv. 150–151

"I do not say, monks, that without being aware of it, there is a wiping out of intentional deeds done and accumulated, and that whether arising in this very life or later or in a succession (of lives). I do not say to you that, without being aware of it, there is an ending of the ill of intentional deeds done and accumulated.

Monks, that ariyan disciple, who is thus without coveting and malevolence, not bewildered but self-possessed and recollecting, with a heart possessed of love abides suffusing one quarter of the world, likewise the second, third, and fourth quarters of the world, likewise above, below, across, everywhere, for all sorts and conditions—he abides suffusing the whole world with a heart possessed of love that is widespreading, vast and boundless, without enmity or malice. He has foreknowledge thus : " Formerly my heart was limited, not made to become, but now my heart is boundless, well made to become. Moreover, whatever deed belongs to what is limited—it does not stay there, it does not stop still there." Now, what do you think, monks ? If from his youth up this young man should make become the freedom of heart that is love, would he do an evil deed ? "

" Surely not, lord."

" If he does not do an evil deed, could he touch anything that is ill ? "

" Surely not, lord. If he does not do an evil deed, how could he touch ill ? "

[1] These sacrifices are also referred to in *S.* i. 76, *A.* ii. 42 (*cf.* p. 135), *It.* p. 21. The " Throwing of the Peg," or " Peg-thrown Site," is explained in the Comys. as the site for an altar, determined by the place where a wooden peg falls when thrown. Hence, it is not, strictly speaking, the *name* of any sacrifice. It is claimed that originally all these were harmless rites, but later they degenerated into blood-sacrifices.

[2] Closely following E. M. Hare's translation in *G.S.* iv. 103–104.

"Indeed, monks, this freedom of heart that is love should be made to become both by women and men. A woman or man cannot take this body and go away. This mortal being is but a between-thoughts. He (or she) has foreknowledge thus : "Whatever evil deed was formerly done by me here with this body born to deeds, it must all be felt and known here, it will not become (something that) follows." Freedom of heart, thus made to become, conduces to a state of non-return for a monk who has wisdom here (but) who has not penetrated to a further freedom.

"Then, again, he suffuses one quarter of the world with a heart possessed of compassion . . . with a heart possessed of joy . . . with a heart possessed of balance, likewise the second, third, and fourth quarters of the world . . . (continue as above reading compassion . . . joy . . . balance for love) . . . not penetrated to a further freedom."   A. v. 299–301

Just as those families which have few women, many men, are hard to molest by robbers and pot-thieves, so that monk who has made become, made much of the freedom of heart that is love is hard to molest by non-human beings. Therefore, monks, you must train yourselves thus : Freedom of heart that is love will be made become by us, made much of, made a vehicle, made a basis, exercised, augmented, and thoroughly set going.   S. ii. 264

He goes on, having suffused the four quarters with a heart possessed of love, of compassion, of joy, of balance, above, below, across, everywhere, he goes on with a heart that is wide-spreading, vast, boundless, without enmity or malice, and that has suffused the whole world everywhere for all sorts and conditions. He has foreknowledge that : "There is this, there is the low, there is the excellent ; there is a further escape [1] from this perception." For him, thus knowing, thus seeing, the heart is freed from the fluxions of sense-pleasures, of becoming, of ignorance. The knowledge comes to be : "In freedom I am freed" ; and he knows : "Destroyed is birth, lived is the Brahma-faring, done is what was to be done, there is no more of being such-and-such." This is called a monk who is washed with an inner washing.   M. i. 38

[1] Cf. Escape section.

Easy to see are others' faults,
those of self are hard to see.
Surely the faults of other men
a man doth winnow as 'twere chaff,
but those of the self he covers up
like crafty gamester losing throw.[1]

Dh. 252

Monks, there are these five ways of putting away malice whereby all malice arisen ought to be put away. What five ? In whatever person malice is engendered, in that person love should be made to become, also compassion, also balance. In whatever person malice is engendered, unmindfulness, inattentiveness to it should be brought about in that person. In whatever person malice is engendered, that person should call to mind the fact that one is responsible for deeds, and think : " This man so-and-so is responsible for deeds, heir to deeds, having deeds for matrix, deeds for kin, to him the deed comes home again. Whatever deed he does, whether good or evil, he will become its heir." In these five ways should malice in that person be put away.   *A.* iii. 185–186

Wrath must ye slay, if ye would happy live,
Wrath must ye slay, if ye would weep no more.
Victor of wrath with its poison-root,
Sweetest intoxicant—Dragon-queller :
That is the slaughter by the ariyans praised,
That must ye slay if ye would weep no more.

S. i. 47

By no-wrath should he conquer wrath ;
unworth by worth should be o'ercome ;
he should o'ercome the stingy by a gift,
by truth him who doth falsely speak.[2]

Dh. 223

Conquest engenders hate ; the conquered lives
In misery. But whoso is at peace
And passionless, happily doth he live ;
Conquest hath he abandoned and defeat.[3]

S. i. 83 ; *Dh.* 201

---

[1] Mrs Rhys Davids, *Min. Anth.* i.
[2] *Ibid.*
[3] *Ibid. K.S.* i. 109.

A man may spoil another, just so far
As it may serve his ends, but when he's spoiled
By others he, despoiled, spoils yet again.
So long as evil's fruit is not matured,
The fool doth fancy " Now's the hour, the chance ! "
But when the deed bears fruit, he fareth ill.
The slayer gets a slayer in his turn ;
The conqueror gets one who conquers him ;
Th' abuser wins abuse, th' annoyer fret.
Thus by the evolution of the deed
A man who spoils is spoilèd in his turn.[1]

S. i. 85

No man by case he settles forcibly
is rightly one " on *dhamma* standing."
But the wise man who into both inquires
what is the case and what is not the case—

In that he settles (case) of other men,
by *dhamma* and by justice, not by force,
warded of *dhamma*, that sagacious man
is (rightly) named " he who on *dhamma* stands." [2]

Dh. 256–257

Lo ! see the folk at strife,
How violence breeds fear !
I'll tell of the dismay,
The terror felt by me.

As fish in shallow pool
I saw man floundering :
I saw the feuds 'twixt men,
And in me entered fear.

All worthless was the world,
All quarters seemed to quake :
Fain for a home, I saw
No shelter for myself.

Feuds as the only end
I saw—and rose my gorge !
Then lo ! I saw the barb,
Heart-propping, hard to see.

From realm to realm runs he
Who by that barb is pierced :
But he who draws that barb
Runs not nor sinketh down.[3]

Sn. 935–939

---

[1] Mrs Rhys Davids, *K.S.* i. 110. *Cf. Revelations* xiii. 10, " He that leadeth
into captivity shall go into captivity : he that killeth with the sword must be
killed with the sword ".
[2] *Ibid. Min. Anth.* i.   [3] E. M. Hare. *Woven Cadences.*

IV. TENDING THE SICK

" Is there, monks, in such-and-such a dwelling-place a monk who is sick ? "

" There is, lord."

" What is his disease ? "

" The venerable one has dysentery, lord."

" But, monks, is there anyone who is tending this monk ? "

" No, lord."

" Why do not the monks tend him ? "

" Lord, this monk is of no use to the monks, therefore they do not tend him."

" Monks, you have not a mother, you have not a father who might tend you. If you, monks, do not tend one another, who is there who will tend you ? Whoever, monks, would tend me, he should tend the sick." [1] *Vin.* i. 302

V. PARENTS

Monks, those families where mother and father are honoured in the home are reckoned like unto Brahmā,[2] they are ranked with the teachers of old ; worthy of offerings are such families. " Brahmā," monks, is a term for mother and father. " Teachers of old " is a term for mother and father. " Worthy of offerings " is a term for mother and father. Why so ? Because mother and father do much for children, they bring them up, nourish them, and introduce the world to them.

> Parents are called " Brahmā," " teachers of old."
> Worthy of gifts are they, compassionate
> Unto their tribe of children. Thus the wise
> Should worship them and pay them honours due,
> Serve them with food and drink, clothing and beds,
> Anoint their bodies, bathe and wash their feet.
> For service such as this to parents given
> In this life sages praise a man, and he
> Hereafter has reward of joy in heaven.[3]
> *A.* i. 132, ii. 70 ; *It.* p. 109

---

[1] Cf. " Inasmuch as ye have done it unto the least of these, ye have done it unto me ".

[2] Governor of the Brahma-world ; not Brahman=Deity.

[3] F. L. Woodward, *G.S.* i. 114-115, ii. 79 ; *Min. Anth.* ii. 192 f.

There are, monks, these four bases of sympathy. What four? Charity, kind speech, doing a good turn, and treating all alike.[1]

> Charity, kind words, and doing a good turn
> And treating all alike as each deserves :
> These bonds of sympathy are in the world
> Like to the linchpin of a moving car.
> Now if these bonds were lacking, mother who bore
> And father who begat would not receive
> The honour and respect (which are their due).
> But since the wise rightly regard these bonds,[2]
> Therefore 'tis theirs the Great Self to win,
> And they become worthy the praise of men.

A. ii. 32

> Who, being rich, supports
> Not parents in their age,
> When gone is all their youth :
>
> And he who parents strikes,
> Doth brother vex with words,
> Wife's mother, sister too :
> Know him as outcast vile.[3]

Sn. 124, 125

And he by *dhamma* should his parents serve.

Sn. 404

VI. DHAMMA FOR THE LAITY

> The rule for householders now will I tell,
> What action best becomes such listeners ;
> For busied much, none can attune himself
> Wholly unto the thing required of monks.
>
> Let him no creatures kill and none incite
> To kill, nor sanction others taking life,
> But put by violence for all that lives,
> For stout of heart and all that trembles here.
>
> Then let the listener awakening
> Wholly refrain from taking things not giv'n,
> And none incite to steal nor sanction theft ;
> Let him refrain from every form of theft.
>
> Let him refrain from all unchastity,
> As wise men shun the burning charcoal pit ;
> If powerless to live in continence,
> Let him not with another's wife transgress.

---

[1] *Cf. A.* ii. 248, iv. 364 ; *D.* iii. 152.
[2] F. L. Woodward, *G.S.* ii. 36 (except last two lines).
[3] E. M. Hare. *Woven Cadences.*

Gone to th' assembly hall or gathering,
Let him not to another falsely speak,
And none incite to lie nor sanction lies ;
Let him refrain from all that is not truth.

Let him not of intoxicants partake,
The householder who doth this *dhamma* choose,
And none incite to drink nor sanction drink,
Knowing that madness is the end of it.

For verily drunken fools commit ill deeds,
And other people gird to wantoning :
Let him avoid this sphere of wrongful deeds,
Maddening, deluding, the delight of fools.

Let him not kill nor take a thing not giv'n,
Let him not lie nor drink intoxicants,
Let him eschew ungodly practices,
Let him not eat untimely food at night.

Let him not garlands wear nor perfumes use,
Let him lie on a mat spread on the ground :
This eightfold is indeed th' observance called,
Made known by the Awake, to ill's end gone. . . .

And he by *dhamma* should his parents serve,
And in accord with *dhamma* ply his trade :
The householder who lives thus earnestly
Goes to the *devas* called self-luminant.[1]

Sn. 393–401, 404

Who fitly acts and toils
And strives shall riches find ;
By truth shall fame acquire ;
By giving, friends shall bind.

And lovers of the home
Who hold in faith these four,
Truth, *dhamma*, firmness, gift,
Hence gone shall grieve no more.

With brahman and recluse,
Prithee, at large this sift ;
Be there here better than
Restraint, truth, patience, gift ?[2]

Sn. 187–189

Plain is the weal in life,
Plain is the suffering :
Prospers who *dhamma* loves,
Suffers who *dhamma* hates.

Who hath bad men as friends,
Nor maketh friends with good,
Who chooseth men's bad ways :
A source of suffering that.

---

[1] E. M. Hare. *Woven Cadences.*   [2] *Ibid.*

When man loves company
And sleep, when he is lax
And slack and known for wrath :
A source of suffering that.

Who being rich, supports
Not parents in their age
When gone is all their youth :
A source of suffering that.

Who with false words deceives
A brahman or recluse
Or other mendicant :
A source of suffering that.

When man of wealth and means,
Of gold and property,
Enjoys its sweets alone :
A source of suffering that.

When man is proud of birth
And purse and family,
And yet ashamed of kin :
A source of suffering that.

When man on woman dotes,
On drink and dice alike,
And all his savings wastes :
A source of suffering that.

Who not content with his,
Is seen with others' wives,
Is seen with harlots too :
A source of suffering that.

When man, passed youth, doth wed
A maid with rounded breasts,
Nor sleeps for jealousy :
A source of suffering that.

When woman or when man,
A spendthrift or a sot,
Is placed in sovran power :
A source of suffering that.

When born of noble clan,
A man is poor and craves
For much and longs to rule :
A source of suffering that.

These sufferings in the world
The wise discern, and blest
With vision ariyan,
They seek the world of bliss.[1]

Sn. 92 ff.

---

[1] E. M. Hare. *Woven Cadences.*

By growing in ten (ways of) growth the ariyan disciple grows in the ariyan growth, and he becomes one to take hold of the essence, to take hold of the best for his person. In what ten ? He grows in landed property, in wealth and granary, in child and wife, in slaves, servants and workmen, in four-footed beasts ; he grows in faith, in moral habit, in what he hears, in generosity, in wisdom.

> Whoso in this world grows in wealth and store,
> In sons and wives and in four-footed beasts,
> Hath fame and worship as a man of means
> From relatives and friends and those that rule.[1]

> But whoso in this world in faith and virtue,
> In wisdom, generosity and lore
> Alike makes growth—a very man like this,
> Keen-eyed, in this life grows alike in both.[2]

A. v. 137

There are these five disadvantages, householders, to one of wrong moral habit, falling away from moral habit. What are the five ? Now, householders, one of wrong moral habit, falling away from moral habit, suffers great diminution of wealth owing to sloth. This is the first disadvantage.

Then again, householders, an evil reputation is noised abroad of one of wrong moral habit. This is the second disadvantage.

Then again, householders, if one of moral habit, falling away from moral habit, approaches any company, whether of nobles, of brahmans, of householders, of recluses, he approaches it diffidently, being ashamed. This is the third disadvantage.

Then again, householders, one of wrong moral habit passes away bewildered. This is the fourth disadvantage.

Then again, householders, one of wrong moral habit, falling away from moral habit, at the breaking-up of the body after dying, arises in the Waste, the Bad Bourn, the Downfall, Niraya Hell. This is the fifth disadvantage to one of wrong moral habit, falling away from moral habit. These are the five disadvantages.

There are these five advantages, householders, to one of moral habit, accomplished in moral habit. What are the five ? Now, householders, one of moral habit, accomplished in moral habit,

---

[1] The latter part of these verses occurs also at *A.* iii. 80 ; *S.* iv. 250. The first part resembles those at *D.* iii. 165.

[2] F. L. Woodward, *G.S.* v. 93 f.

acquires a great mass of wealth owing to zeal. This is the first advantage.

Then again, householders, a lovely reputation is noised abroad of one of moral habit. This is the second advantage.

Then again, householders, if one of moral habit approaches any company, whether of nobles, of brahmans, of householders, of recluses, he approaches it confidently, not being ashamed. This is the third advantage.

Then again, householders, one of moral habit passes away un-bewildered. This is the fourth advantage.

Then again, householders, one of moral habit, accomplished in moral habit, at the breaking-up of the body after dying, arises in a Happy Bourn, in a heaven world. This is the fifth advantage to one of moral habit, accomplished in moral habit.

Vin. i. 227–228 ; *A.* iii. 252–253 ; *D.* ii. 85–86, iii. 235–236 ;
Ud. 86–87

Sāriputta, whatever white-clothed houseman you may know whose deeds are controlled in respect of the five rules of training and who obtains at will, without difficulty, without trouble, the four (ways of) abiding in ease that belong to the mind and are here and now, may, if he so desire, for himself predict of himself : " Destroyed is Niraya Hell for me, destroyed is rebirth as an animal, destroyed is the realm of the departed, destroyed is the Waste, the Bad Bourn, the Downfall, a stream-winner am I, not liable to the Downfall, assured, bound for awakening." And in regard to which five rules of training are his deeds controlled ?

As to this, Sāriputta, a disciple of the ariyans comes to be one who is restrained from onslaught on creatures, restrained from taking what is not given, restrained from wrong conduct as to sense-pleasures, restrained from lying speech, restrained as to the occasions for sloth (engendered by) strong and intoxicating liquors. He comes to be one whose deeds are controlled in regard to these five rules of training. What are the four (ways of) abiding in ease that belong to the mind and are here and now, and which he comes to obtain at will, without difficulty, without trouble ?

As to this, Sāriputta, a disciple of the ariyans comes to be possessed [1] of perfect confidence in the Awakened One, and

[1] At *D.* ii. 93, *S.* v. 357 the four possessions of a stream-winner (as follows) are called the " Mirror of Dhamma ".

thinks : " He indeed is lord, perfected one, fully awakened one, endowed with knowledge and right conduct, well-farer, knower of the worlds, incomparable, charioteer of men to be tamed, teacher of *devas* and men, Awakened one, lord." This is the first (way of) abiding in ease that belongs to the mind and is here and now, and that comes to be won to for purifying a mind that was not purified, for cleansing a mind that was not cleansed.

And again, Sāriputta, a disciple of the ariyans comes to be possessed of perfect confidence in *dhamma*, and thinks : " *Dhamma* is well taught by the lord, it is for the present, it is intemporal, it is a come-and-see thing, leading onwards, it is to be understood individually by the wise." This is the second (way of) abiding in ease. . . .

And again, Sāriputta, a disciple of the ariyans comes to be possessed of perfect confidence in the Order, and thinks : " The lord's Order of disciples fares along well, the lord's Order of disciples fares along uprightly, the lord's Order of disciples fares along in the right manner, the lord's Order of disciples fares along in the proper course—that is to say the four pairs of men, the eight (kinds of) individuals.[1] This Order of disciples of the lord is worthy of honour, worthy of reverence, worthy of offerings, it is to be saluted with joined palms, it is an unsurpassed field for merit in the world. This is the third (way of) abiding in ease. . . .

And again, Sāriputta, a disciple of the ariyans comes to be possessed of the moral habits that are dear to the ariyans, (habits that are) faultless, flawless, spotless, unstained, making for liberty, praised by the intelligent, untarnished, conducive to contemplation. This is the fourth (way of) abiding in ease that belongs to the mind and is here and now, and that comes to be won to for purifying a mind that was not purified, for cleansing a mind that was not cleansed.

A. iii. 211–213 ; cf. S. iv. 271–273

[The householder, Potaliya, tells Gotama that he has given up all trade and common usages. Gotama replies :]

What you, householder, call common usages is one thing, but what is common usage in the discipline for an ariyan is another

---

[1] Those on the four ways to perfection (*arahatta*) and those who have gained the fruit of these four ways.

thing. These eight rules, householder, in the discipline for an ariyan conduce to giving up common usages : through making no onslaught on creatures, onslaught on creatures should be renounced ; through taking what is given, taking what is not given should be renounced ; through speaking truth, lying should be renounced ; through unmalicious speech, malicious speech should be renounced ; through absence of coveting, greed should be renounced ; through absence of angry blame, angry blame should be renounced ; through absence of wrathful rage, wrathful rage should be renounced ; through humility, self-conceit should be renounced. These, householder, are the eight rules, spoken of in brief and not in detailed analysis, which in the discipline for an ariyan conduce to giving up common usages.

When I said that through making no onslaught on creatures, onslaught on creatures should be renounced, I meant this : Suppose, householder, that an ariyan reflects thus : " I am attaining the renunciation and giving up of those fetters because of which I was one who made onslaught on creatures. For indeed, if I were one who made onslaught on creatures, the Self would upbraid me for making onslaught on creatures, intelligent persons, having found out, would censure me for making onslaught on creatures, and at the breaking-up of the body after dying a Bad Bourn would be expected for making onslaught on creatures. This is a fetter, this is a hindrance, that is to say, onslaught on creatures. But those destroying, consuming fluxions which would arise because of onslaught on creatures, come not to be when there is restraint from onslaught on creatures.

It is the same in the case of each one of the seven other rules.

Householder, it is like a dog, weak through hunger and starvation, who might find his way to a slaughtering-place for cows, and to whom the butcher or his apprentice might fling a bare bone absolutely scraped of all meat and with only a trace of blood remaining. Do you think that the dog's hunger would be allayed by such a bare bone ? In the same way, householder, an ariyan disciple reflects thus : " Pleasures of the senses have been likened by the lord to a bare bone, of great suffering, of great tribulation, wherein is further peril " [1]—having by right wisdom seen this as it has really come to be, and having laid aside that indifference which comes from

[1] Six more similes for the pleasures of the senses follow here.

diversity and depends on diversity, he makes become only that indifference which comes from unity and depends on unity and in which all hankerings after the material things of the world are stopped and none remain. . . . To this extent, householder, in the discipline for an ariyan there comes to be in all matters a complete giving up of the common usages.

M. i. 360–367

Therefore, girls, train yourselves thus : To whatever husband our parents shall give us—anxious for our good, seeking our happiness, compassionate, out of compassion—for him we will rise up early, be the last to retire, be willing workers, order all things sweetly and speak affectionately. Train yourselves thus, girls.

And in this way also, girls : we will honour, revere, esteem, and respect all whom our husband reveres, whether mother or father, recluse or brahman, and on their arrival will offer them a seat and water. Train yourselves thus, girls.

And in this way also, girls : We will be deft and nimble at our husband's home-crafts, whether they be of wool or cotton, making it our business to understand the work, so as to do it and get it done. Train yourselves thus, girls.

And in this way also, girls : Whatever our husband's household consists of—servants or messengers or workpeople—we will know the work of each one of them by what has been done and their remissness by what has not been done ; we will know the strength and the weakness of the sick ; we will portion out the solid food and the soft to each according to his share. Train yourselves thus, girls.

And in this way also, girls : The treasure, corn, silver, and gold that our husband brings home, we will keep safe watch and ward over it, and will act as no robber, thief, carouser or wastrel in regard to it. Train yourselves thus, girls.

Indeed, girls, possessed of these five qualities, women, on the breaking-up of the body after dying, arise among the *devas* of lovely form.[1] A. iii. 37–38 ; iv. 265

Brahman, wealth is a noble's goal, wisdom's his ambition, power is his resolve, earth is his want, dominion his fulfilment. A brahman's goal is wealth, wisdom his ambition, mantras

---

[1] Closely following translation in G.S. iii. 29–30.

are his resolve, sacrifices his want, the Brahma-world his fulfilment. A householder's goal is wealth, wisdom's his ambition,
a craft is his resolve, work is his want, perfected work his fulfilment. A woman's goal is man, adornment is her ambition,
a son is her resolve, to be without a rival is her want, dominion
is her fulfilment. A thief's goal is booty, stealing is his ambition,
a caravan his resolve, darkness his want, not to be seen is his
fulfilment. A recluse's goal is patience and forbearance, wisdom
is his ambition, moral habit is his resolve, nothingness his want,
nirvana is his fulfilment.   *A. iii. 363*

Monks, endowed with six things, the householder Tapussa
has gone to fulfilment in the Truth-finder, has seen the Deathless,
and proceeds having realized the Deathless. What are the
six ? Unwavering confidence in the Awakened One, unwavering confidence in *dhamma*, unwavering confidence in the Order,
ariyan moral habit, ariyan knowledge, ariyan freedom.

[The same is then said of a number of other householders and lay
followers.]
                                                          A. iii. 450–451

VII. CASTE

These, sire, are the four castes : the noble, priestly, merchant,
and worker. Of these, two are declared chief : the noble and
the priestly, that is in regard to the way (their members) are
addressed, greeted by standing up and by palms joined in
salutation (of them), and by the way they are treated. There
are these five qualities to be striven after : faith, health, honesty,
output of energy, wisdom. The four castes may be endowed
with the five qualities that are to be striven after, and this would
be for them for a long time a blessing and a happiness. As to
this I do not say that there is a distinction in striving. It is as if
there might be a pair of tamed elephants, horses or steers,
well tamed and trained, and another pair not tamed or trained.
The first pair would be reckoned as tamed and would attain
tamed capacity. The second pair would not. In the same
way, it cannot happen that that which can be attained by faith,
health, honesty, no trickery, the output of energy and wisdom
can be won if there is no faith, poor health, deceit, trickery,

inertia and weak wisdom. In the case of the four castes, if (their members) are endowed with the five qualities that are to be striven after, if they should have right striving, I say that in such a case there is not any difference, that is to say in freedom as against freedom. It is as if four men, one taking a dry stick of brushwood, another a dry stick of sāl-wood, the third a dry stick of mango wood, and the fourth a dry stick of fig wood, were each to make a fire and get it to give out heat. Would there be any difference in the fires produced by the different woods as to their flame, hue or brilliance ? It is the same with the heat kindled by energy and produced by striving. I do not say that there is any difference in freedom as against freedom.

M. ii. 128–130

[Some recluses and brahmans, having heard it said that the recluse Gotama lays down the purity of the four castes, sent a brahman youth, Assalāyana, to refute him. Assalāyana approached Gotama and said :]

" Good Gotama, brahmans say : Just brahmans form the best caste, other castes are low ; only the brahman is a fair caste, other castes are dark ; only brahmans are pure, not non-brahmans ; only brahmans are own sons of Brahma, born of his mouth, born of Brahma, formed by Brahma, heirs of Brahma. What do you say ? "

" But, Assalāyana, brahman women have their periods, conceive, give birth, and give suck. And yet these brahmans, born of women like everyone else, say that only brahmans form the best caste, and so on."

" Although the revered Gotama speaks thus, this is what they think."

" Have you heard that in some of the adjacent districts there are only two ' castes '—masters and slaves, and that (a member of) the master (caste) can become a (member of) the slave (caste), and vice versa ? "

" Yes, sir, I have heard that ; but although the revered Gotama speaks in this way there are brahmans who think that only brahmans form the best caste, and so on."

" Now, would a noble, suppose he made onslaught on creatures or took what was not given, or behaved badly in

regard to the pleasures of the senses, or was a liar or slanderer or
of violent speech, or was one who tattles or covets, or was
malevolent or held a wrong view—would he, at the breaking-up
of the body after dying, arise in The Waste, the Bad Bourn, the
Downfall, Hell ? And would a merchant ? Would a worker ?
But not a brahman ? "

" No, good Gotama. A noble who was like this would arise
after dying as you say. So would a brahman, and also a
merchant and a worker. Indeed (members of) all four castes
who made onslaught on creatures, and so on, would arise in the
Waste, the Bad Bourn, the Downfall, Hell. But although the
revered Gotama speaks in this way there are brahmans who
think that only brahmans form the best caste . . . and are heirs
of Brahma."

" If a brahman refrained from onslaught on creatures, from
taking what is not given, from bad behaviour in regard to
pleasures of the senses, from lying and slandering and violent
speech, from tattling, and did not covet, was benevolent and
held a right view—would he at the breaking-up of the body after
dying arise in a Good Bourn, a heaven world ?—he only, not a
noble, not a merchant, not a worker ? "

" No, good Gotama. If nobles, brahmans, merchants and
workers refrained in all these ways, (members of) all four castes
would, at the breaking-up of the body after dying, arise in a
Good Bourn, a heaven world. But in spite of what the revered
Gotama says, there are brahmans who think that only brahmans
form the best caste, and so on."

" Now, what do you think, Assalāyana ? Is it only a brahman
who, in this district, can make become a heart of love that is
peaceable and kindly—not a noble, not a merchant, not a
worker ? "

" No, good Gotama, (members of) all four castes are able to
do this. But in spite of what you say there are brahmans who
think that only brahmans form the best caste . . . and are heirs
of Brahma."

" What do you think, Assalāyana ? Is it only a brahman who,
taking a string of bath-balls [1] and powder, having gone to a
river, is able to cleanse himself of dust and mud—not a noble,
not a merchant, not a worker ? "

" No, good Gotama. (Members of) all four castes are able to

[1] *Sotti.* So explained in *MA.* ii. 46.

do this, but in spite of what you say there are brahmans who think that only brahmans form the best caste, and so on."

"Now, suppose that a noble who has been anointed king were to assemble a hundred men of varying origins and were to say to them : 'Come, good sirs, those of you who are from noble, priestly, or royal families, take kindling wood of sāl, or of a sweet-scented tree, or of sandal, or of lotus, light a fire and get it to give out heat.' What do you think, Assalāyana ? Would it not be possible for all of these to make a fire and get heat showing flame, hue, and brilliance, no matter which of these woods they used ? But if a fire were lit and heat produced by one belonging to a despised family—a trapper, bamboo-plaiter, cartwright, or scavenger family—suppose him to have taken kindling wood from a dog's trough or a pig's trough or from a trough for dyeing or sticks of a castor-oil shrub—would this fire have neither flame nor hue nor brilliance so that it would not be possible for it to serve the purpose of a fire ? "

"No, good Gotama. It is possible to make all the fires, in regard to flame, hue, and brilliance, serve the purpose of a fire no matter the member of whatever family it was who lit them and no matter whatever was the kind of wood he used. But in spite of what you say there are brahmans who think that brahmans alone form the best caste . . . and are heirs of Brahma."

"Now, Assalāyana, suppose there were two young brahmans, blood brothers, one skilled (in the Vedas) and having received the (brahmanical) education, the other unskilled and uneducated. To which of these would brahmans offer food first at the time of offering to the departed or of sacrifice or of hospitality to a guest ? "

"To the skilled and educated young brahman. For what great result could derive from giving to one who was unskilled and uneducated ? "

"But suppose the skilled and educated young brahman was weak in moral habit and given to evil, while the unskilled and uneducated one was of (good) moral habit and given to what is lovely. To which of these would brahmans offer food first ? "

"To the unskilled and uneducated one who was of (good) moral habit and given to what is lovely. For what great result could derive from giving to one of weak moral habit and given to evil ? "

"First, you, Assalāyana, set off about birth ; you went on to mantras, from there you have come round to the purity of the four castes, which is what I am laying down."

M. ii. 148–154

VIII. DEVAS

" Well, now, good Gotama, are there *devas* ? "

" That is certainly known to me, Bhāradvāja : there are *devas*." [1]

" Is not this vain and false ? "

" There are *devas*, Bhāradvāja. If anyone is asked and should say that there are *devas*, or should say, ' It is certainly known, it is known to me '—this is indeed the conclusion to be reached by intelligent men."

" Why did you not explain this at the beginning, good Gotama ? "

" But this is acclaimed in the world, that is to say, that there are *devas*."

M. ii. 212–213

" Monks, I will teach you about the *devas* belonging to the Gandhabba [2] group. Listen. Which are the *devas* belonging to that group ?

" There are, monks, *devas* inhabiting the scent of roots ; there are, monks, *devas* inhabiting the scent of heart-wood . . . the scent of soft-wood . . . the scent of bark . . . the scent of sap . . . the scent of leaves . . . the scent of flowers . . . the scent of fruits . . . the scent of the tastes . . . the scent of the scents.[3] Monks, these are called *devas* belonging to the Gandhabba group."

" What, lord, is the cause, what the reason why a certain person who is here, at the breaking-up of the body after dying, arises in companionship with the *devas* belonging to the Gandhabba group ? "

" In this case, monks, a certain person walks the good walk in

---

[1] For a list of *devas* see p. 60.

[2] Sanskrit Gandharva. The presence of one of these *devas* was necessary to conception. *M.* i. 265, etc.

[3] According to *SA.* ii. 350 *gandhagandha* is the scent of the scent of the roots, and so on.

body, speech, and thought. He comes to hear : ' The *devas* belonging to the Gandhabba group are of long life-spans, beautiful, abounding in happiness.' He then thinks: ' O might I, at the breaking-up of the body after dying, arise in companion-ship with the *devas* belonging to the Gandhabba group.' On the breaking-up of the body after dying he arises in companionship with them.''

" What is the cause, lord, what the reason why a certain person who is here, at the breaking-up of the body after dying arises in companionship with the *devas* who inhabit the scent of roots ? "

" In this case, monks, someone walks the good walk in body, speech, and thought. He comes to hear : ' The *devas* who inhabit the scent of roots are of long life-spans, beautiful, abounding in happiness.' He then thinks : ' O might I, at the breaking-up of the body after dying, arise in companionship with the *devas* who inhabit the scent of roots.' He becomes a giver of the scent of roots.[1] The person who wishes to arise in companionship with the *devas* who inhabit the scent of heart-wood becomes a giver of the scent of heart-wood (*and so on down to the giver of the scents of the scents*)."

Or again, a monk asks the lord : " What is the cause, lord, what the reason why a certain person who is here, at the breaking-up of the body after dying arises in companionship with the *devas* who inhabit the scent of roots ? "

" In this case, monk, a certain person walks the good walk in body, speech, and thought. He comes to hear : ' The *devas* who inhabit the scent of roots are of long life-spans, beautiful, abounding in happiness.' He then thinks : ' O might I, at the breaking-up of the body after dying, arise in companionship with the *devas* who inhabit the scent of roots.' He gives food, drink, clothes, vehicles, garlands, scents, ointments, sleeping-places, and lamps with the material for lighting them.[2] He, at the breaking-up of the body after dying, arises in companion-ship with the *devas* who inhabit the scent of roots."

(*In an exactly similar way others arise, as they wish, in companionship with the devas who inhabit the scent of heart-wood and so on down to those who inhabit the scents of the scents.*)

S. iii. 250–253

[1] *SA.* ii. 350, such as the scent of the fragrant sandalwood roots.
[2] As at *A.* ii. 85, 203, iv. 239 ; *It.* p. 65, etc.

Wherever a wise man sets up his dwelling,
he invites those of moral habit who are Brahma-farers.

He gives offerings to the *devatās* who may be there ;
revered, honoured by him, they revere and honour him.

Since they have compassion for him, as a mother for her child,
A man, through the *devatās'* compassion, sees good everywhere.

D. ii. 88 ; *Vin.* i. 229 ; *Ud.* 89

Mahānāma, the young man of family, with his riches lawfully
obtained, honours, respects, reveres, and venerates those *devatās*
who are worthy to receive his offerings. Because of this, these
devatās have compassion for him, saying : " Long life, may a
long life-span be protected." Because of the *devatās'* compassion,
growth may be expected for the young man of family, not
decline.   *A.* iii. 77

IX. SACRIFICE

Māgha, make offering, (he said),
But in so doing, cleanse thy heart
In all its ways. To th' offerer
The offering is the help ; by this
Supported, he doth then quit hate.

With passion gone and hate expelled,
Let him in boundless measure then
Quicken a heart of amity,[1]
E'er day and night with zeal suffuse
All quarters to infinitude.

Who offers, Māgha, (he then said)
The offering threefold [2] endowed,
He would make offerings prosperous
By giving to gift-worthy men ;
And rightly minded, offering thus,
The ready almoner doth rise
Unto the world of Brahm, I say.[3]

Sn. 506, 507, 509

---

[1] Elsewhere in this volume translated " love ".

[2] *Cf. A.* iii. 336 where the giver's part is threefold : before the gift he is glad
at heart ; in giving the heart is satisfied ; and uplifted is the heart when he has
given.

[3] E. M. Hare. *Woven Cadences.*

Wherefore, brahman, bend low thine ear, and *dhamma* will I teach :

Ask not of birth but of the faring ask !
From wood is awe-inspiring fire begot :
From lowly clan noble becomes the sage
Who's steadfast and by modesty restrained.

Truth-tamed, endued with temperance, adept
In lore and end, has the Brahma-faring fared :
Timely on him let brahman seeking merit
In sacrifice his offering bestow.

On them who, lusts forsaking, homeless fare,
The well controlled-of-self, as shuttle straight :
Timely on them let brahman seeking merit
In sacrifice his offering bestow.

The passionless with faculties composed
And freed as moon from Rāhu's dark eclipse :
Timely on them let brahman seeking merit
In sacrifice his offering bestow.

Those unattached who wayfare in the world,
The ever mindful, quit of thoughts of " mine " :
Timely on them let brahman seeking merit
In sacrifice his offering bestow.

He who is pleasure-quit, as conqueror fares,
Hath found and known the end of birth-and-death.
Cool man, cool as the waters of a lake,
Oblation-worthy is the Man-thus-come.[1]

Peer with his peers, aloof from crooked men,
Of boundless wisdom is the Man-thus-come,
Unsoiled by anything of here or hence,
Oblation-worthy is the Man-thus-come.

In whom abideth neither guile nor pride,
He who is free of greed and " mine " and hope,
Void of all wrath, exceeding cool-of-self,
A brahman he, with stain of sorrow razed,
Oblation-worthy is the Man-thus-come.

He who hath razed all harbours of the mind,
In whom abides no claim to things whate'er,
He, unattached to things of here or hence,
Oblation-worthy is the Man-thus-come.

---

[1] Elsewhere translated " Truth-finder ".

He who with mind-intent hath crossed the flood
And *dhamma* in the yondmost view hath known,
The cankerless who his last body bears,
Oblation-worthy is the Man-thus-come.

In whom becoming, cankers, all harsh speech,
Are quenched, gone to their end, and are no more
He, lore-adept, released in every way,
Oblation-worthy is the Man-thus-come.

'Mid men of pride, no man of pride himself,
Bond-overcomer who hath no bonds left,
Who understandeth ill, its base and scope,
Oblation-worthy is the Man-thus-come.

Seer of the lone, not trusting here to hope,
Who view and lore of other men hath passed,
He in whom no supports whate'er exist,
Oblation-worthy is the Man-thus-come.

He who hath reached the yon and nigh of things,
So all are ended, quenched and are no more,
Calm man, and in attachment's end released,
Oblation-worthy is the Man-thus-come.

Seer of the end and term of bond and birth,
Who passion's ways hath wholly left behind,
The cleansed, spotless, taintless, without flaw,
Oblation-worthy is the Man-thus-come.

He who perceiveth not self by the self,
Intent-of-mind, straight-goer, poised-of-self,
He truly still, the vital, doubt-free man,
Oblation-worthy is the Man-thus-come.

He with no room for error whatsoe'er,
The seer of knowledge as to all that is,
He who his final body beareth now,
Won to the full awakening, utter bliss,
(Such is the cleansing of that spirit here)
Oblation-worthy is the Man-thus-come.

Not mine t'enjoy fare won from chanting hymns
'Tis not the thing for seers, O brahmana !
Fare won from chanting hymns the Wake reject ;
Where *dhamma* reigns this, brahman, is the rule.

Nay, thou must offer other food and drink
To a great rishi wholly consummate,
The cankerless, untroubled man of calm :
Sure field is that for merit-seeking man.

Him th' unprovokable,
Him of unclouded mind,
Freed of all lustfulness,
Void of all indolence,
Guide of those on the brink,
Master of birth-and-death,
Type of the silent sage,
Perfect in silent lore,
Come to the sacrifice :
Him with thy brows unknit
Venerate with joinèd hands,
Worship with food and drink,
Thus prosper holy gifts.[1]

Sn. 462–478, 480–481, 483–485

Whoever month by month should sacrifice
for a century with a thousand (offerings),
but should venerate even for a moment
one who has made the Self become—
that veneration is better than oblation for a hundred years.

And whoever may tend for a century
the (sacred) fire in the (sacrificial) grove,
but should venerate even for a moment
one who has made the Self become—
that veneration is better than oblation for a hundred years.

Dh. 106–107

Nay, brahman, deem not that by mere wood-laying
Comes purity. Verily that is external
To him who thus purification seeketh.
By things without none is made pure, the wise say.

I lay no wood, brahman, for fires on altars,
Only within burneth the flame I kindle.
Ever my fire burns, ever composed-of-self,
I, perfected, fare the Brahma-faring.

As load of fuel surely is pride, O brahman ;
The altar's smoke, anger ; thy false words, ashes ;
The tongue's the priest's spoon ; and the heart the altar ;
The flame thereon—this is man's self well tamed.

A lake is *dhamma*, with virtue's strand for bathing,
Clear, undefiled, praised by the good to good men,
Wherein in sooth masters of lore come bathing,
So, clean of limb, to the Beyond cross over.

Dhamma is truth, restraint is Brahma-faring,
The Middle Way pursuing, brahman, the way to Brahma-attainment.
Due honour pay thou to the upright-minded.
Whoso doth this, him do I call Tide-rider.[2]

S. i. 169

---

[1] E.M. Hare, *Woven Cadences.*
[2] Similar to version given by Mrs Rhys Davids at *K.S.* i. 212.

Brahman, even before the (animal) sacrifice a man who lays the fire, who sets up the pillar, sets up three swords, evil, ill in yield, ill in fruit. What three? The deed-sword, the word-sword, the thought-sword.

Even before the sacrifice, brahman, a man laying the fire, setting up the pillar, causes such thoughts to arise as : " Let there be slain for the sacrifice so many bulls, so many steers, heifers, goats, rams ! " Thinking to make merit, he makes demerit; thinking to do good, he does evil; thinking he seeks the way of happy-going, he seeks the way of ill-going. Brahman, even before the sacrifice, a man laying the fire, setting up the pillar, sets up firstly this thought-sword, which is evil, ill in yield, ill in fruit.

Again, brahman, even before the sacrifice, a man . . . speaks thus : " Let there be slain so many bulls, steers, heifers, goats, and rams ! " Thinking to make merit, he makes demerit; . . . he seeks the way of ill-going. Brahman, even before the sacrifice, he, laying the fire, setting up the pillar, sets up secondly this word-sword. . . .

Moreover, brahman, even before the sacrifice, a man laying the fire, setting up the pillar, himself first sets on foot the business, saying : " Let them slay bulls, steers, heifers, goats, rams ! " Thinking to make merit, he makes demerit . . . he seeks the way of ill-going. Brahman, even before the sacrifice, he, laying the fire, setting up the pillar, sets up thirdly this deed-sword. These three evil swords are ill in yield, ill in fruit.

Brahman, these three fires ought to be forsaken, shunned, avoided. What three? The fires of passion, hatred, delusion. And why ought these fires to be forsaken, shunned, avoided? With mind impassioned (perverted or deluded), mastered, obsessed by passion (hatred or delusion) he takes a course ill in act, word and thought; and so doing, on the breaking-up of the body after dying, he arises in the Waste, the Bad Bourn, the Downfall, Niraya Hell. Therefore these three fires ought to be forsaken, shunned, avoided.

Brahman, these three following fires when esteemed, revered, venerated, respected, must bring perfect happiness. What three? The fires of the venerable, the householder, the gift-worthy.

And what is the fire of the venerable? Consider, brahman, the man who honours his mother and father—this is called the

fire of the venerable. And why? From this, this veneration
has sprung. Therefore, brahman, the fire of the venerable
when esteemed, revered, venerated, respected, must bring
perfect happiness.

And what is the fire of the householder? Consider, brahman,
the man who honours his sons, womenfolk, slaves, messengers,
workmen—this is called the fire of the householder. Therefore
the fire of the householder when esteemed . . . must bring
perfect happiness.

And what is the fire of the gift-worthy? Consider, brahman,
those recluses and brahmans who abstain from pride and
indolence, who bear things patiently and meekly, each taming
self, each calming self, each making self attain utter nirvana [1]—
this is called the fire of the gift-worthy. Therefore, brahman,
this fire of the gift-worthy when esteemed, revered, venerated,
respected, must bring perfect happiness.   *A.* iv. 42–45

No, brahman, I do not praise every sacrifice. Yet I do not
withhold praise from every sacrifice. In whatever sacrifice cows
are slaughtered, goats and sheep, fowl and swine, and where
divers living creatures come to destruction—such sacrifice,
brahman, as involves butchery, I do not praise. Why is this?
To such a sacrifice, involving butchery, neither perfected ones
nor those who have entered on the way to perfection draw near.
But in whatever sacrifice cows are not slaughtered, nor goats and
sheep, nor fowl and swine, and where divers living creatures
do not come to destruction—such sacrifice, not involving
butchery, I do praise, such as, for example, a long established
charity, an oblation for the welfare of the clan. Why is this?
Because to such a sacrifice which involves no butchery both
perfected ones and those who have entered on the way to perfection draw near.

> The sacrifices called The Horse, The Man,
> The " Throwing of the Peg," the " Drinking Rite,"
> The " House Unbarred " [2] with all their cruelty
> Have little fruit. Where goats and sheep and kine
> Of divers sorts are sacrificed, go not
> Those sages great who've travelled the right way.

---

[1] *parinibbāpenti.* " Taming, calming, making one self attain nirvana," also
at *A.* i. 168, ii. 68, iii. 46 ; *D.* iii. 61. *See* p. 43.

[2] These sacrifices are also referred to at *A.* iv. 151 ; *S.* i. 76 ; *It.* p. 21 ; *see* p. 111
above.

But sacrifices free from cruelty
Which men keep up for profit of the clan,
Where goats and sheep and kine of divers sorts
Are never sacrificed—to such as these
Go sages great who've travelled the right way.
Such should the thoughtful celebrate ; and great
The fruits of such ; profit they bring, not loss.
Lavish the offering ; *devas* therewith are pleased.[1]

A. ii. 42–43 ; verses also at *S.* i. 76

x. ANIMALS

If a monk were to suffuse with a heart of love the four great snake families, he would not pass away if he were bitten by a snake. I allow you, monks, to suffuse with a heart of love these four great snake families for the warding of self, for the guarding of self, for the protection of self :

For the Virūpakkhas my love,
My love for the Erāpathas,
For the Chabbyāputtas my love,
And for the Kaṇhāgotamakas,
For the footless my love,
My love for the bipeds,
For the four-footed my love,
My love for those with many feet.
Let not the footless do me harm,
Nor those that have two feet,
Let not the four-footed ones me harm,
Nor those with many feet.
All creatures, all breathers,
All beings and everything—
May they all see luck,
May none come to evil.

A. ii. 72–73 ; *Vin.* ii. 110

Do you see that fisherman, monks, who, having slaughtered a haul of fish, is selling fish-nets ? I have never seen, monks, nor have I heard of such a fisherman who, as a result of his action, as a result of his mode of living, goes about on an elephant or horse or in a chariot or vehicle, or who feasts at feasts or who lives in the abundance of great wealth. Why is this ? It is because he gloats evilly on fish being slaughtered or brought to the slaughter. It is the same with a butcher who kills and sells

[1] F. L. Woodward, *G.S.* ii. 49 f.

cattle or sheep or swine or game or forest beasts. It is because he gloats evilly on their being slaughtered or brought to the slaughter that he does not go about on an elephant or . . . live in the abundance of great wealth. Indeed, monks, he who gloats evilly on animals being slaughtered or brought to the slaughter shall become neither one who goes about on an elephant . . . nor one who lives in the abundance of great wealth. But he who gloats evilly on a human being being slaughtered or brought to the slaughter—for this there will be woe and sorrow for him for a long time : at the breaking-up of the body after dying he will arise in the Waste, in the Bad Bourn, in the Downfall, in Niraya Hell. *A.* iii. 301

In many a figure could I, monks, talk a talk on animal birth, but this is as far as I go ; it is not easy to describe in full, monks, so many are the woes of animal birth. *M.* iii. 169

How can you, foolish men, dig the ground or get someone else to do so ? For people think that there are living things in the ground. Whatever monk should dig the ground or get some one else to do so, there is an offence of expiation. *Vin.* iv. 32

How can you, foolish men, fell a tree or get some one else to do so ? For people think that there are living things in a tree. There is an offence of expiation for destroying vegetable growth. *Vin.* iv. 34

Whatever monk should intentionally deprive a breathing thing of life, there is an offence of expiation. *Vin.* iv. 124

Whatever monk should make use of water knowing that it contains breathing things, there is an offence of expiation. *Vin.* iv. 125

Whatever monk should sprinkle water that he knows to contain breathing things over grass or clay or get someone else to do so, there is an offence of expiation. *Vin.* iv. 49

Fish and meat are pure in three respects : if it is not seen, heard, or suspected (to have been killed specially for you).

Vin. iii. 172

If a monk should make use of human flesh, there is a grave offence. A monk should not eat the flesh of elephants, horses, dogs, snakes, lions, tigers, leopards, bears, hyenas (even in times of scarcity). Whoever should eat the flesh of any of these animals, there is an offence of wrong-doing. *Vin.* i. 218–220

V. EVOLUTION

1. EVOLUTION

THERE ARE, MONKS, SOME RECLUSES AND BRAHMANS WHO ARE
partially eternalists, partially non-eternalists. They lay
down on four grounds that the self and the world are
partially eternal, partially non-eternal. In regard to what do
they do so ?

Now, monks, there comes a condition when, at some time or
other after the lapse of a long interval, this world involves.[1] As
this world is involving, beings, for the most part, come to be
involved as Radiant Ones. There they become made of mind,
enjoyers of rapture, self-lucid, faring through the sky, abiding in
glory ; they endure for a long, long life-time.

Now, monks, there comes a condition when, at some time or
other after the lapse of a long interval, this world evolves.[1] As
this world is evolving, an empty mansion of a Brahmā appears.
Then some being, either because his life-span is worn away or
because his merit is worn away, having passed away from the
group of the Radiant Ones, arises in the Brahmā's empty mansion.[2] He there becomes made of mind, an enjoyer of rapture,
self-lucid, faring through the sky, abiding in glory ; he endures
for a long, long life-time.

With a self disconcerted at being there alone for a long life-
time, discontent and agitation arise in him, and he thinks : " O
that other beings would also come to this state of things." Then
certain other beings also, either because their life-span is worn
away or because their merit is worn away, having passed from
the group of the Radiant Ones, arise in the mansion of the
Brahmā in companionship with that being. These also are made
of mind . . . they endure for a long, long life-time.

Consequently, monks, it occurs to whatever being arose there
first : " It is I who am a Brahmā, a great Brahmā, Conqueror,
Unconquered, All-seeing, Controller, Lord, Maker, Creator,
Chief, Disposer, Master, Father of all that have and will become.

[1] In accordance with the traditional theory of cycles, more fully expounded
in *Vism.* 414 f. ; *cf.* also *DA.* i. 110.
[2] Like Baka Brahmā, *M.* i. 329, and the Buddha himself, *A.* iv. 89.

These beings were created by me. What was the cause of this ? It occurred first to me : O that other beings would also come to this state of things. And such was my resolution that these beings have come to this state of things. And it also occurs thus to those beings who arose later : " This revered Brahmā is a great Brahmā . . . Father of all that have and will become. We were created by this Brahmā. What was the cause of this ? It is that we see that he arose here first and that we arose after him."

But it may happen, monks, that some being, having passed away from that group, comes to this state of things and goes forth from home into homelessness. When he has done so, it may be that, as a result of ardour, as a result of striving, as a result of application, as a result of earnestness, as a result of right mental work, he touches such mental contemplation, that when the mind is contemplative he recollects that former habitation ; he does not recollect any beyond that. He thinks : " Whatever revered Brahmā is a great Brahmā, Conqueror, Unconquered . . . Father of all that have and will become—we were created by that revered Brahmā. He is permanent, stable, eternal, not liable to change, like unto the eternal in that he will endure. But those of us who were created by that Brahmā, having come to this state of things, are impermanent, unstable, of short life-spans, liable to pass away."

This is the first way in regard to which some recluses and brahmans lay down that the self and the world are partially eternal, partially non-eternal.

Secondly, monks, there are *devas* called " Debauched by Pleasure." During a tremendously long time they live intent upon things of laughter, pleasure, enjoyment. Because of this their memory is confused, and because their memory is confused these *devas* pass away from that group.[1] But it may happen, monks, that, having passed away from that group, some being comes to this state of things and goes forth from home into homelessness. When he has done so . . . (*as above*) . . . he does not recollect any beyond that. He thinks : " Whatever worthy *devas* are not those Debauched by Pleasure, these have not been intent during a tremendously long time on things of laughter, pleasure, enjoyment. Because of this their memory is not confused ; because their memory is not confused, these *devas*

[1] This exactly parallels Plato's formulation in *Phaedrus* 248c.

do not pass away from that group. They are permanent, stable, eternal, not liable to change ; they are like unto the eternal in that they will endure. But those of us who have been intent on things of laughter, pleasure, enjoyment for a tremendously long time—our memory is confused ; because our memory is confused we have passed away from that group, and have come to this state of things. We are impermanent, unstable, of short life-spans, liable to pass away."

This is the second way in regard to which some recluses and brahmans lay down that the self and the world are partially eternal, partially non-eternal.

Thirdly, monks, there are *devas* called "Debauched in Mind." During a tremendously long time they have looked at and thought about one another enviously. Because of this, their minds are polluted in regard to one another, and therefore their bodies are weary, their minds are weary. They pass away from that group. But it may happen, monks, that having passed away from that group, some being comes to this state of things, and goes forth from home into homelessness . . . (*as above*) . . . he does not recollect any beyond that. He thinks : "Whatever worthy *devas* are not those Debauched in Mind, these have not looked at and thought about one another enviously during a tremendously long time. Thus their minds are not polluted in regard to one another, their bodies and minds are not weary. These *devas* do not pass away from that group. They are permanent . . . they will endure. It is those of us who are Debauched in Mind and who have looked at and thought about one another enviously for a tremendously long time, whose minds are polluted in regard to one another, whose bodies and minds are weary, and who, having passed away from that group, having come to this state of things, are impermanent, unstable, of short life-spans, liable to pass away."

This is the third way in regard to which some recluses and brahmans lay down that the self and the world are partially eternal, partially non-eternal.

Fourthly, monks, some recluse or brahman reasons and investigates. He speaks thus from a system of his own devising beaten out by reasoning based on investigation [1] : "Whatever is called eye and ear and nose and tongue and body—this self is im-

---

[1] A position which the Buddha expressly denies as regards himself, *M.* i. 68 f. His knowledge is *a priori*, not inductive.

permanent, unstable, not eternal, liable to change. But whatever is called mind or thought or consciousness—that self is permanent, stable, eternal, not liable to change ; it is like unto the eternal in that it will endure."

This is the fourth way in which some recluses and brahmans who are partially eternalists, partially non-eternalists, lay down that the self and the world are partially eternal, partially non-eternal.

Of this, monks, the Truth-finder has foreknowledge : These speculative tenets, held in this way, stressed in this way, will come to lead to such-and-such a bourne, to such-and-such a future state. Of this the Truth-finder has foreknowledge and he has foreknowledge of more than this. And having foreknowledge of this, he lays no stress on it. As he lays no stress on it, known in him of himself is nirvana ; having known as they really are the arising and the passing away of feelings and their sweetness and their peril and the escape from them, the Truth-finder, monks, is freed without any residuum (for existence) remaining.

D. i. 17–22 ; cf. D. iii. 84

II. THE UNITY OF MANKIND

Vāseṭṭha, (he replied), I will expound
To you in gradual and very truth
Division in the kinds of living things ;
For kinds divide.[1] Behold the grass and trees !
They reason not, yet they possess the mark
After their kind : for kinds indeed divide.
Consider then the beetles, moths and ants :
They after their kind too possess the mark . . .
And so four-footed creatures, great and small . . .
The reptiles, snakes, the long-backed animals . . .
Fish and pond-feeders, water-denizens . . .
Birds and the wingéd creatures, fowls o' the air
They after their kind all possess the mark ;
For kinds divide. Each after his kind bears
His mark.[2] In man there is not manifold.[3]
Not in the hair or head or ears or eyes,
Not in the mouth or nose or lips or brows,
Not in the throat, hips, belly or the back,

---

[1] There is diversity of kind.
[2] I.e. a native mark.
[3] I.e. no variety of native marks.

Not in the rump, sex-organs or the breast,
Not in the hands or feet, fingers or nails,
Not in the legs or thighs, colour or voice,
Is mark that forms his kind, as in all else.
Nothing unique [1] is in men's bodies found:
The difference in men is nominal.[2]

Sn. 600–611

---

[1] Or specific.
[2] E. M. Hare. *Woven Cadences.*

VI. THE TEACHING

1. CAUSALITY

I WILL TEACH YOU *dhamma* : IF THIS IS, THAT COMES TO BE ; from the arising of this, that arises ; if this is not, that does not come to be ; from the ceasing of this, that ceases.[1]

M. ii. 32

Whoever sees uprising by way of cause sees *dhamma* ; whoever sees *dhamma* sees uprising by way of cause.   *M.* i. 190–191

This uprising by way of cause, Ānanda, is profound and has the appearance of being profound. It is through not knowing, not discovering, not penetrating this *dhamma* that this generation, having become entangled like a ball of string, and covered with blight like coarse grass and rushes, cannot overpass the Waste, the Bad Bourn, the Downfall, the Faring-on.

D. ii. 55 ; *S.* ii. 92

And what, monks, is uprising by way of cause ? Conditioned by ignorance are the constructions ; conditioned by the constructions is consciousness ; conditioned by consciousness is name-and-shape ; conditioned by name-and-shape are the six (sense-) spheres ; conditioned by the six (sense-) spheres is contact ; conditioned by contact is feeling ; conditioned by feeling is craving ; conditioned by craving is grasping ; conditioned by grasping is becoming ; conditioned by becoming is birth ; conditioned by birth, old age and dying, grief, suffering, sorrow, despair and lamentation come into being. Thus comes to be the origination of this entire mass of ill. This, monks, is called uprising.

The stopping of the constructions is from the utter fading away and stopping of ignorance ; the stopping of consciousness is from the stopping of the constructions ; the stopping of name-

[1] Aristotle, *Met.* vi. 3. 1, " Will A be or not ? Yes, if B happens ; otherwise not ".

and-shape is from the stopping of consciousness ; the stopping of
the six (sense-) spheres is from the stopping of name-and-shape ;
the stopping of contact is from the stopping of the six (sense-)
spheres ; the stopping of feeling is from the stopping of contact ;
the stopping of craving is from the stopping of feeling ; the
stopping of grasping is from the stopping of craving ; the stopping of becoming is from the stopping of grasping ; the stopping
of birth is from the stopping of becoming ; from the stopping of
birth, old age and dying, grief, suffering, sorrow, depair, and
lamentation are stopped. Thus comes to be the stopping of this
entire mass of ill.   *S. ii. 1–2*

And what, monks, is ageing and dying ? Whatever of this or
that being in this or that group of beings is ageing, decrepitude,
when the teeth are broken, the hair grey, the skin wrinkled, when
the term of life is drawing to its close and the sense-organs are
spent—this is called ageing.

Whatever of this or that being in this or that group of beings
is deceasing and arising, breaking up, disappearance, death and
dying, passing away, a breaking-up of the constructions, a laying-
aside of the carcase—this is called dying. This is what ageing is
and this is what dying is. This, monks, is called ageing and
dying.

And what, monks, is birth ? Whatever of this or that being in
this or that group of beings is birth, origination, being conceived,
coming forth, an appearance of the constructions, acquisition of
the (sense-) spheres—this is called birth.

And what, monks, is becoming ? There are these three kinds
of becoming : becoming in sense-pleasures, becoming in form,
becoming in non-form.

And what, monks, is grasping ? There are these four kinds of
grasping : grasping after sense-pleasures, grasping after view
(i.e. opinion), grasping after rule and rite, grasping after the
theory of " self."

And what, monks, is craving ? There are these six groups of
craving : craving for material shapes, craving for things heard,
smelt, tasted, touched, craving for states of mind.

And what, monks, is feeling ? There are these six kinds of
feeling : feeling which is born from contact with the eye, from
contact with the ear, from contact with the nose, from contact

with the tongue, from contact with the body, from contact with the mind.

And what, monks, is contact ? There are these six kinds of contact : contact with the eye, the ear, the nose, the tongue, the body, the mind.

And what, monks, is the sixfold (sense-) sphere ? The (sense-) sphere of eye, of ear, of nose, of tongue, of body, of mind.

And what, monks, is name-and-shape ? Feeling, perception, striving, contact, attention—this is called name. The four great elements and the shape derived from them—this is called shape. This is name and this is shape. This is called name-and-shape.

And what, monks, is consciousness ? There are these six groups of consciousness : consciousness through eye, through ear, through nose, through tongue, through body, through mind.

And what, monks, are the constructions ? There are these three kinds of constructions : constructions through body, constructions through speech, constructions through thought.

And what, monks, is ignorance ? Whatever is not-knowing concerning ill, its arising, its stopping, the course leading to its stopping—this, monks, is called ignorance.

S. ii. 2–4 ; *cf. M. i.* 49–54

From the arising of ignorance is the arising of the constructions, from the stopping of ignorance is the stopping of the constructions. This ariyan eightfold Way itself is the course leading to the stopping of the constructions, that is to say : right view, right concept, right speech, right doing, right mode of living, right effort, right mindfulness, right contemplation. Inasmuch as an ariyan disciple knows cause thus, knows the uprising of cause thus, knows the stopping of cause thus, knows the course leading to the stopping of cause thus—he, monks, is called an ariyan disciple who is endowed with (right) view, who is endowed with vision, and he has come into this true *dhamma* and he sees this true *dhamma*, and he is endowed with the knowledge of a learner and endowed with the lore of a learner, and he has attained to the stream of *dhamma*, and he has ariyan discriminating wisdom, and he stands knocking at the door of the Deathless.

S. ii. 43

From the arising of birth is the arising of ageing and dying, from the stopping of birth is the stopping of ageing and dying.

This ariyan eightfold Way itself is the course leading to the stopping of ageing and dying, that is to say : right view . . . right contemplation. Inasmuch as the ariyan disciple knows ageing and dying thus, knows their arising thus, knows their stopping thus, knows the course leading to their stopping thus— he, monks, in this case has knowledge of *dhamma* ; he, by this *dhamma* which is seen, discerned, intemporal, won, plunged into, draws the conclusion as to past and future thus : Whatever recluses and brahmans in past times have thoroughly understood ageing and dying, their uprising, their stopping, the course leading to their stopping—all these have thus thoroughly understood (these matters) even as I do now. And whatever recluses and brahmans in future times will thoroughly understand ageing and dying, their uprising, their stopping, the course leading to their stopping—all these will thus thoroughly understand (these matters) even as I do now. This is their knowledge of (logical) connection.

Inasmuch as these two knowledges—knowledge of *dhamma* and knowledge of (logical) connection—are cleansed and purified for the ariyan disciple, he, monks, is called an ariyan disciple who is endowed with (right) view, who is endowed with vision, and he has come into this true *dhamma* and he sees this true *dhamma*, and he is endowed with the knowledge of a learner and endowed with the lore of a learner, and he has attained to the stream of *dhamma*, and he has ariyan discriminating wisdom, and he stands knocking at the door of the Deathless.   *S*. ii. 57–58

II SELF.

(*a*) The Two Selves

The Self is lord of the self, for what other lord could there be ?
                                        Dh. 160

The self is not in Self.   *Dh*. 62

This one, steadfast, released from views,
Is unsmirched by the world, not blamed by Self.

                                        Sn. 913

Desire he should curb for either course [1] . . .
Committing nothing that the Self would blame.

Sn. 778

If one knows the Self as precious, he should guard it well guarded.   *Dh.* 157

Through Self one should urge on the self,
One should restrain the self by Self,
That monk, guarded by Self, mindful,
Will fare along to happiness.

For Self is lord of the self,
For Self is bourn of the self.[2]
Therefore restrain the self
As a merchant thoroughbred horse.

Dh. 379, 380

Material shape is like unto a ball of foam,
Feelings like unto a bubble blown,
Perceptions like a mirage are,
The constructions like a plantain tree,[3]
Consciousness like an illusion :
So has said the Kinsman of the Sun.

However one contemplates it, investigates it thoroughly,
And sees it thoroughly, it is empty, void.
Beginning with this body (as) taught by the very wise :
Material shape is bereft of three things—
Life, heat and consciousness—
See that it is thrown aside.
When the body is cast off
Discarded there it lies, food for others, senseless.
Such is this series, this babbling illusion.
Made known is this murderer, no essence here is found.

Thus should a monk, his energy stirred up,
Regard the constituents, day by day,
Day and night. Mindful, thoughtful,
Let him cast off all fetters,
Let him make of Self a refuge,[4]
Let him fare as if his turban were ablaze,
Aspiring for the path that changes not.

S. iii. 142–143

---

[1] *Anta.* *Cf.* other " dead ends " or " extremes " at pp. 104, 105, 106.
To pursue either of the opposing extremes is a false view, *Vin.* i. 172
[2] *Cf.* " Self of the self, Immortal Leader," *Maitri Up.* vi. 7 ; " self's intrinsic form," *Sn.* 368 ; " self's heart-wood," *S.* iv. 250, and *cf. Dh.* 12.
[3] Its trunk is so soft that the plantain tree has become a symbol of insubstantiality and worthlessness.
[4] As the Buddha himself had done, *D.* ii. 120, *cf.* p. 47.

(b) The Great Self

From earnest contemplation [1] is wisdom born,
From lack of earnest contemplation wisdom wanes,
Knowing this twofold path, by becoming and by de-becoming
He may so give Self a home that wisdom waxes.

Dh. 282

[The wanderer, Vacchagotta, spoke thus to the lord :]

" Now, good Gotama, is there a Self ? " When he had spoken thus, the lord became silent.

" What, then, good Gotama, is there not a Self ? " And a second time the lord became silent. Then the wanderer, Vacchagotta, rising from his seat, departed. Then, soon after his departure, the venerable Ānanda spoke thus to the lord :

" Why, lord, did the lord not answer Vacchagotta the wanderer's question ? "

" If I, Ānanda, on being asked by the wanderer, Vacchagotta, if there is a Self, should have answered that there is a Self, this, Ānanda, would have been a siding-in with those recluses and brahmans who are Eternalists. If I, Ānanda, on being asked by the wanderer, Vacchagotta, if there is not a Self, should have answered that there is not a Self, this, Ānanda, would have been a siding-in with those recluses and brahmans who are Annihilationists.

" If I, Ānanda, on being asked by the wanderer, Vacchagotta, if there is a Self, should have answered that there is a Self, would this have been in accordance with my knowledge that ' all things are not-Self ' ? "

" This would not be so, lord."

" If I, Ānanda, on being asked by the wanderer, Vacchagotta, if there is not a Self, should have answered that there is not a Self, the wanderer, Vacchagotta, already confused, would have been increasingly confused (and he would have thought) : ' Was there not formerly a Self for me ? There is none now.' " [2]

S. iv. 400–401 ; *cf. S.* iii. 99 ; *Ud.* 67

[1] *Yoga.*
[2] Vacchagotta would have assumed that a once-existing Self had now been " annihilated ".

Well said, Sāriputta, well said! Just this, Sāriputta, is the whole Brahma-faring, that is to say friendship, companionship, intimacy with the lovely.[1] Of a monk who has friendship, companionship, intimacy with the lovely, this is to be expected—that he will make the ariyan eightfold Way become, that he will make much of it. . . . Mine, Sāriputta, is friendship with the lovely, owing to which beings liable to birth are freed from birth, those liable to old age are freed from it, those liable to dying are freed from it, and those liable to grief, suffering, lamentation and despair are freed therefrom.

S. v. 3

I do not see any other single condition by means of which the ariyan eightfold Way, if not arisen, can arise, or if it has arisen can be brought to perfection of culture, except by this friendship with the lovely.   S. v. 35

Just as the dawn, monks, is the forerunner, the harbinger of the sun's arising, even so is friendship with the lovely the forerunner, the harbinger of the arising of the seven limbs of wisdom in a monk.   S. v. 101

In regard to factors which are external (to the body), I see no other single factor for the arising of the seven limbs of wisdom except this friendship with the lovely.   S. v. 102

> Now you are like a yellow leaf,
> And Yama's [2] men upon you wait;
> You stand at journey's starting point,
> And provender for you there's none.

> Do you make of the Self a lamp; [3]
> Endeavour swiftly, wise become!
> With flaws blown out, corruptions gone,
> You'll come to *devas'* ariyan plane.

> Now you are brought to close of life;
> To Yama's presence setting out;
> No halting place between for you,
> And provender for you there's none.

---

[1] By the " lovely " can be meant none else than the Great Self.
[2] Yama, lord of the realm of death; *cf.* p. 179.
[3] *Cf. D.* ii. 100; *S.* iii. 42.

Do you make of the Self a lamp ;
Endeavour swiftly, wise become !
With flaws blown out, corruptions gone,
You'll come to birth and ageing not again.[1]

Dh. 235-238

What, Ānanda, does the Order of monks expect that I should
not attain utter nirvana until I have left some instructions
concerning it ? Ānanda, *dhamma* has been taught by me without
making any distinction between exoteric and esoteric ; for, in
respect of truths, Ānanda, the Truth-finder has no such thing as
the closed fist of a teacher, who keeps some things back. Surely,
Ānanda, should there be anyone who harbours the thought that
it is he who should lead the Order or who thinks that the Order
is dependent on him, it is he who should lay down instructions
in any matter concerning the Order. But the Truth-finder,
Ānanda, does not think that it is he who should lead the Order
or that the Order is dependent on him. Why, then, should he
leave any instructions concerning the Order ? I, Ānanda, am
now worn, old, full of years, I have lived my span and am at the
close of my days, I am turning eighty years of age. And just as
a worn-out cart, Ānanda, can be kept going only with the help
of thongs, so, methinks, can the body of the Truth-finder be kept
going only by bandaging it up. It is only when the Truth-finder,
paying attention to none of the things which have signs, abides,
owing to the stopping of every feeling, in the signless contemplation of mind—it is only then that his body is at ease.

Wherefore, Ānanda, go along having Self as lamp, Self as
refuge and none other refuge ; having *dhamma* as lamp, *dhamma*
as refuge and none other refuge. And how, Ānanda, does a monk
go along thus ? In this connection, a monk in regard to body so
looks upon body that he dwells ardent, composed, mindful in
order to control the hankering and dejection in the world ; and
similarly with feelings, and with mind and mental states. It is
in this way, Ānanda, that a monk goes along having Self as lamp,
Self as refuge, and none other refuge ; having *dhamma* as lamp,
dhamma as refuge, and none other refuge. Whoever they are,
Ānanda, either now or after I am no more, who go along having
Self as lamp, Self as refuge and none other refuge ; having
dhamma as lamp, *dhamma* as refuge, and none other refuge, these

[1] Closely following Mrs Rhys Davids, *Min. Anth.* i.

monks of mine will become in the peak of the Deathless—those
who are willing to train.   *D*. ii. 100–101

Go along, monks, having Self as lamp, Self as refuge, and none
other refuge ; having *dhamma* as lamp, *dhamma* as refuge, and
none other refuge. By those going along with Self and *dhamma*
as lamp and refuge, and with none other refuge, the very source
(of things) is to be searched for, thinking : " What is the birth
and origin of sorrow, grief, woe, lamentation and despair ? "
What, then, monks, is the origin of these ?
The uninstructed many folk, not discerning the ariyans, not
skilled in their *dhamma*, untrained in it, not discerning those who
are true men, not skilled in their *dhamma*, untrained in it, these
regard material shape as Self, or Self as having material shape, or
material shape as being in Self, or Self as being in material shape.
But one's material shape alters and becomes otherwise, and
therefore sorrow, grief, woe, lamentation, and despair arise.
But the instructed ariyan disciple thinks : Formerly also, as
well as now, all material shape was impermanent, suffering,
liable to change. By right wisdom, seeing it thus as it really
comes to be, sorrow, grief, woe, lamentation, and despair wane.
He is not troubled at their waning, but untroubled lives at ease,
and so living is called a monk who has attained nirvana in respect
of all that.
So also in regard to feeling, perception, the constructions,
consciousness.   *S*. iii. 42–43

[Ānanda is disconcerted by Sāriputta's death :]

Ānanda, has not this been shown by me already : the coming
to be different, the coming to be without, the coming to be other
of all that is dear and liked ? In this case, Ānanda, how is it
possible to say of that which is born, has become, is composite
and liable to dissolution : " O let not that be dissolved ! " ?
This is a situation that cannot exist.
Ānanda, as one of the larger branches might fall from a great
and stable and pithy tree, even so, Ānanda, has Sāriputta attained
utter nirvana in the great and stable and pithy Order of monks.
As to this, Ānanda, whence is it possible to say of that which is
born, has become, is composite and liable to dissolution : " O
let not that be dissolved ! " ? This is a situation that cannot exist.

Therefore, Ānanda, go along having Self as lamp, Self as refuge and none other refuge ; having *dhamma* as lamp, *dhamma* as refuge, and none other refuge. And how, Ānanda, does a monk go along thus ? In this connection, a monk in regard to body so looks upon body that he dwells ardent, composed, mindful in order to control the hankering and dejection in the world. It is in this way, Ānanda, that a monk goes along having Self as lamp, Self as refuge, and none other refuge ; having *dhamma* as lamp, *dhamma* as refuge, and none other refuge. Whoever they are, Ānanda, either now or after I am no more, who go along having Self as lamp, Self as refuge, and none other refuge ; having *dhamma* as lamp, *dhamma* as refuge, and none other refuge ; these monks of mine will become in the peak of the Deathless —those who are willing to train.

S. v. 162–163 ; *cf. S. v.* 164 ; *D.* ii. 100

Monks, truly this company of mine seems empty. Monks, this company of mine has become empty on the attainment of utter nirvana by Sāriputta and Moggallāna.[1] We cannot tell which is the quarter where Sāriputta and Moggallāna are faring along.

Monks, those who in past times became perfected ones, fully awakened ones, those lords had just such a chief pair of disciples as Sāriputta and Moggallāna were to me. And those who in future times will become perfected ones, fully awakened ones, these lords will have just such a chief pair of disciples as Sāriputta and Moggallāna were to me.

Monks, it is a wonder of disciples, it is a marvel of disciples, that they become doers of the Teacher's bidding, promoters of his instruction. They become affectionate towards the four companies,[2] liked by them, revered, and what they ought to become. Monks, it is a wonder in a Truth-finder, it is a marvel in a Truth-finder that on the attainment of utter nirvana by such a pair of disciples there is for the Truth-finder neither grief nor lamenting. As to this, whence is it possible to say of that which is born, has become, is composite and liable to dissolution : " O let not that be dissolved ! " ? This is a situation that cannot exist.

Monks, as the larger branches might fall from a great and stable and pithy tree, even so, monks, have Sāriputta and Moggallāna

---

[1] Moggallāna died, according to the Commentary, a fortnight after Sāriputta.
[2] Monks, nuns, men and women lay-followers.

attained utter nirvana in this great and stable and pithy Order of monks. As to this, Ānanda, whence is it possible to say of that which is born, has become, is composite and liable to dissolution : " O let not that be dissolved ! " ? This is a situation that cannot exist.

Therefore, Ānanda, go along having Self as lamp, Self as refuge, and none other refuge ; having *dhamma* as lamp, *dhamma* as refuge, and none other refuge. . . .[1]   *S.* v. 164

(c) The Little Self

Evil is done by the self, by the self one comes to grief.
Evil is left undone by the self, by the self one is purified.
The pure, the impure—this is of the self ;
No one can purify another.

Dh. 165

Evil is done just by self, it is born of self, brought into being by self.   *Dh.* 161

The well tamed should (set out to) tame (others),
for they say the self is hard to tame.

Dh. 159

Those whose conduct in body, speech, and thought is bad, to these self is not dear. Even if they should say : " Self is dear to us," nevertheless self is not dear to them. And why ? Because that which the not-dear would do to the not-dear, even that they do of themselves to self. Therefore to these self is not dear. But those whose conduct in body, speech, and thought is good, to these self is dear. Even if they should say : " Self is not dear to us," nevertheless self is dear to them. And why ? Because that which the dear would do the dear, even that they do of themselves to self. Therefore to these self is dear.

Of whom is self guarded ? Of whom is self not guarded ? Those whose conduct in body, speech, and thought is bad, of these self is not guarded. Even should these be guarded by a squadron of elephants, of horses, of chariots, of infantry, nevertheless of these self is not guarded. And why ? This guard is

[1] Continue as in excerpt from *S.* v. 162-163

external, it is not an inner guard. Therefore of these is self not guarded.

But those whose conduct in body, speech, and thought is good, of these self is guarded. Even if these should be guarded neither by a squadron of elephants, nor of horses, nor of chariots, nor of infantry, nevertheless of these self is guarded. And why ? This is an inner guard, this guard is not external. Therefore of these self is guarded.

> The whole world wide we traverse with our thought,
> And nothing find that dearer is than self.
> Since aye the self so dear to others is,
> Let the self-lover harm no other thing.

                    S. i. 71 ff. ; verses also at *Ud.* 47

[Then the lord addressed the group of five monks, saying :]

" Body,[1] monks, is not the Self. Now, were body the Self, monks, this body would not tend to sickness, and one might get the chance of saying in regard to body : Let body become thus for me, let body not become thus for me. But inasmuch, monks, as body is not the Self, therefore body tends to sickness, and one does not get the chance of saying in regard to body : Let body become thus for me, let body not become thus for me.

" Feeling is not the Self . . . perception is not the Self . . . the constructions are not the Self . . . consciousness is not the Self. Now, were consciousness the Self, monks, consciousness would not tend to sickness, and one might get the chance of saying in regard to consciousness : Let consciousness become thus for me, let consciousness not become thus for me. But inasmuch, monks, as consciousness is not the Self, therefore consciousness tends to sickness, and one does not get the chance of saying in regard to consciousness : Let consciousness become thus for me, let consciousness not become thus for me. Now, what do you think about this, monks : Is body permanent or impermanent ? "

" Impermanent, lord."

" And is that which is impermanent painful or at ease ? "

" Painful, lord."

" But, now, is it fit to consider that which is impermanent, painful, liable to change, in this way : This is mine, this am I, this is my Self ? "

[1] *rūpa*, material shape.

" It is not, lord." (*The same questions and answers in regard to feeling, perception, the constructions, consciousness.*)

" Therefore, monks, whatever is body that is past, future, present, subjective or objective, gross or subtle, low or excellent, far or near—all body should be viewed, with right wisdom, as it has really come to be, thus : This is not mine, this am I not, this is not my Self." (*The same repeated for feeling, perception, the constructions, consciousness.*)

" Seeing this, monks, the instructed ariyan disciple disregards body, and disregards feeling and disregards perception and disregards the constructions, and disregards consciousness ; by disregarding he is passionless, by passionlessness he is freed, in freedom the knowledge comes to be : I am freed, and he comes to know : Destroyed is birth, lived is the Brahma-faring, done is what was to be done, there is no more of being such-and-such." [1]

Vin. i. 13 ; *S.* iii. 66 ff.

Material shape is impermanent. What is impermanent, that is suffering. What is suffering, that is not the Self. What is not Self, that is not mine, that am I not, that is not my Self. As it really comes to be, one should discern it thus by right wisdom, and by right wisdom seeing it thus, the mind disregards and is freed from the fluxions with no grasping. From being freed, it is steadfast ; from being steadfast, it is happy ; from being happy, it is not troubled ; from being not troubled, one is individually attained to utter nirvana, [2] and one knows : Destroyed is birth, lived is the Brahma-faring, done is what was to be done, there is no more of being such-and-such. [3]

So also in regard to feeling, perception, the constructions, consciousness.　　　　　　　　　　　　　*S.* iii. 44–45

There may be an occasion, monks, where some foolish man, unintelligent, ignorant, his mind dominated by craving, may think to deviate from the Teacher's instruction thus : " So then you say, material shape is not the Self, feeling . . . perception . . . the constructions . . . consciousness is not the Self. So what Self can not-self-done deeds refer to ? " You, monks,

---

[1] This is the famous Second Utterance. In the *S.* version it is called " The Five," which refers either to the five (first) disciples who heard it, or to the five topics (body . . . consciousness) with which it deals.

[2] *parinibbāyati.*　　　　　　　　[3] *Cf.* below, p. 170.

have been trained by me in causality,[1] everywhere and in every matter.

Material shape and the rest are impermanent, suffering, liable to change. Therefore it should be seen as it really is that no material shape (and so on) is mine, this am I not, this is not my Self. *M.* iii. 19 ; *S.* iii. 103

Monks, everything is burning. And what is everything that is burning ? The eye is burning, material shapes are burning, consciousness through the eye is burning, contact through the eye is burning ; in other words, the feeling which arises from contact through the eye, be it pleasant or painful or neither painful nor pleasant, that too is burning. With what is it burning ? I say that it is burning with the fire of passion, with the fire of hatred, with the fire of delusion ; it is burning with birth, with old age, dying, grief, sorrow, suffering, lamentation, and despair.

The ear is burning, sounds are burning . . . the nose is burning, odours are burning . . . the tongue is burning, tastes are burning . . . the body is burning, tangible objects are burning . . . the mind is burning, mental states are burning, consciousness through the mind is burning, contact through the mind is burning ; in other words, the feeling which arises from contact through the mind, be it pleasant or painful or neither painful nor pleasant, that too is burning. With what is it burning ? I say that it is burning with the fire of passion, with the fire of hatred, with the fire of delusion ; it is burning with birth, with old age, dying, grief, sorrow, suffering, lamentation, and despair.

Seeing this, the instructed ariyan disciple disregards all these sense organs and sense data that I have called " burning." By disregarding he is passionless, by passionlessness he is freed ; in freedom the knowledge comes to be : I am freed, and he knows : Destroyed is birth, lived is the Brahma-faring, done is what was to be done, there is no more of being such-and-such. *Vin.* i. 34

" The sea, the sea," monks, says the uninstructed average person. This, monks, is not the sea in the discipline for an ariyan. Great is this stretch of water, great are the deeps of the water.

The eye, monks, is the sea for a man ; its data are made of material shapes. Whoever overcomes its data, which are made of material shapes, he, monks, is called one who has crossed the

[1] *M. paṭicca,* causality ; *S. paṭipuccha,* have been answered (by me).

sea of the eye with its waves, its whirlpools, with its sharks, its demons—crossed over, gone beyond, the brahman stands on dry land.[1]

The nose, monks, is the sea for a man ; its data are made of odours. . . .

The ear, monks, is the sea for a man ; its data are made of sounds. . . .

The tongue, monks, is the sea for a man ; its data are made of tastes. . . .

The body, monks, is the sea for a man ; its data are made of contacts. . . .

The mind, monks, is the sea for a man ; its data are made of mental states. Whoever overcomes its data, which are made of mental states, he, monks, is called one who has crossed the sea of the mind with its waves, its whirlpools, with its sharks, its demons —crossed over, gone beyond, the brahman stands on dry land.

> Whoso has crossed this sea with its sharks and demons,
> With its fearsome waves, so hard to cross—
> Who is versed in lore and has lived the Brahma-faring,
> " Gone to world's end," " gone beyond " is he called.[2]

S. iv. 157

In the Himalaya, monks, there is a region that is rough and hard to cross, the range of neither monkeys nor human beings. There is a similar region, which is the range of monkeys but not of human beings. There are level and delightful tracts of country, the range of both monkeys and human beings. It is here, monks, that a hunter sets a trap of pitch in the monkeys' tracks to catch the monkeys. Now, those monkeys who are not stupid and greedy, on seeing that pitch-trap, keep far away from it. But a stupid, greedy monkey comes up to the pitch and handles it with one of his paws, and his paw sticks fast in it. Then thinking : I'll free my paw, he lays hold of it with the other paw—but that, too, sticks fast. To free both paws he lays hold of them with one foot, but that, too, sticks fast. To free both paws and one foot he lays hold of them with the other foot, but that, too, sticks fast. To free both paws and both feet he lays hold of them with his muzzle, but that, too, sticks fast.

So that monkey, thus trapped in five ways, lies down and howls, thus fallen on misfortune, fallen on ruin, a prey for the

---

[1] *Cf.* p. 191.   [2] Last two lines as p. 192.

hunter to work his will on him. The hunter spits him and prepares him for eating then and there over a charcoal fire and goes off at his pleasure.

Even so it is with one who goes in wrong pastures, the beat of others. Therefore, monks, do you not so walk. To those who do so, Māra gets access, Māra gets a chance over them. And what, monks, is the wrong pasture, the beat of others? It is the fivefold set of pleasures of the senses. What are the five? Material shapes cognizable by the eye, sounds cognizable by the ear, scents cognizable by the nose, tastes cognizable by the tongue, contacts cognizable by the body, desirable, pleasant, delightful, dear, passion-fraught, inciting to lust. This, monks, is the wrong pasture, the beat of others. Go, monks, in a pasture that is your own native beat, for to those who so go Māra gets no access, Māra gets no chance over them. And what is a monk's pasture, his own native beat? It is the four stations of mindfulness. What are the four? In this connection a monk dwells ardent, attentive, mindful, regarding body as body, feelings as feelings, thought as thought, mental states as mental states, so that he may control the hankering and dejection in the world. This is a monk's pasture, his own native beat.[1] S. v. 148–149

There where one is not born, does not age, does not die, does not pass on (from one rebirth), does not arise (in another)—I do not say that *that* is an end of the world that one can apprehend, see, or reach by walking. . . . But nor do I say that, not having reached the end of the world, an end can be made of ill. For I lay down that the world, its uprising, cessation, and the course leading to its cessation are in this fathom-long body itself with its perceptions and ideas.

> Not to be reached by locomotion is World's End ever :
> Yet there is no release from ill till it has been reached.
> So let a man become a World-knower, World-ender,
> Let him have led the Brahma-faring—
> Knowing World's End, as one now pacified,
> He longs not either for this or another world.

[The monks do not understand and question Ānanda on what Gotama means. He says : " The lord knowing, knows ; seeing, sees ; he has become vision, become knowledge, become *dhamma*, become Brahma ; he is proclaimer, expounder, leader to the goal, giver of the Deathless,

[1] This is a Tar-Baby (Stickfast) story.

dhamma-lord, Truth-finder." Still the monks do not understand, and ask for a further explanation. Ānanda replies : " That by which in the world one has perception of the world, *that* in the discipline for the ariyan is called ' world.' It is through the eye, the ear, the nose, the tongue, the body that, in the world, there is perception of the world, conceit of the world. Each one of these is called ' world ' in the discipline for an ariyan."

[This is corroborated by Gotama. *S*. iv. 93 ff.]

S. i. 61–62 ; *A*. ii. 47–49 ; *cf. S*. iv. 93

Suppose, monks, there were four archers mighty with the bow, well trained, expert, past masters in their art, standing one at each quarter, and a man were to come, saying : " I will catch and bring the shafts let fly by these four archers, mighty with the bow, or ever they touch the ground." What do you think of this, monks ? Would it be enough to call him a swift man possessed of supreme speed ? Now, as is the speed of that man, as is the speed of moon and sun, swifter than he, and as is the speed of those *devatās* who run ahead of the moon and the sun, swifter than that man and swifter than both of these, so even swifter than these is the wasting-away of the components of a life-span. Wherefore you must train yourselves thus : We will live with diligence.   *S*. ii. 265–266

Regard the world as void [1] ; and e'er
Alert, uproot false view of self.
Thus, Mogharāja, thou wouldst be
Death's crosser ; and regarding thus
The world, Death's king doth see thee not.[2]

Sn. 1119

The Sage rejected the aggregate of the components
Of becoming—ponderable and imponderable ;
With inward delight, composed, he burst
Like shell of armour the aggregate of self.

D. ii. 107 ; *A*. iv. 312 ; *S*. v. 263 ; *Ud*. 64

No brahman from another cleansing claims,
Be it by things seen, heard, felt, rule or rite ;
Unsoiled is he alike by good and bad,
Rid of the self, he's not effecting [3] here.

---

[1] I.e. of selfhood, or anything of the nature of a self.
[2] E. M. Hare, *Woven Cadences.*
[3] I.e. not doing deeds and therefore setting up results from them.

The self cast out, ungrasping,
In knowledge even places he no trust ;
Nay, no party-man among the heretics,
Unto view even has he no recourse.

Sn. 790, 800

Not to consider " I am this," that is freedom.

Ud. 74

Rejecting the notion " I am."   *M.* i. 139

What is impermanent, that is ill ; what is ill is not the Self.
What is not Self, that is not mine, that am I not, that is not my
Self. . . . Happy indeed those perfected ones ! The thought
" I am " eradicated, delusion's net is rent.   *S.* iii. 83

When the thought " I am " has been eradicated, the monk is
no more on fire.   *A.* ii. 216

Seeing in what's impermanent the permanent, in what is ill what's well,
In what's not-Self the Self, in what is ugly beauty,
These are the erroneous views of the scatter-brained and unintelligent. . . .
They tread the round of becoming, theirs is the road of birth and death.

A. ii. 52

Happy his solitude who glad at heart
Hath *dhamma* learnt and doth the vision see !
Happy is that benignity towards
The world which on no creature worketh harm.
Happy the absence of all lust, th' ascent
Past and beyond the needs of sense-desires.
He who doth crush the great " I am " conceit—[1]
This, truly this, is happiness supreme.[2]

Vin. i. 3 ; *Ud.* 10

This world of men, given over to the idea " I am the doer,"
bound up with the idea " Another is the doer," do not truly
understand this ; they have not seen the point. But for one who

---

[1] " But now from my forehead I'll quickly erase
     The stamp of the Devil's great ' I '."

                              Shaker Hymn

" Any person would be infinitely happier if he could accept the loss of his
' individual self ' . . . the very mother of illusions " : E. E. Hadley and H. S.
Sullivan in *Psychiatry* 5 [1942] and 1 [1938], p. 134.

[2] Translation taken from F. L. Woodward, *Min. Anth.* ii.

sees this point beforehand, there does not come to be the notion
" I am the doer," nor the notion " Another is the doer." [1]

This folk, possessed of pride, fettered by pride, bound by pride,
Making " activity " (one) among false views, overpasses not the faring-on.
                                                            Ud. 70

Whatever material shape, Rāhula, whatever feeling, whatever
perception, constructions, consciousness, whether past, future,
present, whether gross or subtle, low or excellent, far or near,
which one sees by right wisdom as it really comes to be—that is
to say as " This is not mine, this am I not, this is not my Self "—
knowing it thus, seeing it thus, there does not come to be in
regard to this body, which is informed by consciousness, nor in
any of the features which are external to it, the notion " I am the
doer, mine is the doer, any latent ' I am.' "
         S. ii. 252 ; *cf. S.* iii. 80, 169 (*cf.* BG. xviii. 16 ; iii. 26)

" How, lord, does the mind of one who knows, of one who
sees, come to be without the thought ' I am the doer, mine is the
doer, and the latent " I am " ' in regard to this body which is
informed by consciousness, and in regard to all the features
which are external to it, so that it transcends all distinctions,
is tranquillized, is well freed ? "
    " Whatever material shape, Rāhula, feeling, perception, con-
structions, consciousness is past . . .[2] near, if he thinks, ' This is
not mine, this am I not, this is not my Self,' then having seen by
right wisdom this material shape and so on as they really come to
be, he becomes freed with no residuum (for rebirth remaining)."
                                                    S. iii. 136–137

Monks, if a monk perceive six advantages, they suffice for
him to establish, without reserve, awareness of not-the-Self.
What are the six ? The thoughts : " I will become without

---

[1] There is an apparent contradiction of the above in *A.* iii. 337–338 (*see* p. 166),
where the reality of *attakāra* and *paramkāra* is asserted. This must be resolved in
the light of *Sn.* 661, i.e. in the sense that he is a liar (*abhūtavādin*), a sayer of that
which is not true, who repudiates his agency even at the moment when he *is*
doing something ; such a one is precisely an *akiriyavāda* heretic using the principle
of " inaction " to excuse his vilest actions. That " I am not the doer " is not,
of course, only Buddhist and Brahmanical, but Islamic, Philonic, Taoist, and
Christian (" I do nothing of myself ").
[2] As in previous extract.

desire in regard to the whole world ; and the notion ' I am the doer ' shall be kept in check ; and the notion ' Mine is the doer ' shall be kept in check ; and I will become possessed of knowledge that cannot be [1] imparted ; and cause shall be properly discerned by me, and the causal origination of things."   *A. iii. 444*

It may be, Ānanda, that a monk may acquire contemplation of such a kind that in regard both to this body which is informed by consciousness, and to any of the features which are external to it, there could not be for him the notion " I am the doer, mine is the doer, any latent ' I am ' " ; and whatever freedom of heart, freedom of intellect be entered upon and abided in where there is not the notion " I am the doer, mine is the doer, any latent ' I am ' "—having entered upon that freedom of heart, that freedom of intellect, he would abide in them. For, as to this, Ānanda, it occurs to the monk : " This is peace, this is the excellent, namely the calm of all the constructions, the surrender of all the residuum (for rebirth), the destruction of craving, dispassion, stopping, nirvana."   *A. i. 132–133*

III. DEEDS AND TRANSMIGRATION

It is not the custom for a Truth-finder to lay down " Penalty, penalty." It is the custom for a Truth-finder to lay down " Deed, deed." I, Tapassin, lay down three kinds of deeds for the doing of an evil deed, for the execution of an evil deed, that is to say : deed of body, deed of speech, deed of mind. Deed of body is one thing, deed of speech is another, deed of mind yet another. Of these three kinds of deeds thus classified, thus particularised, I lay down that a deed of mind is the most greatly censurable in the doing of an evil deed, in the execution of an evil deed ; a deed of body is not thuswise, a deed of speech is not thuswise.   *M. i. 373*

Monks, there are these three sources for the origination of deeds. What are the three ? Greed, hatred, delusion is each a source for the origination of deed. Whatever deed is done from greed, born from greed, has its source in greed, its origination in greed, wherever an individuality uprises that deed of his matures,

---
[1] *V.l.* can be.

and when that deed is mature he experiences the result of that deed, either here and now or later or in a succession (of lives). So it is with a deed done in hatred, with a deed done in delusion.

A. i. 134

A deed, monks, must be known, its tie-source, variety, fruit, stopping, and the course leading to its stopping. And wherefore ?

I, monks, say that willing is a deed. Having willed, one does a deed through body, speech, or thought. Contact is the tie-source of deed. Variety in deed are these : they are to be experienced in Niraya Hell, in an animal's womb,[1] in the realm of the departed, in the world of men, in a *deva*-world. The fruit of a deed is threefold : it may arise here and now, or later, or in a succession (of lives). The stopping of a deed is the stopping of contact. This ariyan eightfold Way—right view and the rest—is itself the course leading to the stopping of deed. And in so far as an ariyan disciple has foreknowledge thus of deed, of the tie-source of deeds, of their variety, their fruit, their stopping and the course leading to their stopping, he has foreknowledge that this discriminative Brahma-faring is the stopping of deed.

A. iii. 415

> None is by birth a brahman [2] ; none
> By birth no brahmana ; by deeds is one
> A brahmana, by deeds no brahmana.
> By deeds one is a farmer and by deeds
> An artisan, by deeds a trader too ;
> By deeds one is a servant and a thief,
> By deeds a soldier and a celebrant,
> And even so a rajah is by deeds.
> 'Tis thus in truth the wise perceive the deed.
> Seers of the origin by way of cause,
> Men expert in the result of deeds. The world
> Revolves by deeds, mankind revolves by deeds:
> As pin holds fast the rolling chariot's wheel,
> So beings are in bondage held by deeds.
>
> A brahman one becomes by Brahma-faring,
> By temperance, austerity, restraint :
> This is indeed supreme for brahmanhood.[3]

Sn. 650–655

---

[1] I.e. in a rebirth as an animal.
[2] Here, as often, a " true " brahman, synonym of arahant.
[3] E. M. Hare. *Woven Cadences.*

In sooth to every person born
An axe is born within his mouth,
Wherewith the fool doth cut himself
Whenas he speaketh evilly.

And they who praise the blameworthy,
And they who blame the praiseworthy,
Cull with the mouth the seeds of woe,
Nor from the seeds raise happiness.

Who with the dice-seeds loseth wealth,
Little his woe ; greater for him
The seeds of woe, alike for wealth,
Alike for self, should he beget
Illwill in heart for well-farers.

For a hundred thousand periods,
Thrice twelve, and five, he goes to hell,
Whoso with ill-intent in word
And thought reviles the Ariyans.

The liar and he who does but says
" I did not do it," go to hell,
Degraded both by deeds, in death
Hereafter they become alike.[1]

Who wrongs the man who doth no wrong,
Him cleansed, full-grown, the fleckless man,
That evil turneth on the fool
Even as fine dust windward thrown.

Whoso is prone to coveting
Will speak of others in dispraise—
Mean miscreant, ill-mannered man,
Jealous and set on slandering :

O foul-mouthed, false, ignoble man,
Truth's murderer, ill-doer, vile ;
Thou ill-born, least of men, woe's seed,
Speak here not much ! Hell's man art thou !

Thou spreadest dust unto thy loss,
Transgressor, whom the good revil'st,
Thou who hast fared most evilly,
For long hast gone to steepy pit.

For perishes the deed of none,
Nay ! it becomes his taskmaster ;
Both dullard and transgressor see
Themselves hereafter writhe in pain. . . .

Wherefore in pure, fair, friendly ways
Ward word and thought unceasingly.[2]

Sn. 657–666, 678

---

[1] =Dh. 306.   [2] E. M. Hare, *Woven Cadences.*

[A brahman spoke thus to Gotama :]

" This, good Gotama, is my avowal, this my view : There is no self-agency, there is no other agency."

" Never, brahman, have I seen or heard such an avowal, such a view. Pray, how can one step forwards, how can one step backwards, and yet say : There is no self-agency, there is no other-agency ? What do you think, brahman : is there such a thing as initiative ? "

" Yes, sir."

" That being so, are beings known to initiate (deeds) ? "

" Yes, sir."

" Well, brahman, since there is initiative and beings are known to initiate, this is self-agency among beings, this is other-agency. What do you think, brahman : is there such a thing as stepping away . . . stepping forth . . . halting . . . standing . . . and stepping towards anything ? "

" Yes, sir."

" That being so, are beings known to do all these things ? "

" Yes, sir."

" Well, brahman, since there are such things as stepping away, stepping forth, and the rest, and beings are known to do these things, this is self-agency among beings, this is other-agency. Never, brahman, have I seen or heard such an avowal, such a view as yours. Pray, how can one step away, step forth, and so on, and yet say : There is no self-agency, there is no other-agency ? "

A. iii. 337–338 ; *cf. Dh.* 306

Monks, it is by not awakening to, not penetrating the four ariyan truths that there is thus this long, long faring-on and running-on both for me and for you. What are the four ? Monks, it is by not awakening to, not penetrating the ariyan truth about ill, the ariyan truth about the uprising of ill, the ariyan truth about the stopping of ill, the ariyan truth about the course leading to the stopping of ill that there is thus this long, long faring-on and running-on both for me and for you. But if these four ariyan truths are awakened to and are penetrated, rooted out is the craving for becoming, destroyed is the conduit for becoming, now there is no becoming again.

D. ii. 90 ; *S.* v. 431–432

Incalculable, monks, is the beginning of this faring-on. The earliest point is not revealed of the running-on, the faring-on, of beings hindered by ignorance, fettered by craving. If a man, monks, were to prune out the grasses, sticks, boughs, and foliage in this India and should make a pile of them, saying for each : " This is my mother, this my mother's mother," those grasses, sticks, boughs, and foliage would be used up and ended or ever the mothers of that man's mother were come to an end. Or if a man were to make this great earth into clay balls each only the size of a *kola* kernel and were to lay them down, saying : " This is my father, this is my father's father ", this great earth would be used up and ended or ever the fathers of that man's father were come to an end. . . .

And which is the greater—the flood of tears shed by you crying and weeping as you run-on, fare-on for this long while, united as you have been with those that are not dear, separated from those that are dear, or the waters in the four seas ? The flood of tears shed by you as you have run-on and fared-on is the greater. For many a long day you have experienced the death of mother, of son, of daughter, the ruin of kinsmen, of wealth, the calamity of disease. What is the cause of this ? It is that incalculable is the beginning of this faring-on. . . .

Long is an aeon. It is not easy to reckon how long by saying so many years, so many centuries, so many thousand centuries. But it could be told in a parable. Take where the river Ganges has its source and where it reaches the sea. The sand that lies between, that is not easy to count—so many (grains of) sand, so many hundreds, so many thousands, so many hundred thousand grains of sand. More than that are the aeons that have passed and gone by. But it is not easy to count them—so many aeons, so many hundreds, so many thousands, so many hundreds of thousands of aeons. How is this ? Incalculable is the beginning of this faring-on. The earliest point is not revealed of the running-on, the faring-on of beings hindered by ignorance, fettered by craving. . . .

Not an easy thing it is, monks, to find a being who during this long many-a-day has not at one time been a mother, a father, a brother, a sister, a son, a daughter. How is this ? Incalculable is the beginning, monks, of this faring-on. The earliest point is not revealed of the running-on, the faring-on of beings hindered by ignorance, fettered by craving. Thus have you, monks, for

a long time suffered ill, pain, misery, and the charnel-field has
grown.   *S. ii.* 178 ff. (*condensed*)

This, monks, that we call thought, that we call mind, that we
call consciousness, is that to which the uninstructed many-folk
cleave ; it is that which they stress as " mine," thinking : " This
is mine, I am this, this is my Self." It were better, monks, if the
uninstructed many-folk were to approach this body, rather than
the mind, as Self. Why should this be so ? Monks, this body is
seen enduring for one year, for two years, three, four, five, ten,
twenty, thirty, forty, fifty years, for a hundred years, and even
longer. But this, monks, that is called thought and mind and
consciousness, this by night and day dissolves as one thing and
reappears even as another. As a monkey faring through jungle
and wood catches hold of a bough and, having let it go, takes
hold of another, even so that which is called thought and mind
and consciousness, this by night and day dissolves as one thing and
reappears even as another.   *S. ii.* 94

[Sāti, the fisherman's son, has put forward the false view that " it is
this consciousness itself that runs-on, fares-on, not another."]

In many a figure have I, monks, told you that consciousness
arises by way of cause ; without cause there is no origination of
consciousness. Whatever form of consciousness arises from an
assignable cause, it is known by the name of that (cause) : if
material shape arises because of the eye and there is consciousness,
it is known as visual consciousness ; if sound arises because of
the ear and there is consciousness, it is known as auditory consciousness ; if smell arises because of the nose and there is consciousness, it is known as olfactory consciousness ; if taste arises
because of the tongue and there is consciousnesss, it is known as
gustatory consciousness ; if touch arises because of the body and
there is consciousness, it is known as tactile consciousness ; if
mental states arise because of the mind and there is consciousness,
it is known as mental consciousness. It is like a fire that burns
from some assignable cause : if a fire burns because of wood, it
is known as a wood fire ; if a fire burns because of sticks, grass,
cowdung, husks, rubbish, it is known as a fire of sticks, of grass,
of cowdung, of husks, of rubbish. So it is with the various forms
of consciousness.

Monks, do you see that this has come to be ? Do you see its origination from a particular form of food ? Do you see that what has come to be is liable to stopping from the stopping of its particular food ? Does perplexity arise from the doubt that it has not come to be, or from the doubt that its origination is not from a particular kind of food, or from the doubt that it is not liable to stopping from the stopping of its particular food ? By thoroughly knowing, by seeing as it really is that this has come to be, does that perplexity decline ? By thoroughly knowing, by seeing as it has really come to be that its origination is from a particular food, does that perplexity decline ? By thoroughly knowing, by seeing as it has really come to be that what has come to be is liable to stopping from the stopping of its particular food, does that perplexity decline ? Thinking, " This is what has come to be," have you lack of perplexity ? Thinking, " Its origination is from a particular food," have you lack of perplexity ? Thinking, " What has come to be is liable to stopping from the stopping of its particular food," have you lack of perplexity ? Thinking, " This is what had come to be," is it well seen through right wisdom as it has really come to be ? And so with the other two cases ? If you, monks, should cling to this view, should treasure it, should cherish it, should hanker after it, although it is purified thus, cleared thus, could you, monks, understand that the Parable of the Raft [1] is *dhamma* taught by me for crossing over, not for retaining ? But if you, monks, should not cling to this view, should not treasure or cherish it or hanker after it when it is purified thus, cleared thus, would you then understand, monks, that the Parable of the Raft is *dhamma* taught by me for crossing over, not for retaining ?   *M.* i. 259 ff.

Consciousness is supported by body, feeling, perception, the constructions. . . . It cannot be said that apart from any of these there is any coming or going or future-arising of consciousness. If the passion for these supports has been cast off by a monk, there remains no support for consciousness. Because of freedom he is one whose Self is freed, because of stability he is one whose Self is stable, because of content one whose Self is contented, and therefore he no longer worries, and worrying no more he is individually attained to utter nirvana, and he knows that " Birth

[1] *Cf.* p. 184.

is ended, lived is the Brahma-faring, done is what was to be done,
there is no more of being such-and-such." [1]

S. iii. 55 (condensed)

What the monk, remembering his " former habitations " (past
lives), remembers is the five stems of grasping, or some one of
them ; he thinks, " Such-and-such was my body, or feeling, or
perception, constructions or consciousness " ; and so reflecting,
he becomes indifferent to his past bodies, feelings, etc. For all of
these are impermanent ; and neither of all or any of them can it
be said that " It is mine, I am that, or That is my Self." He
rejects them all, and grasps no more. [2]

S. iii. 86 ff. (condensed)

Do you not see, monks, that steaminess, that murkiness going
even to the eastern quarter, to the western quarter, to the northern,
to the southern, going aloft, going downwards, going to the
intervening points ?   That, monks, is Māra, the Evil One,
searching about for the discriminative consciousness [3] of Godhika,
the clansman, [4] and thinking : " Where is the discriminative
consciousness of Godhika, the clansman, instated ? "   But,
monks, the clansman Godhika has attained utter nirvana without
his discriminative consciousness being (re-) instated.

> He, a seer, possessed of vision,
> A meditator, ever delighting in meditation,
> Given up to it night and day,
> Not desiring life ;
> By overcoming the host of death,
> Not having come to again becoming,
> By conquering craving and its root
> " Godhika " [5] has attained utter nirvana.

S. i. 122

" What is the cause, good Gotama, what the reason why some
beings who are here arise, at the breaking-up of the body after
dying, in the Waste, the Bad Bourn, the Downfall, Hell ? "

---

[1] That is, he is Arahant, Awake, no longer existent in any mode. *Cf.* p. 156.
[2] Note the distinction here between " I " and " my Self" and all that " I "
am not and was not.
[3] *viññāṇa.*
[4] In the narrative leading up to this speech, Godhika is referred to as *āyasmā*,
venerable (monk), before his suicide, but as *kulaputta*, clansman, after it had
taken place.
[5] It is precisely " this man so-and-so " that has gone out like a lamp without oil

" Because of a faring by what is not *dhamma*, an uneven faring, some beings who are here, brahman, arise thus."

" But, good Gotama, what is the cause, what the reason why some beings who are here arise, at the breaking-up of the body after dying, in a Good Bourn, a heaven world ? "

" Because of a faring by *dhamma*, an even faring, some beings who are here, brahman, arise thus."

A. i. 55, v. 301 ; M. i. 285, 291

If, householders, one who fares by *dhamma*, who fares evenly, should desire (one of the following states) : " O that at the break-ing-up of the body after dying I might arise in companionship with rich nobles, with rich brahmans, with rich householders, with the *devas* of the Four Great Regents, with the *devas* of the Thirty-Three, with the *devas* of Yama, with the Happy *devas*, with the *devas* who delight in creating, with the *devas* who have power over the creations of others, with the *devas* in the retinue of Brahmā, with the *devas* of Splendour, with the *devas* of Limited Splendour, with the *devas* of Boundless Splendour, with the Lustrous *devas*, with the Beautiful *devas*, with the *devas* of Limited Beauty, with the *devas* of Boundless Beauty, with the Radiant *devas*, with the Vehapphalā *devas*, with the Avihā *devas*, with the Cool *devas*, with the Fair *devas*, with the Well-seeing *devas*, with the Elder *devas*, with the *devas* who have reached infinity of space, with the *devas* who have reached infinity of consciousness, with the *devas* who have reached self-naughting, with the *devas* who have reached neither-perception-nor-non-perception "—it hap-pens that he may so uprise. Why is this ? Because he is one who fares by *dhamma*, who fares evenly.

If, householders, one who fares by *dhamma*, who fares evenly, should desire : " O that I, by the destruction of the fluxions, having here and now realized by my own super-knowledge that freedom of heart and freedom of intellect that are fluxionless, might abide in them "—it happens that he may so abide. Why is this ? Because he is one who fares by *dhamma*, who fares evenly. M. i. 289

Monks, four advantages are to be looked for from the frequent verbal practice of teachings heard with the ear, considered in the mind, and well penetrated by view. What are the four ?

Herein a monk masters *dhamma*. Those teachings heard with

the ear are often practised verbally, considered in the mind, well penetrated by view. He, passing away with recollection confused, arises in a certain company of *devas*. There the happy ones recite to him *dhamma*-verses. Slow is the uprising of recollection, but thereafter that being quickly reaches distinction. This is the first advantage to be looked for.

Then, again, a monk masters *dhamma* (as before). He, passing away with recollection confused, arises in a certain company of *devas*. There indeed the happy ones do not recite *dhamma*-verses to him, but it may be that some monk of psychic power, won to mastery of thought, is teaching *dhamma* to an assembly of *devas*. Then it occurs to him : " This is exactly the *dhamma* and discipline according to which I formerly fared the Brahma-faring." Slow is the uprising of recollection, but thereafter that being quickly reaches distinction. It is as if a man, skilled in the sound of drums, while going along a high-road should hear the sound of a drum. He would have no doubt or uncertainty as to whether it was the sound of a drum or not, but would at once conclude, " That's the sound of a drum." In the same way, a monk masters *dhamma* (*as before*). . . . This is the second advantage to be looked for.

Yet again, a monk masters *dhamma* . . . and arises in a certain company of *devas*. There indeed the happy ones do not recite *dhamma*-verses to him, nor does any monk of psychic power, won to mastery of thought, teach *dhamma* to an assembly of *devas*. But it may be that some one *deva* is teaching *dhamma* to an assembly of *devas*. Then it occurs to him : " This is exactly the *dhamma* and discipline according to which I formerly fared the Brahma-faring." Slow is the uprising of recollection, but thereafter that being quickly reaches distinction. It is as if a man skilled in the sound of conches . . . would at once conclude : " That's the sound of a conch." In the same way, a monk masters *dhamma* (*as before*). . . . This is the third advantage to be looked for.

Yet again, a monk masters *dhamma* . . . and arises in a certain company of *devas*. There indeed the happy ones do not recite *dhamma*-verses to him, nor does any monk of psychic power, won to mastery of thought, teach *dhamma* to an assembly of *devas*, nor does any one *deva* teach *dhamma* to an assembly of *devas*. But it may be that some one, spontaneously uprisen,[1] is making another

---

[1] Not of the ordinary physical birth from parents.

spontaneously uprisen one recollect, saying : " Do you remember, good sir, how we used formerly to fare the Brahma-
faring ? " Then the other says : " I do indeed remember, good
sir." Slow is the uprising of recollection, but thereafter that
being quickly reaches distinction. It is as if two playmates who
used to play at mud-pies together were to meet some time or
other. Then one of them says to the other : " Say, old man, do
you remember this ? Do you remember that ? " and the other
says : " I do indeed remember." In the same way, a monk
masters *dhamma*. Those teachings heard with the ear are often
practised verbally, considered in the mind, well penetrated by
view. Slow is the uprising of recollection, but thereafter that
being quickly reaches distinction. This is the fourth advantage
to be looked for from the frequent verbal practice of teachings
heard with the ear, considered in the mind, and well penetrated
by view.   *A.* ii. 185–187

Monks, if someone should say : " Just as this man does a deed
that is to be experienced, so does he experience its result "—this
being so, there is the living of the Brahma-faring, opportunity is
manifested for the utter ending of ill.

For example, even a trifling evil deed done by some man leads
him to Niraya Hell. Or, on the other hand, a similar trifling evil
deed of some other person is to be experienced (by expiation) in
this very life, not a jot of it appears hereafter. What is the kind
of man whose trifling evil deed leads to Hell ? He is one who has
not made become (right conduct as to) body, moral habit,
thought, wisdom, who is a limited, small self, dwelling in but
little hardship.[1] But the kind of man whose similar trifling evil
deed is to be experienced in this very life is one who has made
become (right conduct as to) body, moral habit, thought,
wisdom, who is not limited, a great self, a dweller in the
immeasurable.[2]   *A.* i. 249

Monks, I will teach you a disquisition on *dhamma*—a disquisition on crookedness. Beings, monks, are responsible for their
deeds, heirs to deeds, having deeds for matrix, deeds for kin,
to them the deed comes home again. Whatsoever deed they do,
be it lovely or evil, they become its heir. In this connection,

[1] Not putting himself out to progress in the Way.
[2] In him. a " venial sin ".

monks, a certain one makes onslaught on creatures, he is a hunter, bloody-handed, given over to killing and slaying, merciless to all living creatures. He goes crookedly in body, in speech, in thought. If his action in body is crooked, so is that in speech, so is that in thought, his bourne is crooked, crooked is his uprising. For one whose bourn and uprising are crooked, there is one of two bourns : either Niraya Hell, painful in the extreme, or the womb of an animal that goes crookedly : a snake, scorpion, centipede, mongoose, cat, mouse, owl or whatsoever other animal goes stealthily on seeing human beings.

Or again, a certain one takes what has not been given . . . behaves wrongly as to pleasures of the senses . . . is a liar, a slanderer, of bitter speech, of idle babble, covetous, of harmful thoughts, of wrong or perverse views. He goes crookedly in body, speech, and thought . . . or whatsoever other animal goes stealthily on seeing human beings.

But if one abandons onslaught on creatures, abstains from it, lays aside the stick, lays aside the knife, he lives modest, merciful, compassionate towards all living creatures. He is not crooked in body, speech, thought. If his deed in body is upright, so is that in speech and thought, his bourn is upright, upright his uprising. For one whose bourn and uprising are upright, there is one of two bourns : either the heavens, pleasant in the extreme, or uprising in whatsoever families are exalted, such as the families of nobles and brahmans and great and wealthy householders. Thus from a being comes to be the uprising of the being. He uprises according to whatever he does ; (appropriate) contacts touch him when he has uprisen. Thus I, monks, say that creatures are heirs to deeds.

It is the same in the case of one who abandons taking what is not given, of one who abandons wrong behaviour in respect of pleasures of the senses, who abandons falsehood, slander, bitter speech, coveting, of one of harmless thoughts, of right view, of reasonable view. Thus from a being comes to be the uprising of the being. He uprises according to whatever he does ; (appropriate) contacts touch him when he has uprisen. That is why I, monks, say that beings are heirs to deeds. Indeed, beings are responsible for their deeds, heirs to deeds, having deeds for matrix, deeds for kin, to them the deed comes home again. Whatsoever deed they do, be it lovely or evil, they become its heirs.   *A.* v. 288–291

There are four types of persons found existing in the world. What are the four ? There is the dark, faring to darkness ; the dark, faring to light ; the light, faring to darkness ; the light, faring to light.

And who is the person who is dark, faring to darkness ? In this connection someone is born in a low family, he is poor, ill-fed, and in wretched circumstances, distressed and deformed. His conduct in body, speech, and thought is bad, so that at the breaking-up of the body after dying he arises in the Abyss, the Bad Bourn, the Downfall. It is as if a person were to go from blindness to blindness, from darkness to darkness, to one stain of blood from another.

And who is the person who is dark, faring to light ? In this connection someone is born to evil circumstances such as I have just described, but his conduct in body, speech, and thought is good, so that at the breaking-up of the body after dying he arises in a Good Bourn, in a heaven world. It is as if a person were to mount a palanquin from the ground, or were to mount a horse from a palanquin, or were to mount an elephant from the back of a horse, or were to mount a terrace from an elephant.

And who is the person who is light, faring to darkness ? In this connection some person is born into a family of high degree, very wealthy, and with ample aids to enjoyment. But his conduct in body, speech, and thought is bad, so that at the breaking-up of the body after dying he arises in the Abyss, the Bad Bourn, the Downfall. It is as if a person were to descend from a terrace on to an elephant, or from an elephant on to a horse's back, or thence to a palanquin, or thence to the ground.

And who is the person who is light, faring to light ? In this connection a person is born among any of the fortunate circumstances I have just mentioned and whose conduct in body, speech, and thought is good, so that at the breaking-up of the body after dying he arises in a Good Bourn, in a heaven world. It is as if a person were to pass from one palanquin to another, or from the back of one horse to the back of another, or from one elephant to another, or from one terrace to another. So do I illustrate this type of person.   *S.* i. 93–95

Although, Puṇṇa, I did not take up your question, but said : " Enough, Puṇṇa, stop this, don't ask me that," yet I will now answer you. Your question was : " What is the Bourn, the

future state of an unclothed ascetic who for a long time has
meticulously observed the canine practice ? " Take a case, Puṇṇa,
where some one fully and completely makes become the canine
practice, the canine moral habit, the canine mind, the canine
behaviour. Having done so, at the breaking-up of the body
after dying, he arises in the companionship of dogs. But if he
has this wrong view : " I, by reason of this moral habit or
custom or austerity or chastity, will become a *deva* or one in the
retinue of a *deva*," I tell you, Puṇṇa, that for anyone who has
such a wrong view there is one or other of two bourns : either
Niraya Hell or an animal's womb. The canine practice, Puṇṇa,
brings those who prosper to the companionship of dogs, those
who do not prosper to Niraya Hell. (*The same is repeated for the*
bovine practice, *reading* bovine *for* canine, *and* cows *for* dogs.)
Well, then, Puṇṇa, attend carefully and I will teach you *dhamma*
so that you can give up the bovine practice and Seniya can give
up the canine practice.

Puṇṇa, by my own super-knowledge I have realized, and I
proclaim, four kinds of deeds : the dark with the dark result ;
the light with the light result ; the dark and the light with a dark
and a light result ; the neither dark nor light with neither a dark
nor a light result—the deed that conduces to the destruction of
deeds.

What is the dark deed with the dark result ? If some one con-
structs a construction of body or speech or thought that is harmful, he arises in a world that is harmful, hence harmful contacts
touch him, hence, like creatures in Niraya Hell, he experiences
feelings that are harmful, painful in the extreme. Thus from a
being comes to be the uprising of the being. He uprises according to whatever he does ; (appropriate) contacts touch him when
he has uprisen. That is why I, Puṇṇa, say that beings are heirs
to deeds. This is the dark deed with dark result.

What is the light deed with light result ? Here someone, after
constructing a construction of body, speech, or thought that is
harmless, arises in a world that is harmless ; hence harmless
contacts touch him, hence, like the Ever-radiant *devas*, he experiences feelings that are harmless, pleasant in the extreme. Thus
from a being comes to be the uprising of the being . . . beings
are heirs to deeds. This is the light deed with light result.

What is the dark and light deed with the dark and light
result ? Here someone, after constructing a construction . . .

that is both harmful and harmless, arises in a world that is both harmful and harmless ; hence both kinds of contacts touch him, hence, like human beings, some *devas* and some in the Downfall, he experiences feelings that are both harmful and harmless, mixed as to pleasantness and pain. Thus from a being comes to be the uprising of the being. He uprises according to whatever he does ; (appropriate) contacts touch him when he has uprisen. That is why I, Puṇṇa, say that beings are heirs to deeds. This is a deed that is dark and light with a dark and light result.

What, Puṇṇa, is the deed that is neither dark nor light, whose result is neither dark nor light—the deed that conduces to the destruction of deeds ? This is the willing to put away the three foregoing types of deeds. This is called the deed that conduces to the destruction of deeds.   *M.* i. 387 *cf.* ; *cf. A.* ii. 230

[When the lord knew that he had put away various wrong subjective states and that, by making them become he had brought to fulfilment various good states, he gave expression to this dictum :]

> Once it was and then was not ; once it was not, then it was ;
> It was not, nor will it come to be, nor is it now to be found.[1]

Ud. 66

[The lord gave expression to this dictum :]

Had it not been, it were not " mine " ; it will not be, 'twill not be " mine," [2] and added : The monk convinced of this can break the fetters that bind him to lower things. *S.* iii. 55–56

[But to hold :]

Had *I* not been it were not mine ; I will not be, it won't be mine—that is the Annihilationist point of view.   *S.* iii. 99

[Citta, an apostate, maintains : *I* was in the past, *I* shall be in the future, *I* am now ; and that his individuality or selfhood, accordingly, was, will be and is true or real. The Buddha replies that :]

[1] " It " is individuality, selfhood, empirical Ego, all that is "not my Self." The first line states the false view, the second the truth.
[2] I.e. " this is my last body." The novice, misinterpreting in the " Annihilationist " sense of the next extract, laments at the thought ; but the adept understands, his Self is liberated, established, content, he is not distressed, he is despirated, (attained to, or, aware of nirvana), birth is at an end for him.

These three modes of selfhood, past, future, and present, are merely the conventional terms of everyday language. I make use of them myself, but I am not misled by them.

D. i. 178–203 ; *cf. S. i.* 14

Old age, disease, and death, these I have not yet outstripped. . . . But I will achieve, ne'er turning back, the passing over by the Brahma-faring won.   *A. iii.* 75

Countless are the births wherein I have circled and run, seeking for, but never finding, the builder of the house ; ill is this being born again and again !

Now thou art seen, thou builder of the house : never again shalt thou build for me ! All of the rafters are broken, the roof-plate shattered : my heart is freed from all constructions ; the waning-out of thirst has been attained.

J. i. 76 ; *Dh.* 153–154 ; *cf. Thag.* 183–184

And how is a monk a " goer " ? Inasmuch as he is agoing quickly thither [1] where on this long road he has not yet been, there where there is a cessation of all constructions, a relinquishing of all conditions, a waning-away of craving, absence of lust, and arrest (of becoming)—nirvana.[2]   *A. iii.* 164

It is as if there were two houses with doors, and a man with eyes to see were to stand between them and to see people going in and out and passing to and fro—in the same way do I, monks, with *deva*-sight, which is purified and surpasses that of men, see beings as they are deceasing and rising up again ; and I see beings who, according to the consequences of their deeds, are mean, excellent, comely, ugly, in a Good Bourn, in a Bad Bourn, (and know) : These beings, endowed with right conduct as to body, speech, and thought, not scoffing at the ariyans, of right view, acquiring for themselves deeds consequent on right view—these at the breaking-up of the body after dying arise in the Happy Bourn, the heaven world, or they arise among men. Or : But these beings, endowed with wrong conduct as to body, speech,

---

[1] " Thither," *disā yad,* " that region where." In other words, the traveller is on his way to " World's End," a Bourn " within you " and " not to be reached by paces," *A.* ii. 49 (p. 159).
[2] Thus the disciple is " going, going " ; the adept is " gone "—home.

and thought, scoffing at the ariyans, or wrong view, acquiring for themselves deeds consequent on wrong view—these at the breaking-up of the body after dying arise in the Waste, the Bad Bourn, the Downfall, Hell. Him do the wardens of Hell seize by both arms and bring before Yama, the lord (of death), saying :

" Sire, this man had no respect for his mother or father, for recluses or brahmans. He showed no deference to the elders of his clan. Let your majesty inflict punishment on him."

Then Yama, the lord (of death), examines him, closely questions him, and addresses him concerning the first *deva*-messenger : " Now, my good man, have you never seen the first *deva*-messenger manifest among men ? "

He replies : " I have not seen him, sire."

" Have you not, my good man, seen a young new-born babe that can only lie on its back in its own filth ? "

" Yes, sire."

" My good sir, did it never occur to you as one of intelligence and fully grown, that you too were liable to birth, that birth was not overpassed, and that you should (therefore) do what is lovely in deed, speech, and thought ? "

" I was not able to, sire, I was slothful."

Then Yama says to him : " It was through slothfulness, my good man, that you did not do what is lovely in deed, speech, and thought. Indeed they will act towards you in accordance with that slothfulness. For that which is the evil deed—it is yours ; it was not done by your mother, it was not done by your father, nor by brother or sister, nor by friends or relations, nor by recluses or brahmans, nor by *devas*. That evil deed was done by you. It is you yourself who will experience its results."

Passing now to the second *deva*-messenger, Yama questions the man as to whether he has seen this messenger. On the man's replying that he has not, Yama says :

" Have you never seen among human beings, my good man, a woman or a man of eighty or ninety or a hundred years of age, broken down, bent inwards like the rafter of a roof, crooked, bent on a staff, tottering as he goes along, ailing, youth gone, teeth broken, grey-haired or bald, with wrinkled brows and limbs all blotched and spotted ? "

The man acknowledges that he has, but says that he was not able to do what is lovely, although he was liable to old age, with old age not overpassed, because he was slothful. Yama tells him, as in the first case, that the evil deed is his and that it is he himself who will experience its results.

The third *deva*-messenger is a woman or a man who is sick, afflicted, suffering from a sore disease, and who is lying wallowing in his own filth, taken up by some and laid down by others. Yama and the man exchange question and answer as before.

Passing to the fourth *deva*-messenger, when Yama asks the man if he has seen him, the man says that he has not. Then Yama says :

" But did you never see a guilty thief arrested by the authorities and punished in divers dreadful ways ? "

" I did, sire."

" Did it never occur to you, my good man, as one of intelligence and fully grown, that you too are liable to death, that death is not overpassed, and that you should (therefore) do what is lovely in deed, speech, and thought ? "

" I was not able to, sire, I was slothful."

Then Yama says to him : " It was through slothfulness, my good man, that you did not do what is lovely in deed, speech, and thought. Indeed they will act towards you in accordance with that slothfulness. For that which is the evil deed—it is yours ; it was not done by your mother, it was not done by your father, nor by brother or sister, nor by friends or relations, nor by recluses or brahmans, nor by *devas*. That evil deed was done by you. It is you yourself who will experience its results."

M. iii. 178 ff. ; *cf. A.* i. 138 ff. *(three messengers)*

IV. THE WAY

Whoso should walk as taught the Wake to each
Who sought, would go from the not-beyond to the beyond ;
And making the Way supernal to become,
They to the beyond from the not-beyond would go.

Sn. 1129–1130

This is the very Way ; there is
None else for purifying vision ;
Herein do you a-faring go,
This is release from Māra.

Herein when you have faring gone
An end you'll come to make of ill ;
Shown surely was the Way by me,
Who ease from barbs had come to know.

Yours 'tis to swelter at the task,[1]
Truth-finders are showers (only).
Meditators, as they faring go,
From Māra's bonds releasèd are.[2]

Dh. 274–276

Who by a path made by the self,
Sabhiya (said the lord),
Has gone to utter nirvana,
Has conquered (all) desire,
Discarded becoming and de-becoming,
Has lived the life, (and)
Destroyed again-becoming :
He is a " monk."

Sn. 514

Who has crossed over doubt, is barbless,
Delighting in nirvana, uncoveting,
The guide of the world with its *devas*—
Such the Wake call " Way-conqueror."

Who here knows the highest as the highest,
Who here shows *dhamma* and explains it,
This desire-cutter, sage immovable—
The second monk they call " Way-teacher."

Who lives in the path of *dhamma*,
The well-taught Way, restrained, mindful,
Following paths that are faultless—
The third monk they call " Way-liver."

Who, making a cloak of piety,
Is a braggart, brings families into disrepute,[3] is reckless,
A trickster, unrestrained, a babbler,
Faring by appearances—he is " Way-fraud."

Sn. 86–89

Just as if, monks, a man walking through a forest, through a
great wood, should see an ancient way, an ancient road, followed
by men of old,[4] and if he were to go along it he would see an
ancient city, an ancient royal capital, inhabited by the men of

---

[1] *Cf.* p. 54.   [2] *Cf.* Mrs Rhys Davids, *Min. Anth.* i.
[3] As in Samghâdisesa xiii., *Vin.* iii.
[4] *Cf. S.* iv. 118, " this is the way for attaining Brahmā " ; *A.* ii. 26 ; *It.* p. 29.
" this is the Way followed by Great Selves, by Great Seers " ; and *BU.* iv. 4. 8.

old, and having parks, woodlands, pools, the foundations of walls—a goodly spot. And that man ought to tell the rajah or the ministers what he had seen and should ask for that city to be restored. This should be done, and after a time that city should be prosperous and flourishing, populous, crowded with people, grown and expanded.

Even so have I, monks, seen an ancient way, an ancient road followed by the wholly awakened ones of olden times. . . . Along that have I gone, and the matters that I have come to know fully as I was going along it I have told to the monks, nuns, men and women lay-followers, even, monks, this Brahma-faring that is prosperous and flourishing, widespread and widely known, become popular—in short, well made manifest for *devas* and men.   *S. ii. 105–106 ; cf. Miln. 217*

A Truth-finder, monks, one perfected, fully awakened, causes a Way to arise which had not arisen before ; he brings about a Way not brought about before ; he proclaims a Way not proclaimed before ; he is knower of the Way, understander of the Way, skilled in the Way. And now his disciples, monks, are wayfarers who follow after him. This is the distinction, the specific feature which distinguishes a Truth-finder, a perfected one, a fully awakened one, from a monk who is freed by wisdom.
                          S. iii. 66 ; cf. M. iii. 8

Some of my disciples, brahman, being advised thus and instructed thus, succeed in winning nirvana, the ultimate goal ; and some do not. . . . (To explain this, I will ask you a question.) You are conversant with the way to Rājagaha ? Well, then, suppose a man were to come to you and say he wished to go to Rājagaha, and asked you to point out the way. And suppose you were to say : " This is the way to Rājagaha : go along it for a short time and then you will see a village ; a little farther on you will see a township, and still a little farther on you will see Rājagaha with its lovely parks, woodlands, open spaces, and lakes." But, although advised and instructed by you in this manner, he might take a wrong road and turn west. Then a second man might come along, also wishing to go to Rājagaha and asking you to point out the way. You would give him nstructions, as to the first man ; and advised and instructed by you in this manner, he might arrive safely at Rājagaha. Now, how is it that with Rājagaha existing, with the way to Rājagaha existing, and with you existing as an adviser, the one man, although advised and instructed by you, might take the wrong road and turn west, while the other might arrive safely at Rājagaha ?

In the same manner, brahman, nirvana exists, the way to nirvana exists, and I exist as adviser. Yet, although some of my disciples, being advised and instructed by me, succeed in winning nirvana, the ultimate goal, some do not. What do I do in this matter, brahman ? Foreteller of the Way, brahman, is a Truth-finder.   *M. iii. 4–6*

Suppose now, Tissa, there be two men, one unskilled in the way, the other skilled in the way. And the one who is unskilled asks the way of the other who is skilled in the way. And that other replies : " Yes, this is the way, sir. When you have gone by it for a short time you will see that it divides into two paths. Leave the left one and take the one to the right. Go on for a little and you will see a thick forest. Go on for a little and you will see a great marshy swamp. Go on for a little and you will see a steep precipice. Go on for a little and you will see a delightful stretch of level ground."

Such is my parable, Tissa, to show my meaning ; and this is what it means : By the " man who is unskilled in the way " is meant the many-folk. By the " man who is skilled in the way " is meant a Truth-finder, a perfected one, a fully awakened one. By "dividing into two paths" is meant a state of wavering. "The way to the left " means the wrong eightfold way, namely that of wrong view, wrong concept, wrong speech, wrong acting, wrong mode of living, wrong exertion, wrong mindfulness, wrong contemplation. The " way to the right " is a synonym for the ariyan eightfold Way, namely that of right view and so on. The " thick forest," Tissa, is a name for ignorance. The " great marshy swamp " is a name for pleasures of the senses. The " steep precipice " is a synonym for the turbulence of anger. The " delightful stretch of level ground " is a name for nirvana.

Be of good cheer, Tissa. I shall exhort (you), I shall help (you), I shall instruct (you).   *S. iii. 108–109*

These two dead-ends, monks, should not be followed by one who has gone forth. Which two ? That which is among sense-pleasures addiction to attractive sense-pleasures, low, of the villager, of the average man, unariyan, not connected with the goal ; and that which is addiction to tormenting the self, ill, unariyan, not connected with the goal. Now, monks, without adopting either of these two dead-ends, there is a middle course,[1] thoroughly understood by the Truth-finder, making for vision, making for knowledge, and which conduces to tranquillity, to super-knowledge, to awakening, to nirvana. And what, monks, is this middle course ? It is just this ariyan eightfold Way, that is to say : right view, right concept, right speech, right acting, right mode of living, right exertion, right mindfulness, right contemplation.[2]   *Vin.* i. 10

This way is the sole one leading to the purification of beings, to the overpassing of sorrow and grief, to the falling-away of ill and sadness, to the winning of the Method,[3] to the realization of nirvana—that is to say, the four stations of mindfulness.[4]

D. ii. 313 ; *M.* i. 55, 63 ; *S.* v. 167, 185

V. CROSSING OVER

Monks, I will teach you *dhamma*—the parable of the raft—for getting across, not for retaining. Listen to it, pay careful attention, and I will speak. It is like a man, monks, who as he is going on a journey should see a great stretch of water, the hither bank with dangers and fears, the farther bank secure and without fears, but there may be neither a boat for crossing over, nor a bridge across for going from the not-beyond to the beyond. It occurs to him that in order to cross over from the perils of this bank to the security of the farther bank, he should fashion a raft out of grass and sticks, branches and foliage, so that he could, striving with his hands and feet and depending on the raft, cross over to the beyond in safety. When he has done this and has crossed over to the beyond, it occurs to him that the raft has been very useful and he wonders if he ought to proceed taking it with him

---

[1] For other contexts dealing with the " mean " or middle way, *see* p. 104 ff.

[2] Gotama's First Utterance, called the Discourse of Turning the Wheel of *Dhamma*.

[3] Comy. (*MA.* i. 236) calls this the ariyan eightfold Way.   [4] *Cf.* p. 217.

packed on his head or shoulders. What do you think, monks? That the man, in doing this, would be doing what should be done to the raft?

No, lord.

What should that man do, monks, in order to do what should be done to that raft? In this case, monks, that man, when he has crossed over to the beyond and realizes how useful the raft has been to him, may think : " Suppose that I, having beached this raft on dry ground, or having immersed it in the water, should proceed on my journey?" Monks, a man doing this would be doing what should be done to the raft. In this way, monks, I have taught you *dhamma*—the parable of the raft—for getting across, not for retaining. You, monks, by understanding the parable of the raft, must discard even right states of mind and, all the more, wrong states of mind.   *M.* i. 134–135

> Well fashioned was the bonded raft,
> (Thus spake the Master in reply),
> But none's the need of raft for him,
> Crossed and yon-fared, the flood-tide ridden.[1]
>
> *Sn.* 21

> Those cross the deeps, the rivers, by making a bridge spanning the swamps ;
> See ! people tie their rafts—but crossed over are the wise.
>
> *Vin.* i. 230 ; *Ud.* 90 ; *D.* ii. 89

Those who do not live professing disgust for abstinence, not making disgust for abstinence essential, not cleaving to disgust for abstinence—these can become those for crossing the flood. Those who practise purity in body, speech, and thought, those whose way of living is pure—these can become those for knowledge and vision, for the supreme awakening.

It is like a man who wants to cross a river. Taking a sharp axe he would enter a wood. If he should see there a mighty sāl-tree, straight, young, not of crooked growth, he would cut it down at the root. Having done so, he would cut off the top, then he would clear it thoroughly of the branches and foliage. Having done so, he would chip it with axes, then with knives. He would then scrape it with a scraper and smooth it with a ball of stone. Then he would make a boat and would fasten oars and a rudder, and having done so he would get the boat down to the river.

[1] E. M. Hare. *Woven Cadences.*

Do you think, Sālha, that this man can become one to cross the river ?

Yes, lord.

Why is this ?

Why, lord, the sal-tree log is well worked over outside, well cleared out within, it is made into a boat with oars and a rudder fastened to it. This is to be expected of it : the boat will not sink, the man will go safely beyond. *A. ii.* 201

> Hence, ever watchful, man
> Should pleasures shun ; thus rid,
> Their vessels baling out,
> Yon-farers cross the flood.[1]

Sn. 771

Monks, do you see that great log of wood being carried along by the stream of the river Ganges ? Now, if the log does not ground on this bank or on the farther bank, does not sink down in mid-stream, does not founder on a shoal, does not become captured by human or non-human beings, is not caught in a whirlpool, does not become rotten within, that log will float down to the sea, will slide down to the sea, will gravitate towards the sea. And why ? Because the stream of the river Ganges flows down to the sea, slides down to the sea, gravitates towards the sea.

Even so, monks, if you do not ground on the hither shore or on the farther shore, if you do not sink down in mid-stream, if you do not founder on a shoal, if you do not become captured by human or non-human beings, if you are not caught in a whirlpool, if you do not become rotten within, so will you, monks, float down to nirvana, slide down to nirvana, gravitate towards nirvana. And why ? Because right view floats, slides, and gravitates towards nirvana.

The " hither shore " is a synonym for this sixfold subjective sense-sphere. The " farther shore " is a synonym for the sixfold objective sense-sphere. " Sinking down in mid-stream " is a synonym for the delight of passion. " Foundering on a shoal " is a synonym for the latent bias " I am." And how is one " captured by human beings " ? In this case, a householder lives in society, rejoices and sorrows with them that rejoice and sorrow, takes pleasure and suffers with them that take pleasure and

[1] E. M. Hare. *Woven Cadences.*

suffer, and applies himself to such duties and business as arise. And how is one " captured by non-human beings " ? In this case, some one or other fares the Brahma-faring with the hope of (being reborn into) a certain class of *devas*, and thinking : " May I, through this moral habit or practice or austerity or Brahma-faring become a *deva* or one of the *devas*." Being " caught in a whirlpool " is a synonym for the five strands of the pleasures of the senses.[1] And what is being " rotten within " ? In this case, some one is of weak moral habit, given to impure, evil, or sus-picious behaviour, of covert actions, not a true recluse although pretending to be one, not a Brahma-farer although pretending to be one, rotten within, full of desire, a rubbish heap of filth is he.

S. iv. 179–181

Monks, a man terrified of four deadly poisonous snakes, terrified of five murderous foes, terrified of a sixth murderer—a housebreaker—terrified of robbers who plunder villages includ-ing deserted ones, might rush about here and there. He might see a great stretch of water, the hither shore beset with dangers and fears, the farther shore secure and without fears, but with no boat for crossing over, nor any bridge across for going from the not-beyond to the beyond. Seeing this, he might think : " Suppose that I were to gather grass, sticks, branches and foliage, and, having fashioned a raft, were to go to the beyond in safety, striving with my hands and feet and depending on the raft ? " Then, suppose that he does so—crossed over, gone beyond, the brahman stands on dry land.

I have made this simile, monks, to clarify my meaning. This is the meaning here :

The four deadly poisonous snakes, monks,—this is a synonym for the four great elementals : for the earth element, for the water element, for the fire element, for the wind element.

The five murderous foes, monks,—this is a synonym for the five components of grasping : for the component of grasping material shape, for the component of grasping feeling, for the component of grasping perception, for the component of grasp-ing the constructions, for the component of grasping con-sciousness.

The sixth, the murderous housebreaker, monks,—this is a synonym for the delight of passion.

[1] Cf. p 192.

Deserted village, monks,—this is a synonym for the six sub-jective (sense-) spheres. A wise, experienced, intelligent person, if he tests one of them by means of the eye, it seems to be empty, it seems to be deserted, it seems to be void. Similarly, if he tests the other (sense-spheres) by means of the nose, the ear, the tongue, the body, the mind, they seem to be empty, deserted, void.

Robbers who plunder villages, monks,—this is a synonym for the six objective (sense-) spheres. The eye, monks, is destroyed in regard to shapes that are delightful and not delightful, the ear in regard to sounds, the nose in regard to smells, the tongue in regard to tastes, the body in regard to touches, the mind is destroyed in regard to mental states that are delightful and not delightful.

The great stretch of water, monks,—this is a synonym for the four floods : for the flood of pleasures of the senses, for the flood of becoming, for the flood of views, for the flood of ignorance.

The hither shore beset by dangers and fears, monks,—this is a synonym for corporeality.

The farther shore, secure and without fears, monks,—this is a synonym for nirvana.

The raft, monks,—this is a synonym for the ariyan eightfold Way, that is to say, right view . . . right contemplation.

Striving with hands and feet, monks,—this is a synonym for stirring up energy.[1]

Crossed over, gone beyond, the brahman stands on dry land, monks,—this is a synonym for a perfected one.[2]

S. iv. 174–175

Onslaught on creatures is the hither shore ; abstaining there-from is the farther shore. Taking what is not given is the hither shore ; abstaining therefrom is the farther shore. Wrong con-duct as to pleasures of the senses is the hither shore ; abstaining therefrom is the farther shore. Falsehood . . . spiteful speech . . . bitter speech . . . idle babble . . . coveting . . . harm-fulness . . . these are the hither shore and abstinence therefrom is the farther shore. Wrong view is the hither shore, right view is the farther shore.   *A.* v. 252, 253

Wrong view, monks, is the hither shore, right view is the

---

[1] As p. 192.   [2] *Cf.* p. 191.

farther shore. Wrong concept is the hither shore, right concept is the farther shore. Wrong speech is the hither shore, right speech is the farther shore. Wrong acting is the hither shore, right acting is the farther shore. Wrong means of living is the hither shore, right means of living is the farther shore. Wrong effort is the hither shore, right effort is the farther shore. Wrong mindfulness is the hither shore, right mindfulness is the farther shore. Wrong contemplation is the hither shore, right contemplation is the farther shore. Wrong knowledge is the hither shore, right knowledge is the farther shore. Wrong freedom is the hither shore, right freedom is the farther shore.

This, brahman, is the hither shore, this the farther shore.

A. v. 232

Once upon a time, monks, an incompetent herdsman of Magadha, in the last month of the rains in the autumn, without considering either the hither or the farther bank of the river Ganges, made his cattle cross to the farther bank in Suvidehā at a place where there was no ford. Then the cattle, crowding together in the middle stream of the river Ganges, fell into difficulties and misfortune there—all because the incompetent herdsman had not considered either the hither or the farther bank of the river Ganges. Even so, monks, to those who think that they should listen to or put faith in any recluses and brahmans who are unskilled about this world, unskilled about the world beyond, unskilled about Māra's realm, unskilled about what is not Māra's realm, unskilled about Death's realm, unskilled about what is not Death's realm, there will be woe and sorrow for a long time.

Once upon a time, monks, there was a competent herdsman of Magadha who, in the last month of the rains in the autumn, considering both the hither and the farther banks of the river Ganges, made his cattle cross to the farther bank in Suvidehā at a place where there was a ford. First of all he made those bulls who were the sires and leaders of the herd go across—these, having cut across the stream of the Ganges, went safely beyond. Then he made the sturdy steers and cows go across, then the half-grown bull-calves and heifers, then the weaker calves—all these, having cut across the stream of the Ganges, went safely beyond. At that time there was a young new-born calf which, by following the lowing of its mother, also cut across the stream of the Ganges and went safely beyond. They all went safely beyond because the competent herdsman had considered both the hither and the farther banks of the river Ganges. Even so, monks, to those who think they should listen to and put faith in any recluses and brahmans who are skilled about this world, skilled about the world beyond, skilled about Māra's realm, skilled about what is not Māra's realm, skilled about Death's realm, skilled about what is not Death's realm, there will be weal and happiness for a long time.

Monks, like unto those bulls who were the sires and leaders of the herd and who, having cut across the stream of the Ganges, went safely beyond, are those monks who are perfected ones, the fluxions destroyed, who have lived the life, done what was to be done, laid down the burden, attained their own goal, the fetters of becoming utterly destroyed, and who are freed by right profound knowledge. For these also, having cut across Māra's stream, have gone safely beyond.

Monks, like unto those sturdy steers and cows who, having cut across the stream of the Ganges, went safely beyond are those monks who, by destroying the five fetters binding to this world, are of spontaneous uprising and who, being ones who have attained utter nirvana there, are not liable to return from that world. For these also, having cut across Māra's stream, will go safely beyond.

Monks, like unto those half-grown bull-calves and heifers who . . . went safely beyond are those monks who, by destroying the three fetters, by reducing passion, hatred, and delusion, are once-returners who, having come back to this world only once, will make an end of ill. For these, too, having cut across Māra's stream, will go safely beyond.

Monks, like unto those weaker calves who . . . went safely beyond, are those monks who, by destroying the three fetters, are stream-attainers, not liable for the Downfall, assured, bound for awakening. For these, too, having cut across Māra's stream, will go safely beyond.

Monks, like unto that young new-born calf which, by following the lowing of its mother, also cut across the stream of the Ganges and went safely beyond, are those monks who are striving for *dhamma*, striving for faith. For these, too, having cut across Māra's stream, will go safely beyond.

Now I. monks. am skilled about this world, I am skilled

about the world beyond, skilled about Māra's realm, skilled about what is not Māra's realm, skilled about Death's realm, skilled about what is not Death's realm. To those who think they should listen to me and should put faith in me there will be weal and happiness for a long time.

This world, the world beyond, are well explained by one who knows,
One that is accessible to Māra, and one that is not accessible to Death.

By the All-awakened One, foreknowing, thoroughly knowing every world,
Opened is the door of the Deathless; when nirvana has been reached there is security.

Cutting across the stream of the Evil One, shattering and destroying it,
Let there be abundant delight, monks, let security be reached.

M. i. 225–227

VI. RIVERS OF LIFE AND DEATH

Monks, there are these four kinds of persons found existing in the world. What are the four? There is the person who goes with the stream, there is the person who goes against the stream, there is the person who is poised of self, there is the brahman who, crossed over, gone beyond, stands on dry land.[1]

And who, monks, is the person who goes with the stream? In this connection, monks, a certain person indulges in pleasures of the senses and does evil actions.

And who, monks, is the person who goes against the stream? In this connection, a certain person does not indulge in pleasures of the senses, nor does he do evil actions; but with sorrow, with lamentation, with tearful face, he fares the Brahma-faring, which is utterly fulfilled, wholly purified.

And who is the person, monks, who is poised of self? In this connection, a certain person, by the destruction of the five fetters that bind him to this lower world, comes to be of spontaneous uprising, one who is attained to utter nirvana there and not liable to return from that world.

And who is the person, monks, who is the brahman, crossed over, gone beyond, standing on dry land? In this connection, a certain person, by the destruction of the fluxions, having realized here and now by his own super-knowledge the freedom of heart and freedom of wisdom that are fluxionless, abides therein.

[1] *Cf. S.* iv. 174–175, quoted p. 187 ff.

These, monks, are the four kinds of persons found existing in the world.[1]   *A.* ii. 5–6

It is, monks, as if a man were to be carried along by the current of a river that looks pleasant and delightful, and as if a man with vision standing on the bank, having seen him, should call out : " Now, you, my good man, are being carried along by the current of a river that looks pleasant and delightful. But farther down there is a pool with waves and whirlpools, with sharks and demons. When you get there you will encounter death or pain like unto death." Then that man, having heard the other's call, should strive against the current with his hands and feet.

I have made this parable, monks, to clarify the meaning. This is the meaning here :

The current of a river—this, monks, is a synonym for craving.

Pleasant and delightful—this, monks, is a synonym for the six subjective (sense-) spheres.

Pool farther down—this, monks, is a synonym for the five fetters that bind to this lower world.

With waves—this, monks, is a synonym for the turbulence of anger.

With whirlpools—this, monks, is a synonym for the five strands of the pleasures of the senses.[2]

With sharks and demons—this, monks, is a synonym for womenkind.

Against the current—this, monks, is a synonym for renunciation.

Striving with hands and feet—this, monks, is a synonym for stirring up energy.[3]

Man with vision standing on the bank—this, monks, is a synonym for a Truth-finder, a perfected one, a wholly awakened one.

> One should eject pain with sense-pleasures,
> Aspiring for future security from bondage ;
> Rightly knowing, the heart well freed,
> One may gain freedom in this or that.[4]
> Who's versed in lore, who's lived the Brahma-faring,
> " Gone to world's end," " gone beyond " is called.[5]

It. pp. 113–115

---

[1] *See* p. 188.   [2] *Cf.* p. 187.   [3] *Cf.* p. 188.
[4] *tattha tattha*, here and there ; that is, in a way or in the fruit of a way, according to *ItA.* ii. 172–173.   [5] Last two lines *cf.* p. 158.

Should desire be born for the unshown,[1]
And his mind surcharged (with it) be,
And if thought's not fettered to sense-pleasures—
Upstreamer is he called.

Dh. 218

In those following the stream of becoming,
O'ercome by passion for becoming,
Who have attained Māra's realm,
This *dhamma* 's not easily well awakened.

Sn. 764, *S.* iv. 128

For those following the stream of becoming,
Who are overcome by touches,
Proceeding by the false way,
Distant is destruction of the fetters.

Sn. 736

In whom no craving spreads,
In monk who cuts the stream,
Rid of all toils and tasks,
No fret is found or known.[2]

Sn. 715

Who here hath lusts crossed o'er,
Bond in the world so hard
To pass, grieves not nor longs,
Stream-cutter, tie-less he.[2]

Śn. 948

Pure-limbed, white-canopied, one-wheeled, the car rolls on.
See him that cometh : faultless, stream-cutter, bondless he.[3]

Ud. 76 ; *S.* iv. 291

They who have cut the stream, so hard to pass,
Of objects dear and sweet, enslaving,
They attain utter nirvana,
They utterly pass over ill.

It. p. 95

Whatever streams flow in the world,
Ajita, (said the Master then),
The dam for them is mindfulness ;
It is their flood-gate too, I say ;
By wisdom may the streams be closed.[4]

Sn. 1035

---

[1] *anakkhāta,* which according to the Comy. is *nibbāna.*
[2] E. M. Hare, *Woven Cadences.*
[3] F. L. Woodward, *Min. Anth.* ii., p. 92.
[4] E. M. Hare. *Woven Cadences.*

VII. THE GREAT OCEAN

Monks, there are these eight strange and wonderful things in the great ocean, from constantly having seen which *asuras* delight in the great ocean. What are the eight? The great ocean, monks, deepens gradually, slopes gradually, shelves gradually, with no abruptness like a precipice. And, monks, that the great ocean deepens gradually, slopes gradually, shelves gradually with no abruptness like a precipice—this, monks, is the first strange and wonderful thing in the great ocean from constantly having seen which *asuras* delight in the great ocean.

And again, monks, the great ocean is stable, it does not overflow its margins. And, monks, that the great ocean is stable, that it does not overflow its margins—this, monks, is the second strange and wonderful thing. . . .

And again, monks, the great ocean does not associate with a dead body, a corpse. Whatever dead body, corpse, there may be in the great ocean, that it just quickly forces ashore and pushes on to the dry land. That the great ocean, monks, does not associate with a dead body, a corpse, . . . this, monks, is the third strange and wonderful thing. . . .

And again, monks, all the great rivers, that is to say, the Ganges, the Jumnā, the Aciravatī, the Sarabhū, the Mahī—these, on reaching the great ocean lose their former names and identities and are reckoned simply as the great ocean. That all the great rivers . . . this, monks, is the fourth strange and wonderful thing. . . .[1]

And again, monks, those streams which in the world flow into the great ocean, and those showers from the sky which fall into it—yet is neither the emptiness nor the fullness of the great ocean affected by that. That those streams which in the world . . . this, monks, is the fifth strange and wonderful thing. . . .

And again, monks, the great ocean has one taste, the taste of salt. That the great ocean, monks, has one taste . . . this, monks, is the sixth strange and wonderful thing. . . .

And again, monks, the great ocean has many treasures, divers

---

[1] This old Brahmanical formula descriptive of the attainment of man's last end of liberation from himself recurs in Christian, Islamic, and Taoist as well as Buddhist contexts.

treasures ; these treasures are there, that is to say : pearl, crystal, lapis lazuli, shell, quartz, coral, silver, gold, ruby, cat's-eye. That the great ocean, monks, has many treasures . . . this, monks, is the seventh strange and wonderful thing. . . .

And again, monks, the great ocean is the abode of great beings ; these beings are there : the *timis*, the *timangalas*, the *timitimangalas*, *asuras*, *nāgas*, *gandharvas*. There are in the great ocean individualities a hundred *yojanas* long, two hundred, three hundred, four hundred, five hundred *yojanas* long. That the great ocean, monks, is the abode of great beings ; that these beings are there : *timis* . . . individualities five hundred *yojanas* long—this, monks, is the eighth strange and wonderful thing from constantly having seen which *asuras* delight in the great ocean. These, monks, are the eight strange and wonderful things in the great ocean from constantly having seen which *asuras* delight in the great ocean.

In exactly the same way, monks, in this *dhamma* and discipline there are eight strange and wonderful things from constantly having seen which monks delight in this *dhamma* and discipline. What are the eight ?

Even, monks, as the great ocean deepens gradually, slopes gradually, shelves gradually with no abruptness like a precipice, even so, monks, in this *dhamma* and discipline there is a gradual training, a gradual (doing of) what is to be done, a gradual course,[1] with no abruptness, such as penetration of profound knowledge. And, monks, that in this *dhamma* and discipline there is a . . . gradual course with no abruptness, such as penetration of profound knowledge, this, monks, is the first strange and wonderful thing from constantly having seen which monks delight in this *dhamma* and discipline.

And even, monks, as the great ocean is stable and does not overflow its margins, even so, monks, whatever course of training has been laid down by me for disciples, my disciples will not transgress it even for life's sake. And that, monks, my disciples will not transgress even for life's sake a course of training laid down by me for disciples, this, monks, is the second strange and wonderful thing. . . .

And even, monks, as the great ocean does not associate with a dead body, a corpse, but whatever dead body, corpse, there may be in the great ocean, that it just quickly forces ashore and pushes on to the dry land, even so, monks, whatever individual is of bad

[1] *Cf. M.* i. 479 (p. 60).

moral habit, of depraved character, of impure and suspicious behaviour, of concealed actions, not a recluse although pretending to be one, not a farer of the Brahma-faring although pretending to be one, rotten within, filled with desire, filthy by nature—the Order (of monks) does not live in communion with him, but having assembled quickly suspends him ; and although he is sitting in the midst of an Order of monks, yet he is far from the Order and the Order is far from him [1] . . . this, monks, is the third strange and wonderful thing. . . .

And even, monks, as those great rivers, that is to say the Ganges, the Jumnā, the Āciravatī, the Sarabhū, the Mahī, on reaching the great ocean lose their former names and identities and are reckoned simply as the great ocean, even so, monks, (members of) these four castes : noble, brahman, merchant, and worker, having gone forth from home into homelessness in the *dhamma* and discipline proclaimed by the Truth-finder, lose their former names and clans and are reckoned simply as recluses, sons of the Sakyans . . . this, monks, is the fourth strange and wonderful thing. . . .

And even, monks, as those streams which in the world flow into the great ocean and those showers which fall into it from the sky, yet neither the emptiness nor the fullness of the great ocean is affected by that—even so, monks, even if many monks are attained to utter nirvana in a condition of nirvana with no residuum remaining, not by that is the emptiness or fullness of the condition of nirvana affected . . . this, monks, is the fifth strange and wonderful thing. . . .

And even, monks, as the great ocean has one taste, the taste of salt, even so, monks, has this *dhamma* and discipline one taste, the taste of freedom . . . this, monks, is the sixth strange and wonderful thing. . . .

And even, monks, as the great ocean has many treasures, divers treasures ; these treasures are there, that is to say : pearl, crystal, lapis lazuli, shell, quartz, coral, silver, gold, ruby, cat's-eye—even so, monks, does this *dhamma* and discipline have many treasures, divers treasures ; these treasures are there, that is to say : the four stations of mindfulness, the four right efforts, the four bases of psychic potency, the five faculties, the five powers, the seven limbs of awakening, the ariyan eightfold Way . . . this, monks, is the seventh strange and wonderful thing. . . .

[1] *Cf. It.* p. 91 (p. 198) : the monk is far from me.

And even, monks, as the great ocean is the abode of great beings ; these beings are there : *timis* . . . individualities five hundred *yojanas* long—even so, monks, this *dhamma* and discipline is the abode of great beings ; these beings are there : the stream-attainer, the one going along to the realization of the fruit of stream-attainment, the once-returner, the one going along to the realization of the fruit of once-returning ; the non-returner, the one going along to the realization of the fruit of non-returning, the perfected one, the one going along to perfection. And that, monks, this *dhamma* and discipline is the abode of great beings ; these beings are there : the stream-attainer . . . the one going along to perfection . . . this, monks, is the eighth strange and wonderful thing in this *dhamma* and discipline from constantly having seen which monks delight in this *dhamma* and discipline. These, monks, are the eight strange and wonderful things in this *dhamma* and discipline from constantly having seen which monks delight in this *dhamma* and discipline.

Vin. ii. 237–239 ; *A.* iv. 206 ; *Ud.* 53–56

VIII. DHAMMA.

Dhamma, I will declare to thee,
Mettagu, (said the Master then),
A thing seen here, not lore come down,
The which who finds and knows, and fares
Alert, may cross the world's foul mire.[1]

Sn. 1053

Whoso hath doubts here, Dhotaka,
Not him I come to liberate :
When *dhamma* thou dost know supreme,
Then mayest thou thus cross the flood.[1]

Sn. 1064

He should arise, he should not heedless be,
by *dhamma* of well-faring let him fare.
Happy the *dhamma*-farer lives,
both in this world and that beyond.

By *dhamma* of well-faring let him fare ;
not that which is ill-faring let him fare.
Happy the *dhamma*-farer lives,
both in this world and that beyond.[2]

Dh. 168–169

---

[1] E. M. Hare, *Woven Cadences.*   [2] Mrs Rhys Davids, *Min. Anth.* i.

Let man revere, as *devas* king,
Him from whom he doth *dhamma* learn ;
Then that great listener revered,
With faith in one, makes *dhamma* plain.

Who heedful, rapt, makes that his goal,
Dhamma by *dhamma* practising,
A knower, clear and full, becomes,
Who follows such a man with zeal.

But whoso serves the little fool,
Jealous, who hath not reached the goal,
Dhamma not having quickened here,
Dies without crossing over doubt.

The man who plunges in the spate,
Flooding and turgid, swift of flow,
He, borne along the current's way,
How can he others help to cross ?

Who *dhamma* hath not quickened here,
Nor heeds the goal of listeners great,
Himself not knowing, doubt not crossed,
How can he others help to muse ?

As one who boards a sturdy boat,
With oars and rudder well equipt,
May many others then help cross—
Sure, skilful knower of the means :

So the self-quickened lore-adept,
Listener imperturbable,
By knowledge may help others muse,
The eager-eared adventurers.

Hence surely follow men-of-sooth,
Great listeners of lucid mind :
Who moves with knowledge to the goal
And *dhamma* knows, he joy obtains.[1]

Sn. 316–323

Monks, even if a monk should take hold of the edge of my outer cloak and should walk close behind me, step for step, yet if he should be covetous, strongly attracted by pleasures of the senses, malevolent in thought, of corrupt mind and purpose, of confused recollection, inattentive, not contemplative, scatter-brained, his sense-faculties uncontrolled, then he is far from me and I am far from him.[2] But, monks, if that monk should be

[1] E. M. Hare, *Woven Cadences.*
[2] *Cf. Vin.* ii. 239, etc. (p. 196) : the monk is far from the Order.

staying even a hundred *yojanas* away, yet if he be not covetous, not strongly attracted by the pleasures of the senses, not malevolent in thought, of incorrupt mind and purpose, his recollection firmly set, attentive, contemplative, his thoughts one-pointed. restrained in his sense-faculties, then he is near me and I am near him. Why is this ? Monks, that monk sees *dhamma* ; seeing *dhamma* he sees me.　　　　　　　　　　　　*It.* p. 90–91

Hush, Vakkali. What is there for you in seeing this vile body of mine ? Whoever, Vakkali, sees *dhamma* sees me ; whoever sees me sees *dhamma*. For, Vakkali, one seeing *dhamma* sees me ; seeing me he sees *dhamma*.　　　　　　　　　　*S.* iii. 120

> The royal chariots wear out,
> and so too the body ages ;
> the true *dhamma* does not age.
> 　　　　　　　*S.* i. 71 ; *Dh.* 151

> *Dhamma*, I say, is the charioteer.
> 　　　　　　　　　　*S.* i. 33

By this means, Vāseṭṭha, it may be understood that *dhamma* is the best among folk both in what is here and now and in a future state. King Pasenadi of Kosala knows : The recluse Gotama has gone forth from the neighbouring Sakyan clan. But the Sakyans have become vassals of King Pasenadi : they render him homage and respectful salutation, they rise and do obeisance to him and treat him with ceremony. Now, just as the Sakyans treat King Pasenadi, so does he treat the Truth-finder. For he thinks : " Is not the recluse Gotama of pure birth ? I am not. He is strong, I am weak. He is comely, I am ugly. The recluse Gotama is of great esteem, I am of little esteem." It is because the king respects *dhamma*, reveres *dhamma*, thinks highly of *dhamma*, honours *dhamma* that, venerating *dhamma*, he renders homage and respectful salutation to the Truth-finder, rising and doing him obeisance and treating him with ceremony. By this means may it be understood that this *dhamma* is the best among folk both in what is here and now and in a future state.

You, Vāseṭṭha, have gone forth from home into homelessness, from different births and names, from different clans and families. On being asked : " Who are you ? " you may reply, " We are recluses, sons of the Sakyans." He, Vāseṭṭha, whose faith in the

Truth-finder is settled, rooted, established, firm, not to be dragged down by a recluse or brahman or *deva* or a Māra or a Brahmā or by anyone in the world, he may well say : " I am the lord's own son, born of his mouth, born of *dhamma*, formed by *dhamma*, heir of *dhamma*," And why ? Because this, Vāseṭṭha, is a synonym for a Truth-finder : belonging to *dhamma* and belonging to Brahma ; *dhamma*-become and Brahma-become.

D. iii. 83–84

It is possible, Ānanda, to lay down in this *dhamma*-discipline a procedure towards Brahma.[1] This, Ānanda, is a synonym for this ariyan eightfold Way : " procedure towards Brahma " ; also " procedure towards *dhamma* " ; also " the matchless victory in the struggle." [2]

S. v. 5

I, monks, am a brahman, one to ask a favour from, ever pure-handed, bearer of my last body, matchless physician and surgeon. You are my own true sons, born of my mouth, born of *dhamma*, formed by *dhamma*, heirs of *dhamma*, not heirs of material things.

It. p. 101

Monks, become heirs of *dhamma* in me, not heirs of material things. I have sympathy with you and think : " How may my disciples become heirs of *dhamma*, not heirs of material things ? " If you, monks, should become heirs of material things, not heirs of *dhamma*, not only may you become in consequence those of whom it is said : " The Teacher's disciples are heirs of material things, not heirs of *dhamma*," but I also may become in consequence one of whom it is said : " The Teacher's disciples are heirs of material things, not heirs of *dhamma*." But if you, monks, should become heirs of *dhamma* in me, not heirs of material things, not only may you become in consequence those of whom it is said : " The Teacher's disciples are heirs of *dhamma*, not heirs of material things," but I also may become in consequence one of whom it is said : " The Teacher's disciples are heirs of *dhamma*, not heirs of material things." Therefore, monks, become heirs of *dhamma* in me, not heirs of material things.

[1] *Brahma-yāna*, or Brahma-vehicle, *yāna* being both the going and the vehicle which takes you.
[2] Over passion, hatred and delusion.

Take a case where I have eaten and have had as much as I please, and some of my alms-food is over and is to be thrown away. Two monks may arrive worn out with exhaustion and hunger. If I should tell them that I have finished my meal and should say : " Do eat if you so desire [1] ; if not, I will throw the remainder of my alms-food away where there is no grass or I will drop it into water that has no living creatures in it," [2] it may occur to the first monk : " But this was said by the lord : ' Monks, become heirs of *dhamma* in me, not heirs of material things.' But this is a material thing, that is to say, alms-food." And he may decide not to eat the food. The second monk, however, decides to eat it. For me the first monk is more to be honoured and more to be praised. What is the reason for this ? It is, monks, that it will conduce for a long time to that monk's desiring little, to his contentment, to his expunging (evil), to his ease in supporting himself, to his putting forth energy. Therefore, monks, become heirs of *dhamma* in me, not heirs of material things.

M. i. 12–13

Whoever, monks, in speaking aright, should say : " He has attained to mastery, he has attained to perfection in the ariyan moral habit, in the ariyan contemplation, in the ariyan wisdom, in the ariyan freedom," even so, in speaking aright of Sāriputta, he would say : " He has attained to mastery, he has attained to perfection in the ariyan moral habit, in the ariyan contemplation, in the ariyan wisdom, in the ariyan freedom." Whoever, monks, in speaking aright should say : " He is the lord's own son, born of his mouth, born of *dhamma*, formed by *dhamma*, heir of *dhamma*, not heir of material things," even so, in speaking aright of Sāriputta, he would say : " He is the lord's own son, born of his mouth, born of *dhamma*, formed by *dhamma*, heir of *dhamma*, not heir of material things."

Monks, Sāriputta rolls on aright the incomparable wheel of *dhamma* set rolling by the Truth-finder.   M. iii. 28–29

I do not know, monks, of any other single person who so rightly keeps arolling the incomparable wheel of *dhamma* set rolling by the Truth-finder as does Sāriputta. Sāriputta, monks,

---

[1] Monks may eat food that is left over, *Vin*. iv. 81 ff.
[2] *Cf. Vin*. iv. 125, quoted p.. 137.

rightly keeps arolling the incomparable wheel of *dhamma* set
rolling by the Truth-finder.   *A.* i. 23

As the eldest son, Sāriputta, of a wheel-rolling monarch rightly
keeps arolling the wheel rolled by his father,[1] so do you, Sāriputta, rightly keep arolling the incomparable wheel of *dhamma*
set rolling by me.   *S.* i. 191

" Whatever king, monks, is a turner of the wheel,[1] a *dhamma*-
man, a *dhamma*-king, he indeed does not set rolling a wheel that
has no king."
A monk then asked the lord : " But who, lord, is the king of
the king who is the turner of the wheel, the *dhamma*-man, the
dhamma-king ? "
" *Dhamma*, monk. In this case a king who is a turner of the
wheel, a *dhamma*-man, a *dhamma*-king, depending on *dhamma*
only, honouring *dhamma*, revering *dhamma*, esteeming *dhamma*,
with *dhamma* as his standard, *dhamma* as his banner, with mastery
as to *dhamma*, provides a *dhamma*-guard and bar and protection
for those within his realm . . . for warriors, camp-followers,
for brahmans and householders, for town and country people, for
recluses and brahmans, for beasts and birds. Having done so,
he rolls on the wheel by *dhamma* only ; that wheel becomes one
not to be rolled back by the hand of any hostile person."
In like manner, monks, does a Truth-finder, perfected one,
wholly awakened one, a *dhamma*-man, a *dhamma*-king, depending on *dhamma* only, honouring *dhamma*, revering *dhamma*,
esteeming *dhamma*, with *dhamma* as his standard, with *dhamma* as
his banner, with mastery as to *dhamma*, provide a *dhamma*-guard
and bar and protection for monks, nuns, men and women lay-
followers, saying : " Such-and-such a deed of body, speech, or
thought is to be resorted to, such-and-such is not ; such-and-such
a way of living is to be resorted to, such-and-such is not ; such-
and-such a village or little town is to be resorted to, such-and-
such is not." When the Truth-finder . . . has thus provided a
dhamma-guard and bar and protection for monks, nuns, men and
women lay-followers, he rolls on, by *dhamma* only, the incomparable wheel of *dhamma* ; that wheel becomes one not to be
rolled back by a recluse or brahman or *deva* or a Māra or a
Brahmā or by anyone in the world.   *A.* i. 109 ; iii. 149

[1] I.e. the wheel of government.

This *dhamma* penetrated by me is deep, difficult to see, difficult to understand, peaceful, excellent, beyond dialectic, subtle, intelligible to the wise. But this is a creation delighting in desire, delighted with desire, rejoicing in desire. So that for a creation delighting in desire . . . rejoicing in desire, this were a matter difficult to see, that is to say : causal uprising by way of cause. This, too, were a matter very difficult to see, that is to say : the calming of all the constructions ; the renunciation of all attachment ; the destruction of craving ; passionlessness, stopping, nirvana. But if I were to teach *dhamma* and others were not to understand me, that would be a weariness to me, a vexation to me.

> This that through many toils I've won—
> Enough ! why should I make it known ?
> By folk with lust and hate consumed
> Not this a *dhamma* that's understood.
> Leading on against the stream,
> Deep, subtle, difficult, delicate,
> Unseen 'twill be by passion's slaves
> Cloaked in the murk of ignorance.

But now, to whom should I first teach *dhamma* ? Who will understand this *dhamma* quickly ? [1]

Vin. i. 4 ; *S.* i. 136 ; *D.* ii. 36 ; *M.* i. 167

I, monks, am freed from all snares, both those of *devas* and those of men. And you, too, monks, are freed from all snares, both those of *devas* and those of men. Walk, monks, on tour for the blessing of the many-folk, for the happiness of the many-folk, out of compassion for the world, for the welfare, the blessing, the happiness of *devas* and men. Let not two of you go by one way. Monks, teach *dhamma* which is lovely at the beginning, lovely in the middle, lovely at the ending. Explain with the spirit and the letter the Brahma-faring which is completely fulfilled, wholly pure. There are beings with little dust in their eyes who, not hearing *dhamma*, are decaying, but if they are learners of *dhamma*, they will grow. And I, monks, will go along to Uruvelā, to the Camp township in order to teach *dhamma*.

Vin. i. 20–21

It may be, Ānanda, that some of you will think : " The word

---

[1] This is the "Hesitation." Parallels are found in the lives of all the great Heroes, e.g. Agni, Christ.

of the Teacher is ended ; we have no teacher." But it is not to be regarded in this way. That *dhamma* (and discipline) taught and laid down by me, this is to be your teacher after my passing on. . . . Come now, monks, all component things are liable to decay ; call up diligence to accomplish your aim.

D. ii. 154, 156

Whatever monk teaches *dhamma* to others with a mind such as this : *Dhamma* is well propounded by the lord, it relates to the here and now, it is intemporal, it is a come-and-see thing, leading on, it may be known by the wise subjectively, and says : Indeed you should hear my *dhamma*, for having heard it you would understand *dhamma*, and when you have understood it you would be on the road to suchness (truth)—it is in this way that he teaches to others *dhamma* well in accordance with *dhamma*, he teaches *dhamma* to others out of pity, out of mercy, because of compassion. The teaching of *dhamma* by a monk such as this is very pure.   *S*. ii. 199

Monk, take the case of a monk who masters *dhamma* : the Discourses in prose, in prose and verse, the Expositions, the Verses, the Utterances, the Quotations, the Birth Stories, the Miracles, the Miscellanies.[1] He spends the day in *dhamma*-mastery, he neglects solitary meditation, he does not devote himself to subjective tranquillity of thought. Monk, he is called a monk who is intent on mastery, (but) not one who goes along by *dhamma*.

And again, monk, a monk teaches others *dhamma* in detail as he has heard it, as he has mastered it. He spends the day in this convincing (others) of *dhamma*, he neglects solitary meditation, he does not devote himself to subjective tranquillity of thought. Monks, he is called a monk who is intent on convincing, (but) not one who goes along by *dhamma*.

And again, monk, a monk studies *dhamma* in detail as he has heard it, as he has mastered it. He spends the day in this study, he neglects solitary meditation, he does not devote himself to subjective tranquillity of thought. Monk, he is called a monk who is intent on study, (but) not one who goes along by *dhamma*.

[1] These nine parts or "limbs" of *dhamma* also mentioned at *A*. ii. 7, *M*. i. 133, *Vin*. iii. 8.

And again, monk, a monk in thought ponders and scrutinizes *dhamma* and considers it mentally as he has heard it, as he has mastered it. He spends the day in this *dhamma*-pondering, he neglects . . . subjective tranquillity of thought. Monk, he is called a monk who is intent on pondering, (but) not one who goes along by *dhamma*.

Take the case, monk, of a monk who masters *dhamma* : the Discourses in prose, in prose and verse . . . the Miscellanies. He does not spend the day in *dhamma*-mastery, he does not neglect solitary meditation, he devotes himself to subjective tranquillity of thought. Such, monk, is a monk who is one going along by *dhamma*.

In this way, monk, is " intent on mastery " taught by me, is taught " intent on convincing," is taught " intent on studying," is taught " intent on pondering," is taught " going along by *dhamma*." Whatever, monk, is to be done by a Teacher out of compassion for his disciples, for their welfare, that, monk, from compassion have I done for you. These roots of trees, monk, are " empty houses " (for you). Meditate, monk, do not be negligent, do not let there be remorse for you later. This is my instruction to you.   *A.* iii. 86–87

[The Gotamid, Pajāpatī the Great, approached the lord and said to him :]

" Lord, it were well if the lord would teach me *dhamma* in brief so that I, having heard the lord's *dhamma*, might live alone, aloof, zealous, ardent, self-resolute."

" Whatever are the states of which you, Gotami, may know : these states lead to passion, not to passionlessness, they lead to bondage, not to the absence of bondage, they lead to the piling up (of rebirths [1]), not to the absence of piling up, they lead to wanting much, not to wanting little, they lead to discontent, not to contentment, they lead to sociability, not to solitude, they lead to indolence, not to the putting forth of energy, they lead to difficulty in supporting oneself, not to ease in supporting oneself —of such states you should know with certainty, Gotami : this is not *dhamma*, this is not discipline, this is not the Teacher's instruction.

" But of whatever states you may know (that they are the

[1] According to *AA*.

opposite of these things that I have told you)—of such states you should know with certainty, Gotami : this is *dhamma*, this is discipline, this is the Teacher's instruction."   *Vin.* ii. 258

[A village headman spoke thus to the lord :]

" Is a Truth-finder compassionate towards all living breathing creatures ? "

" Yes, headman," answered the lord.

" But does the lord teach *dhamma* in full to some, but not likewise to others ? "

" Now, what do you think, headman ? Suppose a farmer had three fields, one excellent, one mediocre, and one poor with bad soil. When he wants to sow the seed, which field would he sow first ? "

" He would sow the excellent field, then the mediocre one. When he has done that he might or might not sow the poor one with bad soil. And why ? Because it might do even for cattle fodder."

" In the same way, headman, my monks and nuns are like the excellent field. It is to these that I teach *dhamma* that is lovely at the beginning, lovely in the middle, lovely at the ending, with the spirit and the letter, and to whom I make known the Brahma-faring utterly fulfilled and purified. And why ? It is these who dwell with me for light, with me for shelter, with me for stronghold, with me for refuge.

" Then my men and women lay-followers are like the mediocre field. To these, too, I teach *dhamma* . . . and make known the Brahma-faring utterly fulfilled and purified. For they dwell with me for light, me for shelter, me for stronghold, me for refuge.

" Then recluses, brahmans, and wanderers of other sects than mine are like the poor field with the bad soil. To these, too, I teach *dhamma* . . . and make known the Brahma-faring utterly fulfilled and purified. And why ? Because if they were to understand perhaps even a single sentence, that would be a happiness and a blessing for them for a long time."

S. iv. 314–316

[Once the lord when he was staying in the Simsapā Wood took up a few simsapā leaves in his hand and addressed the monks, saying :]

" Now, which do you think are more, these few simsapā leaves that I am holding in my hand or those overhead in the Simsapā Wood ? "

" Few in number are the simsapā leaves that the lord is holding in his hand, many more are those overhead in the Simsapā Wood."

" In the same way, monks, many more are those things which through my super-knowledge I do not make known to you, few are those things which I make known. And why do I not make these things known ? Monks, they are not connected with the goal, they are not fundamental to the Brahma-faring, they do not conduce to disregard, to passionlessness, to stopping, to tranquillity, to super-knowledge, to awakening, to nirvana. That is why I have not made them known.

" Then what is it, monks, that I have made known ? That this is ill, that this is the uprising of ill, that this is the stopping of ill, that this is the course leading to the stopping of ill. And why do I make these things known ? Monks, they are connected with the goal, they are fundamental to the Brahma-faring, they conduce to disregard, to passionlessness, to stopping, to tranquillity, to super-knowledge, to awakening, to nirvana. That is why I have made them known."   *S. v. 437–438*

To this extent, Nigrodha, is austerity attained to the height and attained to the pith. So when you say to me : " What is this *dhamma* of the lord's in which he trains disciples and which, when they are so trained and attained to confidence, they acknowledge as their support and as fundamental to the Brahma-faring ? " then I say to you, Nigrodha, that there is a further and a finer matter in which I lead my disciples and which my disciples, when led by me and attained to confidence, acknowledge as their support and as fundamental to the Brahma-faring. . . .

Has it never occurred to you, Nigrodha, who are intelligent and advanced in years, " The lord is an Awakened One, he teaches *dhamma* for awakening ; he is tamed, he teaches *dhamma* for taming ; he is calmed, he teaches *dhamma* for calming ; he is crossed over, he teaches *dhamma* for crossing over ; he has attained utter nirvana, he teaches *dhamma* for utter nirvana ? "

I say this to you, Nigrodha : Let a man who is intelligent,

honest, candid, and upright come to me and I will instruct him,
I will teach him *dhamma*. If he proceed as he is instructed, then
having realized here and now by his own super-knowledge that
unsurpassed goal of the Brahma-faring for the sake of which
young men of family rightly go forth from home into homelessness, he will abide in it. . . . I do not speak to you thus,
Nigrodha, because I am anxious to obtain pupils or to make you
fall away from your rule or mode of living or because I wish to
confirm you in wrong states of mind or draw you away from
right ones. It is for the sake of destroying wrong states of mind
that are not destroyed, that are connected with the obstructions,
with becoming again, with pain, that are ill in result and make for
birth, old age, and dying in the future that I teach *dhamma*. If
you proceed according to this, these wrong states of mind will
perish, states making for purity will grow exceedingly, and you
will attain to and abide in complete and abounding wisdom,
having realized it here and now by your own super-knowledge.

D. iii. 52, 54–57

This is a case where a monk, having seen by right wisdom in
regard to all material shape as it has really come to be—whether
it is past, future, or present, subjective or objective, gross or
subtle, low or excellent, distant or near—that " This is not mine,
I am not this, this is not my Self," comes to be freed without
grasping. And the same in regard to feeling, perception, the
constructions, consciousness. To this extent a monk becomes a
perfected one, the fluxions destroyed, having lived the life, done
what was to be done, laid down the burden, won his own goal,
the fetter of becoming quite destroyed, freed by right profound
knowledge.

The heart thus freed, the monk comes to be endowed with
three incomparable things : with incomparable vision, with incomparable practice, with incomparable freedom. Thus freed,
the monk respects, reveres, esteems, and honours the Truth-
finder, thinking : " This lord is an Awakened One, he teaches
dhamma for awakening ; this lord is tamed, he teaches *dhamma*
for taming ; this lord is calmed, he teaches *dhamma* for
calming ; this lord is crossed over, he teaches *dhamma* for
crossing over ; this lord has attained utter nirvana, he teaches
dhamma for utter nirvana."   M. i. 234–235

IX. ESSENCE

They who deem essence [1] in what's not essence,
and who see what is not essence in essence,
They go not on to essence ;
wrong concept is their pasture.

But they who know essence as essence,
and what is not essence as not essence,
They go on to essence ;
right concept is their pasture.

Dh. 11, 12

Monks, there are these four essences. What are the four?
The essence of moral habit, the essence of contemplation,[2] the
essence of wisdom,[3] the essence of freedom.[4]   *A.* ii. 141

Goodly are words when one has grasped their pith ;
To grasp the heard is pith of mind-intent :
But in the violent and slothful man
No wisdom and no hearing ever grows.

Peerless in word, in thought, in deed, they who
Delight in *dhamma*, known to ariyans,
They, poised in calm and bliss of mind-intent,
The pith of hearing and of wisdom win.[5]

Sn. 329, 330

Thus it is, brahman, that the Brahma-faring is not for advantage in gains, honour, and fame ; it is not for advantage in
undertaking the moral habits, it is not for advantage in undertaking contemplation, it is not for the advantage of knowing
and seeing. But whatever, brahman, is unshakable freedom of
heart, it is this that is the goal of the Brahma-faring, this the
essence, this the consummation.   *M.* i. 197, 204–205

Comport yourselves towards me, Ānanda, in friendliness, not

---

[1] *Sāra*, literally " hard wood " or " heart-wood " (*cf.* " heart of oak "), pith.
Translated " pith " in the extracts from the *Sn.* contained in this section.
[2] *Cf. Sn.* 329, 330, where *samādhi*, contemplation, is rendered " mind-intent "
[3] *Cf. Sn.* 329, 330.
[4] *Cf. A.* ii. 244 (p. 65), and *cf. A.* iv. 385. *Cf.* also " essence of the self "
p. 53 ; " essence of *dhamma*," p. 216.
[5] E. M. Hare. *Woven Cadences.*

in hostility. That will come to be for a long time for your welfare and happiness. I do not deal with you as a potter with mere wet clay. I, Ānanda, will constantly speak to you restraining [1] and cleansing (you). What the essence [2] is, that will persist.   *M.* iii. 118 ; *J.* iii. 368

> Who in " becomings " finds no pith [3]
> As seeker in fig-trees no flowers,
> That monk quits bounds both here and yon
> As snake his old and worn-out skin. [4]

Sn. 5

> Who in affections seeks no pith,
> Curbs wish and passion to possess,
> He, trusting not, whom none can lead,
> Rightly he in the world would fare. [4]

Sn. 364

X. ESCAPE.

Because, monks, there is satisfaction in the world, beings are attached to the world. Because there is peril in the world beings are disgusted by the world. Monks, if there were not an escape from the world, beings could not escape from the world. But because, monks, there is an escape from the world, therefore beings escape from the world. [5] . . . When beings have fully come to know as it really is the satisfaction in the world as satisfaction, the peril as peril, the escape as escape, then they fare along escaped, detached, freed, the barriers of the mind done away with. Whatever recluses and brahmans fully know as it really comes to be the satisfaction in the world . . . the escape as escape, these, monks, are recluses and brahmans, or among recluses they are reckoned as recluses, or among brahmans they are reckoned as brahmans, and these venerable ones, having by their own super-knowledge here and now realized the goal of recluseship and the goal of brahmanhood, entering thereon abide therein. *A.* i. 260 ; *cf. S.* ii. 172–173 ; iii. 69–71 ; iv. 10–11

---

[1] Or reproving.

[2] *MA.* iv. 167 calls this the essence of the ways and the fruits.

[3] *Cf. S.* iii. 143 (p. 148) no essence or pith in the series : material shape . . . constructions.

[4] E. M. Hare, *Woven Cadences.*

[5] *Cf. Ud.* 80, p. 218 ; also *cf.* " further escape from this perception," p. 112.

These, monks, are three elements making for escape. What are the three ? This is the escape from the pleasures of the senses, that is to say renunciation. This is the escape from material shapes, that is to say, immateriality. Whatever has come to be, is composite, has uprisen by way of cause, its arrest is the escape from it.

> Knowing the escape from the pleasures of the senses,
> And transcending material shapes,
> Reaching quietude as to all that is composite,
> Ardent in all ways—
> He is indeed a monk who rightly sees.
> When he is thus released,
> Master of super-knowledges, calmed,
> He is indeed a sage who's passed the bonds.

It. p. 61

Monks, there are these five elements making for escape. What are the five ?

In this case, monks, a monk pays attention to pleasures of the senses, but although his heart does not leap up among pleasures of the senses, yet it is not calm, not composed, not freed. But whose heart, while he pays attention to renunciation, is calm, composed, freed—that heart is well-gone, well made to become, well removed, well freed, well unbound from the pleasures of the senses. And whatever fluxions arise, caused by pleasures of the senses, painful and burning, he is freed from these—nor does he experience that feeling. This is shown to be the escape from pleasures of the senses.

And again, monks, a monk pays attention to ill-will . . . hurt . . . material shape . . . (*as above, reading* ill-will, hurt, material shape *instead of* pleasures of the senses). . . . This is shown to be the escape from ill-will . . . hurt . . . material shape.

And again, monks, a monk pays attention to his own body, but although his heart does not leap up at (the thought of) his own body, yet it is not calm, not composed, not freed. But whose heart, while he pays attention to the stopping of his own body, is calm, composed, freed—that heart of his is well-gone, well made to become, well removed, well freed, well unbound from his own body. And whatever fluxions arise, caused by his own body, painful and burning, he is freed from these—nor does he experience that feeling. This is shown to be the escape from one's own body.   *A.* iii. 245–246

"Do you think, Ānanda, that there in that first station [1] for consciousness, namely that of differing bodies, differing perceptions such as (among) human beings and certain *devas* and certain of those in the Downfall—that for whoever has foreknowledge of this (state), and has foreknowledge of its uprising and foreknowledge of its fading away, and foreknowledge of its satisfaction and foreknowledge of its peril, and foreknowledge of the escape from it, that it is fitting for him to rejoice in it?"

"No, lord."

"When, Ānanda, a monk has known as they have really come to be the uprising and fading away and satisfaction and peril of this state of consciousness, and the escape from it, he comes to be freed without any residuum (for life remaining). He, Ānanda, is called a monk who is freed by wisdom."   D. ii. 69–70

There are, monks, these four releases. [2] What are the four? Release from the bondage of sense-pleasures, release from the bondage of becoming, release from the bondage of view, release from the bondage of ignorance.

And what, monks, is the release from the bondage of sense-pleasures?

In this case, monks, a certain one has foreknowledge of, as they really come to be, the uprising and fading away and satisfaction and peril of the sense-pleasures, and the escape from them. Whatever is, among sense-pleasures, the passion for, the delight in, the affection for, the greed, the thirst, the fever for, the clinging to, the craving for pleasures of the senses, it does not obsess him who knows these things as they really come to be. This, monks, is called release from the bondage of sense-pleasures.

[Release from the bondage of becoming and release from the bondage of view are similarly expounded.]

And what, monks, is the release from the bondage of ignorance?

In this case, monks, a certain one has foreknowledge of, as they really come to be, the uprising and fading away and satisfaction and peril of the six spheres of contact. Whatever is, among the six spheres of contact, ignorance, not-knowing, it does not

---

[1] Seven of these *thitis* are mentioned here.
[2] *Visaṃyoga.*

obsess him who knows these things as they really come to be. This, monks, is called the release from the bondage of ignorance.

Released from evil wrong states which conduce to the corruptions, to again-becomings, to distress, to the maturing of ill, to birth, old age, and dying in the future, therefore is he called one who is secure from bondage.   *A.* ii. 11–12

XI. NIRVANA

Monks, there are these five sense-organs, of different sphere and different domain, which do not separately enjoy the sphere and domain of one another. They are the sense-organs of the eye, ear, nose, tongue and body. Of these five sense-organs, of different sphere and different domain, the mind is the repository. Mindfulness is the repository of mind. Freedom is the repository of mindfulness. Nirvana is the repository of freedom. But if you ask what is the repository of nirvana, this question goes too far and is beyond the compass of an answer. The Brahma-faring is lived for immergence in nirvana, for going beyond to nirvana, for consummation in nirvana.   *S.* v. 218

Where material shape is, Rādha, there would be Death,[1] or a slayer, or at all events what is perishing. Wherefore see material shape as death, see it as a slayer, see it as perishing, see it as a disease, an imposthume, a barb, see it as misery, as identical with misery. They who see it thus see it rightly. And the same is to be said of feeling, perception, the constructions, consciousness. Rightly seeing is for the sake of disregard, disregard is for the sake of passionlessness, passionlessness is for the sake of freedom, freedom is for the sake of nirvana. But if you ask what nirvana is for—this question goes too far and is beyond the compass of an answer. The Brahma-faring, Rādha, is lived for immergence in nirvana, for going beyond to nirvana, for consummation in nirvana.   *S.* iii. 189

If a monk, by disregard, by dispassion, by stopping, is freed from old age and dying without any residuum (for rebirth) remaining, it suffices to call him a "monk who has attained

[1] *Māra.*

nirvana in this very life." If a monk, by disregard, by dispassion, by stopping, is freed from ignorance without any residuum (for rebirth) remaining, it suffices to call him a "monk who has attained nirvana in this very life."   *S.* ii. 18

Just as these that are great rivers—the Ganges, Jumnā, Aciravatī, Sarabhū, Mahī, all tend, slide, and gravitate towards the East, towards the sea, so do monks, by making become the ariyan eightfold Way, by increasing it, tend, slide, and gravitate towards nirvana.   *S.* v. 39, 40

" Those recluses and brahmans, Māgandiya, who have fared or who do or who will fare with longing gone, their minds calmed in regard to what is subjective, do so because, knowing as they have really come to be the arising and the ending and satisfaction and peril of the pleasures of the senses and the escape from them, they have destroyed the craving for pleasures of the senses, have driven off the fever of the pleasures of the senses.

> Health is the highest gain, nirvana the highest bliss,
> And of Ways the eightfold leads to undying security.

In regard to that which you, Māgandiya, have heard spoken of as by generations of past wanderer-teachers :

> Health is the highest gain, nirvana the highest bliss,

what is that health, what is that nirvana ? "
The wanderer, Māgandiya, stroked his limbs with his hands, and said : " This is that health, this is that nirvana. At present I, Gotama, am well and blissful, I have no ailments whatever."
" Māgandiya, it is like a man blind from birth, who cannot see dark and light things, or green, yellow, red, and crimson things, or what is even and uneven, or the stars, moon or sun. Do you think that a man blind from birth would have taken a greasy grimy cloth had he known it and seen it, would have put it on and proudly declare : ' Indeed this is a beautiful, white, clean, spotless garment '—or did he have confidence in the man who had his sight (and who fobbed off the garment on him) ? In the same way, wanderers belonging to other sects, blind and without vision, not knowing health, not seeing nirvana, nevertheless speak this verse :

> Health is the highest gain, nirvana the highest bliss.

This verse, Māgandiya, was spoken by the perfected ones, the fully awakened ones of old :

> Health is the highest gain, nirvana the highest bliss,
> And of Ways the eightfold leads to undying security.

This has now gradually come down to the ordinary people. Now, Māgandiya, this body is a disease, a pustulence, a barb, a misery, a trouble. But yet you say of it : ' This is what health is, this is what nirvana is.' For you have not the ariyan vision by which you might know health, might see nirvana. I might teach you *dhamma*, saying : ' This is what health is, this is what nirvana is " ; but this might be a trouble and a vexation to me. But if I were to teach you *dhamma* in this way, with vision uprising in you, you would eject that passionate desire for the five components of grasping. Moreover you would think : ' For a long time I have been cheated, tricked, deluded by the mind, myself grasping I grasped after material shape, feeling, perception, the constructions, consciousness. Because of grasping there was becoming for me ; because of becoming birth ; because of birth there was ageing and dying ; because of ageing and dying, grief, sorrow, suffering, lamentation, and despair came into being. Thus there came to be the originating of this entire mass of ill.' Therefore, Māgandiya, consort with those who are true men ; if you will consort with these you will hear true *dhamma* ; if you will hear true *dhamma* you will fare along in accordance with *dhamma* ; if you will fare along in accordance with *dhamma* you will know for yourself, you will see for yourself : ' These are diseases, pustulences, barbs. Such things are to be stopped here and now with nothing remaining. By the stopping of grasping after these there is the stopping of becoming ; by the stopping of becoming there is the stopping of birth ; by the stopping of birth there is the stopping of ageing and dying ; by the stopping of ageing and dying, grief, sorrow, suffering, lamentation and despair can be stopped. Thus there comes to be the stopping of this entire mass of ill.' "   *M.* i. 508–512

I say that nirvana is the destruction of old age and death.
                                                           Sn. 1094

The stopping of becoming is nirvana.
                                                       S. ii. 117

Monks, if a monk perceive six advantages they suffice for him to establish, without reserve, awareness of suffering. What are the six ? The thoughts : Among all the constructions, awareness of nirvana will come to be set up for me, like a slayer with a drawn sword ; and my mind will remove itself from the whole world ; and I will become one who sees peace in nirvana ; and latent tendencies in me will come to an end ; and I will become one who performs his duties ; and the Teacher shall be served by me with love.   *A.* iii. 443

XII.   THE DEATHLESS

Whatever, monks, is the destruction of passion, the destruction of hatred, the destruction of delusion, this is called the Deathless. This ariyan eightfold Way itself is the Way leading to the Deathless, that is to say right view, right concept, right speech, right acting, right mode of living, right exertion, right mindfulness, right contemplation.   *S.* v. 8

> When from this, from that, he grasps the rise and fall
> Of the components,[1] he acquires the joy and rapture
> Of those apprehending the Deathless That.
>
> *Dh.* 374

I have attained to the Deathless.   *Vin.* i. 9 ;   *M.* i. 172

I have sounded the drum-roll of the Deathless.

M. i. 171

The gates of the Deathless have been opened.

Vin. i. 7 ;   *M.* i. 168

> Who, desiring merit, standing firm in the good,
> Makes become the Way for attaining the Deathless,
> He, winning to *dhamma's* essence, delighting in destruction,[2]
> Trembles not to think " Death's king will come."
>
> *S.* v. 402

---

[1] The components of personality.
[2] I.e. of the *kilesas*, obstructions, corruptions, or *āsavas*, fluxions.

For whom craving exists not,
Who knows and does not doubt,
Who has attained immergence in the Deathless,
Him I call a brahman.

Dh. 411

These, monks, are the four stations of mindfulness. Herein, monks, a monk goes along regarding body as body ; he is ardent, composed, mindful so as to control the hankering and dejection in the world. For him who goes along regarding body as body, whatever is desire as to the body, this is got rid of ; by getting rid of desire the Deathless comes to be realized.

[It is the same with the three other stations of mindfulness : feelings, the mind, mental states.]

S. v. 181–182

Fare along, monks, your minds well stationed in the four stations of mindfulness ; but let that not be for you the Deathless.

S. v. 184

Possessed of six conditions the householder Tapussa has reached fulfilment in the Truth-finder, he has seen the Deathless, and he goes on his way having realized the Deathless. What are the six ? He has unwavering confidence in the Awakened One, unwavering confidence in *dhamma*, unwavering confidence in the Order, he has ariyan moral habit, ariyan knowledge, ariyan freedom.

A. iii. 450–451

Monks, these seven awarenesses, if made to become, if made much of, come to be of great fruit, of great advantage, immerging in the Deathless, consummating in the Deathless. What are the seven ?

Awareness of impurity, awareness of dying, awareness of aversion for material food, awareness of distaste for the whole world, awareness of impermanence, awareness that in the impermanent there is ill, awareness that in ill there is not-the-Self.

A. iv. 46

XIII. THE INCOMPOSITE

There is an unborn, unbecome, unmade, incomposite, and were it not for this unborn, unbecome, unmade, incomposite no escape could be shown here from birth, becoming, making, composition. But because there is this unborn, unbecome, unmade, incomposite, therefore an escape can be shown from birth, becoming, making, composition.[1]   *Ud.* 80

I will teach you, monks, the incomposite and a way that leads to the incomposite. What is the incomposite ? Whatever is the destruction of passion, the destruction of hatred, the destruction of delusion, this is called the incomposite. And what is a way that leads to the incomposite ? Mindfulness relating to body. And (another) way that leads to the incomposite is tranquillity and insight. Thus, monks, have I taught you the incomposite and a way that leads to the incomposite. Whatever may be done by a teacher, out of compassion, seeking the welfare of his disciples, that have I, through compassion, done for you.

S. iv. 359

Monks, there are these three composite-characteristics of the composite. What are the three ? Uprising is to be seen, destruction is to be seen, alteration in that which exists is to be seen. [2]

Monks, there are these three incomposite-characters of the incomposite. What are the three ? No uprising is to be seen, no destruction is to be seen, no alteration in that which exists is to be seen.   *A.* i. 152

Ānanda, whatever material shape is past, perished, altered, whatever feeling, whatever perception, whatever constructions, whatever consciousness is past, perished, altered, if its arising was discerned, if its destruction was discerned, if alteration in that which exists was discerned, then it was of these things that arising, destruction and alteration in that which exists was discerned.

Whatever material shape is (as yet) unborn, unmanifested,

---

[1] *Cf. A.* i. 260, etc., p. 210.

[2] The Five Stems of individuality, and even the highest contemplative " states," are all composite, *M.* iii. 244.

whatever feeling, perception, constructions, consciousness is (as yet) unborn, unmanifested, if its arising, destruction, if alteration in that which exists shall be discerned, then it is of these things that the arising, the destruction, the alteration in that which exists will be discerned.

Whatever material shape is born, manifested, whatever feeling, perception, constructions, consciousness is born, manifested, if its arising is discerned, if its destruction is discerned, if alteration in that which exists is discerned, then it is of these things that the arising, the destruction, and alteration in that which exists is discerned. *S. iii. 39–40*

VII. TRANSCENDENT

1. TRANSCENDENT

SINCE A TRUTH-FINDER, EVEN WHEN ACTUALLY PRESENT, IS incomprehensible, it is improper to say of him—of the Uttermost Person, the Supernal Person, the Attainer of the Supernal—that after dying the Truth-finder becomes ; that he does not become ; that he both becomes and does not become ; that he neither becomes nor does not become.

S. iii. 118 ; iv. 384 ; cf. S. iii. 112 ; M. i. 140

To hold that he becomes after dying, that he does not, that he both becomes and does not become, that he neither becomes nor does not become, is to view the Truth-finder as body, as feeling, as perception, as the constructions, as consciousness. That is the reason, that the cause why this (matter) is not revealed by the lord.   S. iv. 384–386

The wanderer, Vacchagotta, asks Gotama where a monk (by which he means a Truth-finder) arises (or, is reborn) when he is freed in heart.   Gotama says :
" Arises does not apply."
" Then he does not arise ? "
' Not arises does not apply."
" Then he both arises and does not arise ? "
" Arises-and-not-arises does not apply."
" Then he neither arises nor does not arise ? "
" Neither-arises-nor-does-not-arise does not apply."
" I am at a loss, Gotama, I am bewildered."
" You ought to be at a loss and bewildered, Vaccha, for this dhamma is hard to see and to understand, it is rare, excellent, beyond dialectic, subtle, to be comprehended by the intelligent. To you it is difficult—who have other views, another persuasion, another belief, a different allegiance, a different teacher.   So I will question you in turn.   If there were a fire burning in front of you, would you know it ? "
" Yes, good Gotama."

" If you were asked what made it burn, could you give an answer ? "

" I should answer that it burns because of the fuel of grass and sticks."

" If the fire were put out would you know that it had been put out ? "

" Yes."

" If you were asked in what direction the put-out fire had gone, whether to the east, west, north or south, could you give an answer ? "

" That does not apply. Since the fire burnt because of the fuel of grass and sticks, yet because it received no more sustenance in the way of grass and sticks, then, lacking sustenance, it went out."

" In the same way, Vaccha, all material shapes, feelings, perceptions, constructions, consciousness, by which a Truth-finder might be made known have been destroyed by him, cut off at the root, made like the stump of a palm-tree, so utterly done away with that they can come to no future existence. A Truth-finder is freed of the denotation of ' body,' and so on, he is profound, measureless, unfathomable, even like unto the great ocean."

M. i. 486–487 ; cf. S. iv. 374 f.

Monks, the world is fully comprehended by a Truth-finder. From the world a Truth-finder is released. The arising of the world is fully comprehended and is abandoned by a Truth-finder. The stopping of the world is fully comprehended and is realized by a Truth-finder. The practice going to the stopping of the world is fully comprehended by a Truth-finder ; the practice going to the stopping of the world is made to become by a Truth-finder.

Monks, whatever in the whole world, with the world of Māras, of Brahmās, together with the host of recluses and brahmans, of devas and mankind, is seen, heard, sensed, cognized, attained, searched into, pondered over with the mind—all that is fully comprehended by a Truth-finder. That is why he is called a Truth-finder. Moreover, whatever a Truth-finder utters, speaks, and proclaims between the night of his awakening and the night on which he is attained to utter nirvana—all that is just so and not otherwise. Therefore he is called a Truth-finder.

Monks, as a Truth-finder speaks, so he does ; as he does, so he speaks. That is why he is called a Truth-finder.

D. iii. 135 ; *A.* ii. 23 ; *It.* p. 121

Whatever is seen, heard or sensed is clung to by others deeming it to be the truth.
One such as I could not take as the highest the truth or lies of those who are convinced.[1]
And having already seen this barb [2] whereon mankind is hooked, is hung,
I know, I see that for Truth-finders there is not this clinging.

A. ii. 25

A Truth-finder does not say anything that he knows to be not a fact, untrue, not connected with the goal and which is also displeasing and disagreeable to others ; he does not say anything that he knows to be a fact, true, but not connected with the goal and also displeasing and disagreeable to others. But if a Truth-finder knows something to be a fact, true, connected with the goal, although it is displeasing and disagreeable to others, then he knows the right time when it may be stated. A Truth-finder does not say anything that is not a fact, untrue, not connected with the goal even if it is pleasing and agreeable to others ; and he does not say anything that is a fact, true, but not connected with the goal and which is pleasing and agreeable to others. But if a Truth-finder knows something to be a fact, true, connected with the goal and which is pleasing and agreeable to others, then the Truth-finder knows the right time when it may be stated. What is the reason ? A Truth-finder has compassion for beings.

M. i. 395

Whose victory is not turned to defeat,
Nothing conquered by him follows him in the world—
That one, the Wake, whose range is infinite,
the trackless—by what track will you lead him ?

Dh. 179

Monks, the lion, king of beasts, at eventide comes forth from his lair. Having done so, he stretches himself and then surveys the four quarters in all directions. He then three times roars his lion's roar, and sallies forth in search of prey. What is the cause of that ? (He roars with the idea :) Let me not bring destruction to tiny creatures wandering astray.

[1] *sayasaṃvutesu*, called at *AA.* iii. 41 those who have taken up views, *diṭṭhigatikā*
[2] Here, according to *AA.* iii. 41, the barb of views (i.e. of opinions) and not, as sometimes, the barb of self.

As for the word " lion," monks, that is a term for a Truth-finder, a perfected one, a fully awakened one. For inasmuch as he teaches *dhamma* in an assembly, this is his lion's roar.

There are these ten powers of a Truth-finder possessed of which he claims leadership, roars his lion's roar in assemblies and sets rolling the Brahma-wheel. What are the ten ?

A Truth-finder has foreknowledge of, as it really comes to be, the causal occasion and what is not the causal occasion of (a thing) as such. Inasmuch as he has foreknowledge thus, this is a power of a Truth-finder because of which he claims leadership. . . .

Then again, a Truth-finder has foreknowledge of, as it really comes to be, the acquiring of deeds for oneself, past, future, and present, both in their causal occasion and their result. Inasmuch as he has foreknowledge thus . . .

Then again, a Truth-finder has foreknowledge of, as it really comes to be, the course leading to all bourns. Inasmuch as he has foreknowledge thus . . .

Then again, a Truth-finder has foreknowledge of the world as it really comes to be with its various and divers features. Inasmuch as he has foreknowledge thus . . .

Then again, a Truth-finder has foreknowledge of, as they really come to be, the divers characters of beings. Inasmuch as he has foreknowledge thus . . .

Then again, a Truth-finder has foreknowledge of, as they really come to be, the state [1] of the faculties of other beings, of other persons. Inasmuch as he has foreknowledge thus . . .

Then again, a Truth-finder has foreknowledge of, as they really come to be, the defilement, the purification, the uprising of attainments in meditation, freedom, and contemplation. Inasmuch as he has foreknowledge thus . . .

Then again, a Truth-finder remembers his manifold former abodes, that is to say : one birth, two births, three births and so on . . . up to a hundred thousand births ; likewise the divers involutions of aeons, the divers evolutions of aeons, the divers involution-evolutions of aeons, (remembering) : At that time I had such-and-such a name, was of such-and-such a tribe, of such-and-such a clan, was thus nourished, experienced this and that pleasure and pain, had such-and-such a span of life. As that one I, deceasing thence, rose again in such-and-such an existence. Then, too, I had such-and-such a name, was of such-and-such

---

[1] Or the arising and passing away ; *cf. MA.* ii. 130.

a tribe . . . had such-and-such a span of life. As that one I, deceasing thence, rose again here. Thus with all details and features he can remember his former abodes. Inasmuch as a Truth-finder has foreknowledge thus . . .

Then again, a Truth-finder sees beings with his *deva*-sight which is purified and surpassing that of men ; he has fore-knowledge of beings that, according to the consequence of their deeds they are deceasing and rising up again, they are mean, excellent, ugly, comely, gone to a bad bourn, gone to a good bourn (and he knows) : Indeed these beings, endowed with wrong conduct in body, speech, and thought, scoffing at the ariyans, of wrong view, acquiring for themselves deeds con-sequent on wrong view—these at the breaking-up of the body after dying, arise in the Waste, the Bad Bourn, the Downfall, Hell. Or (he knows) : But these beings, endowed with right conduct in body, speech, and thought, not scoffing at the ariyans, of right view, acquiring for themselves deeds consequent on right view—these, at the breaking-up of the body after dying, arise in the Good Bourn, the heaven world. Inasmuch as he sees beings with his *deva*-sight . . . he has foreknowledge of beings according to their deeds. Inasmuch as a Truth-finder has fore-knowledge thus . . .

And again, a Truth-finder, by the destruction of the fluxions, and having in this very life attained by his own super-knowledge to the freedom of heart, the freedom of wisdom that are fluxion-less, abides therein. Inasmuch as he does so, this is a power of the Truth-finder, possessed of which he claims leadership, roars his lion's roar in assemblies, and sets rolling the Brahma-wheel.

A. v. 32–36

VIII. DEDICATION

FOR RASILA,

WHOSE EFFORTS TO RECOVER FROM BRAIN and bodily injuries incurred by a drunken, hit-and-run driver are a testimony to the strength of the human spirit and the power of the prayers, meditations, blessings and healing energy poured into her by family and friends.

While still partially in a coma as her previous individual self was struggling to re-emerge, she was asked, "What do you perceive to be the greatest problem in the world today?" Rasila replied, "To see life as a series of problems rather than relax in a non-problem state of being where there are merely occurrences to deal with."

When the storms of life sweep over us
And seas with mighty waves churn,
We're guided to refuge by the healing light:
Red, Right, Return.